*f*P

THE SKIN WE'RE IN

Teaching Our Children to Be:

EMOTIONALLY STRONG
SOCIALLY SMART
SPIRITUALLY CONNECTED

JANIE VICTORIA WARD, Ed.D.

THE FREE PRESS

New York   London   Toronto   Sydney   Singapore

THE FREE PRESS
A Division of Simon & Schuster, Inc.
1230 Avenue of the Americas
New York, NY 10020

THE FREE PRESS and colophon are trademarks of Simon & Schuster, Inc.

Designed by Kyoko Watanabe

Manufactured in the United States of America

10 9 8 7 6 5 4 3 2 1

Library of Congress Cataloging-Publication-Data

Ward, Janie Vctoria.
      The skin we're in : teaching our children to be emotionally strong, socially smart,
spiritually connected / Janie Victoria Ward.
          p.   cm.
      Includes bibliographical references and index.
      1. Child rearing—United States.   2. Afro-American parents.   3. Afro-American children.
I. Title
HQ769.W27 2000
649'.1'08996073—dc21   00-031546

ISBN 978-0-684-85929-3

ACKNOWLEDGMENTS

It was my good fortune to have had the chance to travel all over the country and talk with African American teenagers and parents of teenagers in a variety of contexts. We talked about their lives, how they were raised, and how as parents they are now raising the next generation. They said so much that was interesting, that seems critical to share with others, and that I believe all parents can learn from. What was most compelling to me was what they said about placing faith in our history of resistance, and of drawing from it our individual and collective strengths. It reminds me of a kind of bamboo plant that I once read about. The plants bloom only once every hundred years, but somehow they all manage to do it at the same time, all over the world. And so this notion of resistance bloomed through our talks, all over the country, and I awakened to its force and power.

I wish to thank the many friends and colleagues who helped my ideas to bloom. I began designing this project with the support of the Simmons College Fund for Research. My study took shape at The Center for the Study of Black Literature and Culture at the University of Pennsylvania in 1990 where I was awarded a Rockefeller Foundation Postdoctoral Research Fellowship in the Humanities. Then under the direction of Professors Houston Baker and Manthia Diawara, associates at the Center provided me with a home away from home for which I am most grateful. Several years later I was able to envision a first draft of my work as a Visiting Research Scholar at the Centers for Research on Women at Wellesley College. Under the leadership of Susan Bailey, there too I enjoyed the sustenance I received from a community of scholars whose suggestions and constant reinforcement kept me focused and sane.

This project has been many years in the making and at each step of the way I have felt the steady and unwavering support of a number of very special people. My most heartfelt appreciation is extended to the following friends without whom this book would not have been completed. First, thank you to all of the families who invited me into their homes and were willing to share their lives so that others might learn. Thank you to Carol Gilligan who taught me how to truly listen and to make sense of what I hear. Thanks also to the Reverend Doctor Katie Cannon for all those deliciously rich and wondrous conversations about our racial realities that always keep me wanting for more. I am enormously indebted to my Interpretive Community, Jill Taylor, Tina Verba, and Dorothy Smith, for their guidance, energy, and careful comments on draft after draft as my ideas took form. Thanks especially to Jill for her editorial excellence, her friendship, and her ability to keep all things in perspective. Cindy Ness was a Godsend; though she joined the project late, she quickly proved herself invaluable, and I am deeply appreciative of the honest and clear-headed clinical insights she provided that helped to move me along. Assistants who pitched in with data analysis and library research were especially helpful: April Adjai, Jennifer Rosenbloom, and students in my African American Studies classes at Simmons College. And I owe much thanks to Marie McHugh for her photographs and administrative aid in my time of need.

To my friends and family: Judy, Joanne, Barby, the Nathans, Cohens, and Tennermanns, who provided much needed child care during the long summer months and over all those school vacations I had to work through, thank you muchly. And thanks too to Art and Betty Bardige for supplying me with a room of my own where I could read, write, and spread out my interviews with little distraction. I gratefully acknowledge all of the assistance I received from my agent, Kristen Wainwright, and my editor at The Free Press, Philip Rappaport. Philip was instrumental in organizing my thoughts, shaping my ideas, and bringing to the world a book on black children that is filled with the love, passion, and care that they deserve. My writing coach, Kerry Tucker, gets extra thanks. Her smart words, tight edits, and editorial wisdom were always right on the money.

Finally, I couldn't have finished this book without the humor, encouragement, moral support, and constant strength that were offered to me in tremendous abundance by my "sisters," Linda, Kat, and Tracy. My love for you all is as deep as it is unending. I dedicate this book to my son, Eli, who knows how to make me laugh and from whom I expect great and glorious things, and to the memory of Lillian and Monroe Ward. Thanks Mom and Dad for dispensing the kitchen table wisdom that still keeps me emotionally strong, socially smart, and spiritually connected.

Although the sentiments and the stories presented in this book are all real, the names and other identifying characteristics have been changed. The vast majority of the quotes used are drawn primarily from the interview data. However, in a very few cases dialogue was re-created from my own personal experiences and was on two occasions drawn from stories recounted in newspapers, periodicals, and on broadcast television.

CONTENTS

PART FOUR

INTRODUCTION

It is easier to build strong children than to repair broken men.
—FREDERICK DOUGLASS

Just a handful of years ago we celebrated the 40th anniversary of the integration of Central High School in Little Rock, Arkansas. The footage that television news shows broadcast to commemorate the event was dated, of course, but the black children's faces, suffused with courage, dignity, determination, and spirit as they climbed the school steps toward equal education, opportunity, and justice, transcend time. As I watched them I wondered if, as a child, I would have been able to muster the kind of strength and hope that moved those children forward, through the phalanx of state troopers, past the godless gaze of white supremacists, into history. I wondered if I could marshal the courage now, as an adult. I wondered, too, if we, as African Americans, have lived up to the dream that the Little Rock children held so close as they mounted those steps. Have we done all that we can? What have we done wrong? Can we right it? What have we done right? Can we do it better? How can we best help our youth to be strong, self-confident, and resilient? How can we fortify them to resist racism when they experience it firsthand and when they witness discrimination against others?

Black parents across the country struggle with these questions every day. And every day they invent new ways to help their children feel confident of their racial identity—both personally and as part of the African American community—and to recognize and name racism and oppose it in healthy ways. With a confidence born of their own childhoods and shaped by their experiences in the civil rights movement, they are teaching their children to be strong and resilient, and to stand up for what is right and against what is wrong. They are fusing what their own parents taught them with "black folks' truth," the collective wisdom of African Americans. And they are refining, adapting, and reinforcing that knowledge to help their own children counter the obstacles and pressures they face today, including covert racism—at school, in the workplace, and in the community—and unbridled media distortions and influence. They are preparing their children to be emotionally strong, socially smart, and spiritually connected. And they are anxious to share what they have learned with other parents.

In my travels to talk with the families whose wisdom and experience fill this book, the children told me, over and over and in no uncertain terms, of the value of this preparation. Gina, a 15-year-old from Raleigh, North Carolina, said,

> I've been warned that racism still exists—that even though segregation is gone, racism is still here. So sometimes there have been things said or done that I did not realize were racist, and I went back and told my parents, and we went over whatever had happened. And they pointed out to me where racism could have been the issue. Like I've said, I've been warned. And because I've been prepared for it, it doesn't bother me as much. I know people are going to be people. Racism has existed for many years. I don't want to say I accept it, but I don't have the hostility I might have had if I hadn't been taught about it before.

Reality is that today's black children are burdened by the facts of their lives. They are poorer on average than their white counterparts; they face discrimination and racism, both overt and subtle; they are judged by double standards; they all too frequently must come of age in unhealthy communities, with decaying surroundings, increasing crime, and substandard services, and within unhealthy families. Our children are also burdened, as all contemporary children are, by a glut of media information—from magazines, newspapers, advertisers, song lyrics, movies, and TV—that purports to tell them about the social world and their place in it. And the grip the media has on their attention is tighter, and starts earlier, than ever before. As a middle-aged girlfriend of mine told me, when she was growing up she didn't know she was a Negro or poor until told by a white girl in a newly integrated elementary school. But black children today are told early and often about their devalued racial and social-class status, and the demeaning and disheartening messages depress and derail them just at the point in their lives when they are constructing a sense of who they are and making choices that will determine where they want to be.

The media information that black children must decipher is particularly onerous and unfair: they must thread their way through portrayals of blacks as disproportionately violent (as in portrayals of young black males), disproportionately promiscuous (as in portrayals of young black women), and disproportionately lazy, cool, or athletic. It's even more confusing today, because from hip-hop to basketball, black youth culture has become the model for white culture. In fact, since the electronic media is often their primary source of reference, the way our black youth make sense of their lives and determine who they are is shaped by the images that the media project. Black parents today are faced with the formidable task of helping their children interpret information developed and delivered by a system that was in its infancy when they themselves were children, that continues to develop at breakneck speed, and that can have a staggering influence on their children's lives—in fact, some experts say, as much or more influence than a parent or schoolteacher. The truth is that although the lives of our youth are becoming increasingly complicated and increasingly filled with media messages, our children are receiving less and less direct attention from their parents (10 to 12 fewer hours per week since the 1960s, according to one study). The costs of the decline in parental focus are particularly high for black teenagers, who need all the adult guidance and support they can get in understanding the changed nature of racism and how to overcome it. If concerned parents find it hard to help their children decode the media—to understand what is and isn't true about media portrayals of their lives—what will become of children who are left on their own to make sense of this information?

We must also summon our strength and stamina to help our children know how to recognize and resist what I call the "new racism." By this I mean the covert, subtle, institutionalized racism that has replaced much of the overt racism—separate schools and entrances, discrimination in housing and employment—that was made illegal after the civil rights movement. The sobering reality is that racism that was once individualized is now institutionalized as a system of privilege and control. The new racism is hard to recognize and just as hard to counter. Sometimes the perpetrator is not a person at all, but a company, a school, the police department, or a financial institution.

Too many of our teenagers are angry and frustrated. In addition, too many are complacent—about inferior education opportunities, negative stereotyping, and injustice—or they are simply apathetic. Some have given up altogether, surrendering to feelings of fatalism and despair, sure that they will never obtain work that will pay well or a chance to advance; sure that racism will always exist and that they will always be victimized; sure that they have no allies; sure that the boat they're in is leaky and sinking fast. What has happened? Why aren't more of our youth thriving?

The biggest problem is that almost no one is talking to African American teenagers about racial matters in meaningful ways. What we read in the press and hear politicians say tends to obscure, distort, ignore, or belittle racial matters. Politicians and journalists in the popular press are keen to promote the notion of "color blindness," as though saying that race doesn't make a difference will somehow make it true. But this is intellectually and historically unsound, minimizing as it does the existence of race-based attitudes and behaviors that are deeply entrenched and institutionalized in American culture. Anthropologists critique the very idea of race as an arbitrary, abstract concept with little biological support, a hot potato that needs to be abandoned as quickly as possible. Some social scientists, such as Stephan and Abigail Thernstrom, the authors of *America in Black and White,* argue that the social conditions of African Americans, the attitudes of white Americans, and race relations overall have improved to such an extent that racism will soon become a thing of the past. Others, following the lead of William J. Wilson in *The Declining Significance of Race,* maintain that social class, not racial membership, is now the sole impediment to social advancement for African Americans. Still others criticize African American civil rights leaders for focusing so much on racial barriers, refusing to acknowledge, so they say, the gains made by blacks over the past few decades. Or they criticize those who advocate heightened racial consciousness, alleging that it "unfairly infringes on individual autonomy."

The politicians, social scientists, and popular journalists who speak about race in these ways provide little guidance regarding what we say at home to our children about racism and race-related issues. Their focus, instead, is on race relations—on interactions between groups: whites and blacks, blacks and Koreans, Jews and blacks, Latinos and blacks, and so on. They say precious little about intraracial issues, for example, what it's like to be a member of the diverse group known as African Americans. And they fail even to speculate about what it might take to help our black youth become healthy and confident, secure in their personal and racial identities, resilient and resistant, in a society that incessantly devalues them because of their race. They do nothing to help black male teenagers understand why they are met in public spaces with suspicion and fear, or are picked up repeatedly by the police for the offense of "driving while black." They do nothing to help the young black girl who is struggling to understand why the standardized test scores of students in her urban high school are consistently so near the bottom of the scale. And they do nothing to help black teenagers understand why so many black youths in their neighborhoods have "papers"—a juvenile file at the police station or courthouse. Our social scientists, pundits, and politicians offer no instruction or advice about how to stay connected to the black community and promote the collective good, or about what it means to take your place in the world as a responsive, responsible black adult.

What is loudest is the silence about racial matters, a silence that is insidious because it can lead to the belief that racial injustice doesn't exist and therefore demands no reform, a silence that can lead to abdication and survivalism. Our challenge today is to break that silence, to speak the unspeakable, to bring issues of race to the forefront for discussion—in public debate, in our schools, and in our homes. For the parenting of a black child in America today cannot be color blind or silent. We cannot afford to forget, or neglect, or refuse to talk about race with our children. Talking about race challenges misinformation—media distortions that confuse our children about who they are and what they can aspire to—and clarifies racial reality. Talking about race also provides a forum for identifying and planning ways to counter racism. And talking about race with our children, consistently and thoughtfully, with all our patience and energy, directly challenges the widespread denial of African Americans' lived experiences.

We black baby boomers remember when resistance was sweaty, tangible, and in the street. Now it is in the mind. Even though it can't be seen, it can be taught. And now, more than ever, it must be taught.

The African American family can provide a safe and loving context—a "home space"—in which our adolescents can question the social inequities they see. Within the security of the home and community, teenagers can observe and question models of African American identity that successfully integrate the best of both cultures: the dominant culture and our traditional black culture. Here is where they can learn ways of bicultural living that are honest, that will allow them to feel whole, that will make it possible for them to remain at once independent yet connected to others of their race, and that allow them to build on the best of African American history, our struggles and truths, our tragedies and triumphs.

What I set out to discover is how the tasks of parenting converge with the forces of racism. I looked for answers to the following: How can we help our children form a positive racial identity while at the same time preparing them for the possibility of victimization based solely upon their skin color? How do black families foster in their children a sense of commitment to the social and economic progress of the race itself? Are there identifiable messages that parents pass on to their children that allow them to stand tall in a world that would drag them down? And how do we middle-aged baby boomers stand tall ourselves, providing the role models our children so sorely need?

There are more than enough studies of why African Americans fail. I wanted to understand why we succeed. I wanted to discover what African Americans tell their children they need to survive. What would fill our own children with the kind of strength, hope, and courage to dream that illuminated those children in Little Rock as they climbed the steps of Central High School?

The greatest lesson I learned is that black teenagers need to develop the ability to resist racism effectively. The resistance I'm talking about isn't knee-jerk, and doesn't look for a quick fix. It isn't resistance by withdrawal, defiance, or disrespect. It isn't resistance simply for survival. The resistance I'm talking about is thoughtful, intelligent, responsible, and starts from within. It involves the mind and emotions, the heart and the soul. It is healthy and life-affirming and taps into moral beliefs about justice and caring for others of the group, despite those who dismiss such attachments as retrograde "identity politics" in a global economy and society. In order to resist responsibly and effectively, our teenagers need both psychological strength and social knowledge. And they need caring adult guidance to help them understand what they are facing and how best to deal with it. They need adults who will listen to them, support them, calm them, and teach them practical skills, like the four-step model Read It, Name It, Oppose It, Replace it, which I describe in this book.

Without adult guidance our youth are left to resist and flounder on their own. They are particularly vulnerable to retaliation, and not just the kind of public humiliation that goes on in places like department stores, public transportation, and on the streets, but also behind closed doors, in places like school offices where tracking, suspension, and grading policies are decided. Our black children are disproportionately labeled and tracked; they are subject to policies created by criminal justice systems to monitor and control black teens, particularly black males; and they are routinely denied access to valued resources. Although the urge to fight back reflexively, mindlessly, and aimlessly is sometimes understandable, it is not the answer. The answer is to imbue our teenagers with a sense of mission and purpose, strengthened by spiritual beliefs and made vibrant by unshakable hope. With our help and the help of other experienced, responsible, trusted adults, they must take warmth and fire from the knowledge gained and sustained by their African American parents and forbears.

Silence is destructive, even deadly. Failure to recognize and confront racism leads to a sense of ineffectiveness and worse. It even takes a toll on our bodies. Research on hypertension suggests that college-educated African Americans who faced racism in their lives and on the job and fought against it, had the lowest blood pressure. The group that didn't think they were affected by racism or failed to challenge unfair treatment had the highest blood pressure.

Research on African American students and academic achievement suggests that black students who are aware of racial barriers and are comfortable in their own ethnic identity do better in school. In my own research, young black women who recounted receiving messages of strength, perseverance, and resistance against the odds, of being reminded of the blacks who had come before them and the blacks today who aren't fortunate enough to share their advantages, showed a higher frequency of leadership activities as adults. Several of the women had achieved positions in class government and in local social-service agencies such as Big Sister organizations.

African American parents who are willing to take the time and thought to talk about racial matters with their children, no matter how painful the task may be, are precisely the kind of parents our black youth need. Parents who articulate a stance against racism, sexism, and social-class bias—who are able to understand what discrimination is and how it has shaped their lives and can effectively strategize around it—are parents who pass on to their teenagers the tools necessary to negotiate adulthood in this society.

Several years ago I began a research study in which I invited black teens and parents to talk with me about racial socialization and how it is transmitted. To find these stories I decided to go where black people really are—into the living rooms and dining rooms and kitchens of everyday families. I was curious to hear about diverse perspectives and wanted to assemble a sample that would capture the heterogeneity of African Americans. In order to make sure I talked with families in urban, rural, southern, and racially isolated settings, I aimed my sights at Boston, Philadelphia, Raleigh, and Albuquerque. Friends and colleagues in these cities provided me with names and addresses of African American parents who were either in the process of parenting teenagers, or had recently done so.

I visited these generous parents in all kinds of situations: in their homes, at their work sites, after church services, and once even during a child's softball game. To interview black teenagers I made contacts through public school teachers and counselors, church youth leaders, and again, through friends of friends. I interviewed the teenagers in their homes, in school libraries, and in one case, in a McDonald's over lunch.

In general, the parents, who were 35 and older, and the teens, between 13 and 20, were not related to each other. They came from the middle or working classes and low-income groups. They also came from a variety of family configurations. While most were two-parent families when we spoke, some were, or had been single or separated or divorced, and several of the teenagers were young parents themselves. Their education levels varied widely as well, from less than a high-school diploma to doctoral degrees.

As an African American mother and educational psychologist I know well how tired black parents are of hearing everyone outside the black community explain us to ourselves. Social scientists, especially traditional child and adolescent psychologists, still define African American teenagers by their adversities. On the rare occasion when a social scientist does address racial matters, it is most often with the assumption that racism only affects blacks. Researchers who interview African Americans often start with the negatives: "What are the worst problems confronting black youth?" "Why are so many black teenagers killing others, selling illegal drugs, getting pregnant?" Although I knew I could rely on questions like these to jolt a conversation into motion, I instead asked both the parents and the teenagers to talk about who they are as African American women, men, boys, and girls. Many were surprised and mystified at first. Nobody had asked them these kinds of questions before.

Black culture's vitality and vibrancy came through in the telling, retelling, and embellishment of stories, in the host of cultural understandings, metaphors, symbols, and traditions about race that I and the people I interviewed recognized and enjoyed in each other. Sometimes the conversations flowed easily, lubricated by our intimately shared experiences of race. Other times our talks were inhibited by our differences in age or in our educational or regional backgrounds. It can be exhausting to engage in debates with white colleagues about the existence, prevalence, degree of influence, and relevance of racism. The conversations that we as blacks can have with one another, and with our children, are a necessary and welcome respite. We say to one another, "Of course it matters. Of course it exists. We aren't crazy!"

My research was about stories: the oral tradition that has always been a key part of our culture. As Henry Louis Gates Jr. has said, "Telling ourselves our own stories—interpreting the nature of the world to ourselves, asking and answering epistemological and ontological questions in our own voices and on our own terms—has as much as any single factor been responsible for the survival of African Americans and their culture." That tradition, I found, is alive and thriving today in black families across the country. It is the everyday anecdotes and stories we blacks tell one another that help all of us—children, teenagers, and adults—connect to the past, make sense of the present, and prepare for the future. These stories form the backbone of this book, the base that allows me to move from the purely descriptive to the actively prescriptive.

Parenting is about aspirations, about working toward an ideal even when we aren't always sure of the path. Although black parents aren't always in agreement about the best ways to reach the ideal, we are unified to a remarkable degree as regards our parenting concerns and goals. We worry about what we feel our teenagers must learn to resist, and what we think they should be motivated to stand up for. These are all themes I explore in the following pages.

When I began my research I hoped that I would meet some African American mothers and fathers empowering their teenagers with lessons from their own lives, lessons that would respect the past and guide the future. What I found, in fact, was a multitude of such people. I found teenagers with an overwhelming hunger for such messages, and adults with an overwhelming desire to share them. And I found many, many African Americans—men, women, and children—who are struggling to make the best of themselves and their families in a confusing world in constant flux. It is for them that I have written this book.

This is a book about race and about raising children in a society where, despite arguments to the contrary, race still matters. In the conversations I had with parents and teenagers that form the foundation of this book, there was a necessary simplification of racial issues, with the result being that I present a dichotimization of the world that is not altogether correct. Ours is a diverse, multicultural world, with as many gradations of skin color and ethnic origin as there are stars in the sky. However, when most of us talk about race, we talk in terms of black and white, not Latino or Asian or others. This is most likely because when we talk about race we are talking about power dynamics, and in this country, power has historically been in the hands of whites and continues to be. It might be helpful to keep in mind that sometimes we use the word *white* as a kind of proxy, a stand-in for any person who isn't black and who fails to treat us with the fairness and dignity we are due.

General Colin Powell is fond of saying, "Abraham Lincoln freed the slaves, but Martin Luther King Jr. freed the American people." It is now up to those of us who came of age under Dr. King's tutelage to liberate our own children from the myths of equality and meritocracy, and the false notion that the life of an African American is anything other than a struggle—but a struggle out of which strength can be born. By helping African Americans reconnect with the lessons and messages, the collective lore and group values that have always sustained and fortified us, we can replace the tyranny of racism with an exhortation of individual and group affirming racial expectations. I hope that the following pages will illuminate the way.

In Part One, parents of black teenagers share their experiences growing up black in the 1950s and 1960s against a backdrop of dramatic social resistance and political change. Reflecting upon the lessons about race that they received as children, black parents explain how and why they are modifying the messages of the past to fit the challenges faced by their teenagers today. I present a model that parents can use to teach strategies for developing healthy and responsible resistance in racially charged situations. In Parts Two and Three, parents and teenagers explore a variety of issues black youngsters must negotiate during the adolescent years, including gender socialization, racial identity formation, dating, financial responsibility, and moral development. Part Four is a discussion of two enduring institutions that have great impact on the lives of black children: schools and the church. School-based conflicts call for especially thoughtful and deliberate resistance strategies, such as those proposed here. In the final chapter, black parents and teenagers share what they have learned about the importance of developing a spiritual life as a source of strength and purpose, both of which are critical components of healthy resistance.

PART ONE

SPANNING TWO CULTURES

Coming of Age in the Era of Civil Rights

When I was 8, an older cousin—she was 17 or 18 at the time—was sent by her family in South Carolina to live with mine in the Northeast. Many northern blacks can tell similar stories of black kids sent south to live with grandparents when our own parents hit economic hard times. In the case of my cousin, my auntie said she was sent because she was too outspoken, too assertive—or, as the family sometimes put it, because Karen had a big mouth. I remember whispered telephone calls between our families as we prepared for her arrival, whispered undercurrents of fear for her life. This cousin was just too forward, too bold, they said. She showed too little deference to the white system of dominance.

My cousin's challenge to the system posed a threat, I knew that much. This was the early 1960s. Many, many changes were occurring all over America, particularly in the South. But some Negroes, as we were known then, were not happy with the pace of that change—not happy with what we had endured in the past from white folks—and didn't care who knew it. The girl's family was concerned about her future, so they sent her north for "safety reasons."

I was reminded of my cousin's story when I heard a similar tale from a dad in New Mexico. He had grown up with strong messages from his parents and grandparents about not talking back to white folks. He knew from an early age about the serious consequences that could befall black men and women who were outspoken, who didn't know their place. He fled the South in the late 1950s, he said, while he was still a teenager, after getting into fights with white people. He knew his mother would miss him terribly, but she wanted him to go. This man's mother wanted to protect and save him; she wanted him to survive to create another generation. But to do so she had to rein in the resister lest he be destroyed.

A Growing Sense of Change

Along with this sense of fear for growing children who were too bold, too outspoken, there was also a sense—an exciting one to those of us just becoming teenagers—of cultural change. With television and transistor radios, music that used to be thought of as "Negro" began to enter the mainstream. Our music had long been "covered" by white artists who usually got the money and the fame. But now, Fats Domino, Chuck Berry, Little Richard, and the Platters, and crossover artists like Nat King Cole and Johnny Mathis slowly invaded the *Billboard* top ten. There was a growing feeling among blacks that our stake was becoming larger, that something was happening. The "jerk," the "dog" (provocatively raunchy, evoking an expressive freedom that drove our folks crazy), and the "slow drag" were the black dances that started in the South and snaked their way up the East Coast, to D.C., Baltimore, Philly, New York. Eventually, if we were lucky, Boston blacks would be introduced to the beat.

Visiting cousins showed us the latest steps—we cha-cha'd to the Shirelles in our bedrooms, way past bedtime—and couldn't pass up the chance to chide us backward Bostoners for our lack of black cultural knowledge. Even with visiting cousins, plenty of songs and dances never made it to B Town, and thus Boston blacks were considered woefully out of touch. I developed mixed feelings about the South: pity and fear for black cousins still living under Jim Crow, and envy of their cultural sophistication. As painful as it was for me to admit, they possessed that highly desirable adolescent trait: they were undeniably, unabashedly hip.

As a child growing up in the Northeast in the early 1960s I was beginning to hear the rumblings of the civil rights movement, yet it took a while before I fully understood what was going on. My parents, like most of the black folks I knew, read and talked about the sit-ins, the bus boycotts, and, of course, the growing influence of Reverend Martin Luther King. Everyone recognized his courage, his strength, his extraordinary ability to lift a crowd with words alone. Everyone felt certain that he was destined to greatness, that people were responding to him. Everyone, blacks and whites included, had a sense that now things were finally, and really, gonna change.

I remember when Dr. King came to speak at a church in Boston. Listening to other parents, similar in age, sharing similar memories of the past, I was reminded of the events that shaped and molded my own emerging political consciousness of the time. One mom reminded me of the time in April 1965 when, at the urging of local activists involved in the early stages of the struggle to desegregate the Boston public schools, Dr. King was invited to speak at a rally on Boston Common. As it turns out, we were both there with our parents. We both remember the energy of the crowd—Dr. King's presence and words charging his audience—a feeling that we had gathered to watch a rocket take off.

Those of us with relatives in the South were filled with both wild anticipation and fear. Youngsters like my cousin Karen posed a particular challenge to her family. Not only was she unable to be reined in, but her spirit was being broken. Life in the segregated South was destroying that critical feistiness that black women invoke to deal with each other, their kids, and other family members, that they use to navigate the world on a daily basis. The plan was to send her to a place where she would stay alive, where someone, like my mom, could preserve that spirit while eliminating the brash, disrespectful edge that so offended the racial etiquette of the South.

My cousin wasn't the only guest in our house. For many summers our home was like a black folks' summer camp, with my family informally adopting kin and friends, all focused on nurturing our collective survival, fostering cooperation, interdependence, and responsibility for one another. Sometimes what was requested was emotional and financial aid from family members like my dad, who was doing a little better than others. Other times what was needed was a home away from home where the message was that here it is safe to be who you are, even if you are one who challenges authority, dreams of a better life, asserts yourself, fights back, or refuses to acquiesce. It's true the South was changing, but there was no guarantee that the change would be fast enough to give someone like my cousin a chance not just to survive and grow, but to flourish.

Growing up in Cambridge, just outside of Boston, I was spared the degrading visual signs of racial domination. Not that racism was nonexistent in the North—far from it. In Boston in the 1950s and 1960s racism included residential segregation and a cold, unfriendly curious mix of Boston Brahmins, the intellectually conceited, the Irish, the Italians, and any number of ethnic groups each living in their own ethnic enclaves, and old-time Yankees, with and without money. As Gloria Wade-Gayles, who came to Boston from Memphis in 1959 to attend graduate school, wrote in her autobiography, *Pushed Back to Strength:*

> In the South we knew what to expect. We saw the signs which were brighter than neons, flashing "colored." Which meant, "Black folks need not apply, enter or even approach." Boston needed no signs. The city's behavior said it all: we, too, hate blacks. Whites moved away from us on the train. They took their "blessed time" serving us in restaurants. They made us wait forever in department stores. And those who were not "refined" enough, or phony enough, to pretend, hurled racist epithets that won a close first with lynching language associated only with the South.

It wasn't until the summer my family traveled south for vacation that I saw firsthand the physical manifestation of the laws of southern segregation: the splintering Whites Only and Coloreds Only signs swaying from broken hooks over rest-room doors and water fountains near Myrtle Beach, South Carolina, hanging by their rusty fingertips through the last years of legal segregation. I have read in many memoirs of the powerful, sorrowful feelings evoked by first sightings of these signs. I think I was too young to appreciate at first glance their chilling implications. But I do remember the look of embarrassment that crossed over my mother's face, the sudden rush my dad seemed to be in, ushering us kids back to the pseudosafety of the Chevy station wagon with the Massachusetts license plates, and my own sense of unease, and somehow, too, of loss.

I grew up in a family that, like most families, collected embarrassing childhood stories for simple entertainment or for petty revenge at family gatherings. My mother had a favorite story, about traveling through Florida in the early sixties. She would pull it out at family gatherings, unwrapping it slowly and taking great pleasure in the suspenseful drama she created, like someone unpacking a fragile, priceless family treasure. As the story goes, we were in a five-and-dime type store in rural Florida. At the checkout counter the white lady cashier shortchanged me. Old enough to make change myself, I discovered the mistake and spoke up. "Excuse me, ma'am, but you shortchanged me." She asked me to repeat myself. "Say that again?" And I did. She looked at me hard. Was it the accent? The vocabulary? The audacity to speak up? She called the other workers over to her register to see this little Negro girl. All I remember is the crowd of faces looking at me, the silence—and that time stood still. Then suddenly, astonishingly, everyone started laughing, asking me to repeat what I had said. They all wanted to hear the little Negro girl speak her mind. No matter how many times my mother told the story, this was always the cue for her to burst out laughing.

Looking back on it I now realize this was one of those moments in which things could have gone in a number of ways. Given where we were in rural Florida, the situation could have quickly turned ugly. From what I had heard, talking back to white people had brought an early end to any number of black children uninitiated to the tensions just below the surface of black-white relations. Fortunately, this time it didn't. This was one of those classic "waiting-to-exhale" moments, when everyone holds their breath for a second to see what will happen. When it's okay, you can exhale, go on about your business. As a black woman, I've come to learn that black folks have many of these moments, especially when it comes to race—when someone makes a racial faux pas, worries that they've said something they shouldn't have, treading just a bit too close to the borders of racial propriety.

Lots of people today talk about the fifties as being a relatively benign time in our nation's history, a time of shared conservative cultural values that emphasized conformity to social norms—a Donna Reed, don't-rock-the-boat, American-as-apple-pie kind of existence. Not for African Americans. We've always had a love/hate relationship with social norms in this nation. Many of our fathers had returned from fighting Nazis in Europe all fired up. First-class soldiers tired of second-class citizenship at home, they were ready to do battle on their own turf. It took a while—a good decade or so—but gradually the civil rights protests began to take hold, igniting the pent-up passion and frustration of a generation of black people. Things started slowly at first, with Rosa Parks and the Montgomery Bus Boycott in Alabama in December 1955, and later the Woolworth's lunch-counter sit-ins led by black college students in Greensboro, North Carolina, in February 1960. But as the sixties began, even those of us without telephones, televisions, and daily newspapers were hearing the stirrings of a revolution. It was unavoidable, even for the children.

Like me, the African American parents that I interviewed were for the most part black baby boomers, children born into a period in which the earth was shifting under their feet. In the 1950s and 1960s, our everyday lives as black children had been interrupted by the ripples of a movement; the racist systems of structural inequalities that had dominated the lives of African Americans until then were shaken at the root. Some black children grew up in families that were connected to and involved in the movement; some followed the movement through the news accounts on the radio and on TV. "Negro" people discussed it everywhere, from barbershops to Sunday morning church services. And eventually, as the movement picked up momentum, everyone would know.

But until then, African American families did what they have always done: they focused on the tasks of parenthood, the day-to-day work of raising children. And those tasks are countless: providing discipline, health care, and financial support; getting everybody off to school; keeping the household going; trying to make sure each child develops the skills that make the most of his or her abilities; negotiating their increasing autonomy. All the time working to instill moral values, and all the time preparing them to leave the safety of home, live independently, eventually raise children of their own. And always the important task of teaching them how to deal with other people—authority figures outside of the home and even outside of the community—often including whites.

A primary job of black parents is to prepare our children for the realities they must face in America, including racial and economic discrimination. What with racial segregation, economic discrimination, low wages, and the black unemployment rate (which, since World War II, has been double the white rate), black family income lags significantly behind whites. The parents of the black baby boomers in my study had to prepare their kids for what they might be up against. They had to illuminate a frightening and potentially harmful reality in ways that helped their children comprehend the social limits that constrain them. At the same time they needed to take on the continuing, awesomely complex task of helping their children imagine a self that is larger, greater, and more loved than it may seem to be in a segregated, devalued reality.

GROWING UP BLACK IN THE 1950S AND 1960S: PARENTS TELL THEIR STORIES

> What we call family is constructed through memory—what we remember and pass on becomes an essential part of family.
> —MARY HELEN WASHINGTON

The way we raise our children—how we discipline, the beliefs we transmit to them, the strategies we pass on to them to help them navigate life—is shaped by how we ourselves were raised. We often try to pass on what we felt was best about how our parents treated and taught us, and we reject what we feel was wrongheaded or thoughtless. How we raise our children is also informed by the experiences we have had and the political and social landscape that we have passed through as teenagers and adults.

Mary Helen Washington says, "We, too, become artists, recreating our family in an imaginative act, retrieving what is lost by reconstructing our own "memory of kin." I asked parents to "recreate"—to recall what they remembered hearing about race, racial discrimination, and race relations when they were growing up. How had they been oriented to the social and political realities of the 1950s and 1960s? How had it affected their parents' child-rearing practices? And how does it affect their own parenting strategies today?

Childhood for most of the parents I interviewed was in the largely segregated South of the fifties and sixties. Many said that their own parents had been sharecroppers, subsistence farmers, tailors, postal workers, and porters. A few grew up solidly middle class; their parents had midlevel management jobs, or were schoolteachers or principals. Younger parents remembered their parents gaining access to higher-level jobs or to trade unions in the 1960s, when society opened up. The average age of the parents was 42, with a range of 35 to 60.

At his home in Philadelphia, I asked Mr. Lawrence, a man in his late forties, "What does it mean to you to be a black man?"

Among other things, responsibility. There is an enormous parental responsibility in black America. There are a number of people who, for any number of reasons, expect and have already set you up for some type of failure. You won't make it because you don't have the intelligence. You won't make it because of drugs and your ability to sway into the negative situations. You won't make it because you're just plain lazy from the beginning. Any number of things have already been predisposed against me, such that I am not supposed to survive and be productive in society. Now, that's aside from simply trying to grow up and get rid of the acne, run faster than the guys next to me, the normal things of being a male. Add to that this extra burden, to be a black male in America today is a heavy burden of responsibility to yourself, your family, your community, etc. So much is expected of you, both negative and positive.

The interview was long. As we spoke, drinking cup after cup of coffee, the sun began to sink beneath the horizon, and the colors of the sunset filled the large patio window. I asked Mr. Lawrence how the meaning of being a black man had changed for him over time, and whether he had always felt this sense of responsibility.

No. Initially there were the expectations for failure, but there were none for success when I started out. When I was born, on my best day, I was colored, and anything after that, we don't even want to get into. The literal law of the land was that I could be lynched, beaten, deprived of everything, and have virtually no recourse as a result. So that when I started out, segregation was the norm, prejudice and reprisal were everyday facts of life; the fact that you couldn't go here, you couldn't do that. You couldn't aspire to thus and so. It wasn't questioned. If you want to be something, the most you're going to be is a teacher, a preacher, or a laborer. You can forget about dreaming to be a senator, head of a company, etc.

Men and women of Bob Lawrence's generation were raised by humble, God-fearing black folks, some only one, maybe two generations away from slavery. We grew up in northern and southern cities and rural counties. Some of us were raised in racially segregated neighborhoods; some in integrated ones. Some of us moved around when growing up. And some of us lived in families that migrated to the Southwest in the fifties and sixties to escape the Jim Crow South, and later, in the seventies, for jobs.

In the home is where children first learn how to make sense of racism and prejudice when they encounter it and where they develop attitudes toward their own ethnicity and toward the world at large. Most of the parents I interviewed could recall growing up in families in which race was discussed. But Rose Martin, a mother I talked to in Boston, surprised me. It wasn't so much that she could hardly remember anything said in her family while she was growing up about being black. Nor was she the first mother to tell me how she had consciously made the decision to raise her own daughter in an overtly race-conscious manner. But it wasn't until I heard this story of retaliation and retreat that the pieces of her racial socialization began to come together.

She began with a story about her grandfather—how he had fled north from the Deep South with his family in the dead of night, undercover, in a desperate attempt to escape the lynching he was sure to face for having killed a white man after that man had pushed his wife off a sidewalk onto the street. Still maintaining that her family had seldom talked about race, she explained that family members retold the story as an example of an enduring family trait: ferocious tempers possessed by several members of the family who shouldn't be provoked because of how crazy they could get. When I expressed surprise that this story, though often retold in her family, was never seen as a story about race, she stood firm, assuring me more than once that lessons of race were never dispensed.

But surely they were. In *Black Sheep and Kissing Cousins*, Elizabeth Stone says that in some families, "beliefs go unchallenged by everyone involved in spite of the reality distortion which they may consciously imply." That is, families develop myths about key family events, and these myths help them to maintain equilibrium and to feel better about themselves. The mom who told me this story said that when she was growing up her family never talked about race—not about the racial climate that forced the confrontation between the white man and her grandfather, or the desperate escape from the lynch mob. The racism her grandfather faced was so fearful, so awful that the fear shut the family down. They refused to acknowledge the existence of a hatred so deep that it could cause a loved one to take another man's life. This fact was too dangerous to imagine, much less pass down through the generations. Thus, this family cultivated a myth, one powerful enough to reduce the complex phenomena of race, rage, and retribution to one single comprehensible cause—we have short tempers—as though by doing so it would make the terror disappear. Like many families, this one created its own way of talking about a pivotal event that shaped their lives, without fully comprehending its nature. Rose's story helped me understand that families have many ways to talk about painful racial matters. We talk about them directly and indirectly, and even when some of us say our families don't talk at all, the information may still be there, concealed beneath the surface.

When we black baby boomers were growing up, our own parents' agenda was fiercely focused on protecting us from the effects of overt racism, including psychological and physical pain. We were raised to be cautious, suspicious, and fearful so that we could literally survive in a climate where the balance of power between whites and blacks was clearly and enormously unequal. When we were children, those of us parenting today were quickly, and in no uncertain terms, made to know the negative attitudes and values attached to our skin color the moment we stepped outside the safety of our neighborhoods and homes.

Pain and Protection

Stories from our childhood are at times chilling to share and hear, especially those about growing up in the South. Older parents recalled dehumanizing stories of being forced to step into the street to allow a white person to walk down the sidewalk. I caught glimpses of what life was like for their domestic day-working moms, who cooked for and cleaned up behind white families, all the while knowing that the children they were paid to care for were raised to consider them invisible and inferior, existing solely for their convenience. They also told stories about the difficulty of reconciling the posture of deference their parents had to adopt in the work world with their own knowledge that their parents deserved far more than their racial status allowed.

There was a disturbing matter-of-factness in the retelling. Blacks in the shadow of Jim Crow couldn't go to this pool, see a movie in that theater, eat a meal in this restaurant. White folks lived over there, they said; we lived over here. Blacks had been living within this apartheid for centuries and had learned to adapt. They worked, coped, and brought up their children within a legally sanctioned second-class citizenship. They watched their parents struggle to support their children—often on starvation wages—growing tobacco and other crops, trying to scratch a decent living out of the land.

As Bob Roberts said, "My dad was a sharecropper. He did what the white man told him for survival. We didn't ask questions; we knew better." Another father in North Carolina remarked, "You knew how to act with white people. You had to defer to white people. Anything whites did was right and you had to learn to live with that." It wasn't just whites who put fear in black children; they learned to be fearful from their parents at the earliest age. And as one black father remarked, "Many black people have that fear today. We can't get rid of it."

Abbey Simpson's parents often told her horrific stories about blacks killed by white people—cautionary tales of psychic horror whose purpose was to teach black children that whites have control and that bad things could happen to you if you broke the rules or overstepped your place. She remembers, too, being taught that you had to get along with white people at all costs.

Racial socialization can be thought of as encompassing two component parts. First, it entails socializing children toward the sociopolitical environment in general. Second, it entails socializing children to what it means to be a black person and a member of the black race, or racial identity. When we are talking about raising children, racial identity has a moral aspect as well. We are talking about transmitting a moral perspective that allows a child to become a black person who can transcend—on a daily basis—the psychic threats that accompany constant devaluation.

In the 1950s and 1960s, before today's focus on multiculturalism and its exploration and assertion of ethnic identity, we lived a bipolar existence. The world back then was black and white. As a dad in North Carolina explained, there might have been Greeks, Italians, and Jews living near him, but in the fifties they had to come down on one side or the other. The color of their skin allowed them easy entry to the world of power. And nobody who didn't have to be, wanted to be black. A Boston mother remembered that the European immigrants who moved into her neighborhood moved in "different," in language, customs, their view of the world. But as soon as they got a sense of the racial reality—who had the power and who didn't— they rapidly became socially, psychologically, and politically whte.

Black children were taught the futility of immediate, overt resistance. One North Carolina man remembered having no choice but to shop in a particular white grocery where black people had to enter through the back door. When he asked for an explanation, begging his dad to talk more about this painfully unfair and degrading practice, his father simply said sadly, "That's just the way it is." Of course, the interviewee told me with a sigh, his father would never explain further. After all, he didn't need to.

These codes of racial etiquette were in place not just in the South. De facto segregation was practiced across the nation. In Philadelphia, certain restaurants and hotels refused to serve blacks, and many neighborhoods were closed to black homeowners. A mom, Nina Snow told me of how similar messages of racial superiority and entitlement were conveyed:

My father had a tailor shop and a cleaners. My father was the best tailor in the area. He could stitch anything. He made tailor-made suits and stuff like that, but still he had to take shit. On Saturdays we would be able to wait on customers, write tickets, tack things up and stuff like that. I remember this white lawyer coming in and calling, saying to me, "Where's my boy at?" He was referring to my father.

She paused for a moment, as though she was surprised to be learning something new from a story she'd told many times.

> You know, these things are deep. My father was always the man around our house, and I heard myself say to this white man, "My father's not no boy." And there was my dad running out and he said, "What you all saying like that for?" He was actually getting on me about interfering with his customers.

Nina Snow's father was furious and reprimanded Nina for interfering with his customers, jeopardizing his ability to make a living. Rigid racial segregation and isolation went on for so long that blacks and whites both had learned how to live and flourish within this bizarre, obscene social structure, accepting demeaning cross-racial interactions as commonplace.

Mr. Snow knew that his white customers wouldn't like being confronted about racial disrespect. And they especially wouldn't like to hear it from the likes of a black child. Black children like Nina had to learn an important lesson: that it was dangerous to upset or provoke white people. Her father, feeling the need to show the white customer that he could socialize his child properly, chastised Nina for stepping out of her place.

— In the America of our childhood, racism was ideology given the force of law. Notions of black inferiority, and of blacks as dirty, ignorant, and unworthy, were the norm. Black people were told repeatedly in a multitude of ways that they have no rights that white people were bound to respect. We learned early on that there is something dangerous about being black. As children we understood when things were unfair, yet we were expected to extinguish our feelings of anger. And where did all this suppressed anger— anger that must never be unleashed, certainly not toward whites—finally go? Sometimes, we discovered as we grew older, it was turned inward: into alcoholism, family and community violence, self-hatred, and rejection. But that was the risk our parents had to take, the burden we necessarily had to bear, to socialize their children to obey the rules of oppression in order to ensure their survival.

Many blacks have worked so hard to keep their real thoughts about their dehumanization out of their consciousness that only extraordinary circumstances will bring them to talk about it. For many, silence has become a survival technique that allows them to cope, to go about their everyday tasks without succumbing to anguish. When they finally do speak, their children learn powerful, often unintentional, lessons about racism and the costs of silence.

Michael, a friend of mine, told me that when he was a child, his father, after drinking heavily, would call him and his siblings into the kitchen. After they had assembled, he would slam a bottle of scotch and a glass down on the table, turn to the kids, and say, "Boys. Let me tell you about white folks."

Michael can't remember these conversations ever taking place when his father was sober. His father simply couldn't talk about how he felt about his treatment as a black man at the hands of whites unless he was drunk and his guard was down—when he was psychologically free to allow painful thoughts to surface. It was during these unlikely moments that many black children, like Michael, whose parents were ordinarily silent about racial subordination and racism or downplayed the extent of it and its effect on their sense of personhood, became witness to how their parents truly felt.

Some black parents were silenced by a pain rooted in repressed rage. I understood the silence because many of the stories were hard for me to hear. As I listened to these black adults talk, imagining them as frightened, vulnerable children, I saw physical manifestations of the pain and suffering they had to live through and remember. Their shoulders slumped; they sighed a lot and shifted in their seats. Many lowered their voices, embarrassed for their parents, when they described their loved ones' submission. Telling their stories, these parents expressed a sense of powerlessness at what their parents had endured. They brought me back to the embarrassment I saw in my father's eyes at Myrtle Beach.

Michael and I and other black parents that I interviewed (or talked with) experienced a meeting of emotions, one that brought us to a deeper level of communication and understanding and took us out of our roles as researcher and subject; we were simply black children, vulnerable, confused, and wanting better. The more we talked, and learned, and understood, the more we were buoyed by a sense of urgency as parents raising teenagers today, when our children our expected to grow up far too fast, too often in poverty and in fractured communities lacking the social supports that black communities once had, and assaulted by media messages that shape and distort their sense of who they are. Most important, we understood together that the racism our children face is often unacknowledged and denied, and that equipping them to deal with an unseen enemy is a difficult task indeed.

Appearances and Respectability

When I talk with black baby-boomer parents like myself about the lessons in living that shaped and guided our upbringing, folks readily recall receiving strong messages about respectability and social decency. It was important to look decent and be presentable so folks would see you cared about yourself, that your family were good, upstanding people. When these parents were growing up, children were expected to refer to adults as "Ma'am" and "Sir." You didn't simply say "Yes" or "No"; it was "Yes, Auntie," or "No, Grampa." Children were taught to show respect to adults, especially black adults in the family and community. This behavior was about respecting and maintaining unequal status between adults and children, but it was also linked to instilling a sense of personal dignity in people for whom dignity was so often ignored. These kids were, as one mom put it, "raised to think of themselves as somebody." Parents taught their children to imagine a different sense of themselves than that held by the larger world.

The focus on appearance in those days was strong. Mrs. Perkins remembers,

> We had to dress a certain way. We were always on time. It was a very strict upbringing. We were properly dressed. If we went to the train station to meet someone, we'd see the white kids and they'd have on blue jeans. That's how I wanted to dress. My mother would say, "It's because they're white." Or you'd go to the supermarket and the white kids would be running up and down the aisles, and my mother—we were so afraid of her. I mean we would never do anything. And then she'd sit around with her friends, and I could hear her saying stuff like, "Well you know these white people. They don't discipline their kids at all."

White people, black children were warned, were often wild and crazy, undisciplined. But they could behave that way. The same behavior exhibited by black kids would be considered much worse. Whites think we are wild and undisciplined already. If we act that way, it will confirm their negative beliefs about us. So black children couldn't behave badly because of the negative stereotypes that followed us around. We had to avoid their reproach. We had to prove them wrong.

Black children were told they had to work harder, jump higher, walk faster. Prepare yourself—your time will come. Children started to sense that their parents were seeing doors open for their children that had been closed in the past. They wanted to make sure that they would be ready—or at least look the part—when blacks were finally granted their rights.

Children from middle- and working-class families striving toward assimilation and upward mobility were being prepared for integration. Messages in their families took on greater insistence for blacks who were in positions to imagine increased contact with white people. For them blacks should look worthy of acceptance and respect. Black parents today face a far more complicated task: we must try to instill respect among black children in a society where callousness and disrespect, especially among our youth, are increasingly popular and pervasive.

Religion and Coping with Racism

As one father in North Carolina explained, his staunchly religious grandmother was "the ambassador of love." She taught her children that they were never supposed to argue, hold a bad thought, or commit an evil deed against another. In his home, as in many of our homes, religion was the backbone of everything. Sunday church service was the primary, often the only, event of the day. Saturday was spent getting ready for Sunday church. For black folks, Sunday, the Lord's day, was serious. Family dinner was mandatory and everyone, particularly the girls, was expected to help with the preparations. Mom would read and tell stories; the children learned to recite poetry and sang hymns. You couldn't listen to the radio, you couldn't clean house, you couldn't play outside or run in the streets. The kids who did were not the kind of kids good Christian children should commune with anyway. This was family time, quiet, contemplative, a time to give thanks, eat well, and enjoy one another's company. It was also a time when parents picked up where the preacher left off, bringing the Bible stories home, both figuratively and literally, expanding on the messages of goodness, perseverance, faith, resistance, and liberation. These were moral lessons black parents and their children would remember and hang on to fervently as the battle for our civil rights began to unfold.

Another dad, whose family had moved from Texas to New Mexico, picked up on the theme of religious values underlying the coping skills that had been passed on to him. His Pentecostal father was a forgiving man who seldom talked about how bad things were for black men in the part of Texas they had fled. He would shrug it off with few details. His coping style was to smile and just get through it.

But it is hard to reconcile forces as incompatible as racial polarization and the ethic of love, especially in the face of direct oppression. Perhaps this is why so many black families place great emphasis on general moral values like honesty, hard work, education, and especially religion and its role in coping with devaluation. Clearly their parents didn't want to teach hate; they knew that their children would learn that emotion on their own. The trick was to figure out how not to *allow* their children to hate. Religion played an important role in this process. Participation in a church community also gave blacks a sense of cohesiveness—of being bound together—and a sense of responsibility to oneself and to others. Blacks in the church community had much in common: we all felt poor and working class, we had common goals and struggles. The church taught basic moral precepts like how to love and take care of one another. Churches that had schools associated with them offered more general education as well, and another dose of community.

The church provided us with much as we were growing up, including moral guidance, community, and—especially in the 1960s—a springboard for social protest. Most important, it taught us to use our spirituality to cope with and endure racial prejudice and devaluation. But today we know that the spiritual coping strategies we teach our children must be about more than just endurance. The nature of racial oppression has changed. Now many of our children, even though they feel the effects of racism, don't know it when they see it. As parents we have a critical task of teaching our children to analyze and deconstruct their racial reality. We must teach them the model I'll be describing throughout this book: to learn to read racism, name it, oppose it, and replace it. Once they can identify and label the toxic forces that threaten to devalue their sense of self-worth and derail their psychological health, they will be able not just to endure, but to resist effectively, to stand against negative forces, and to take a stand for what is self-affirming.

Racial Pride

Racial pride is almost always a significant subject for African Americans. We remember the way Africa and African heritage was depicted by the white world when we were growing up: Africa, the "dark continent," populated by little black Sambo savages, ignorant pickaninnies, helpless, pitiful figures—images designed to create embarrassment and shame, not a sense of pride, courage, or self-respect. Two of the parents I talked to grew up in families that had immigrated to the United States from the Cape Verde Islands and from nations in the West Indies. These adults grew up surrounded by traditional practices and Africanisms. When in the late sixties everyone was rushing to buy dashikis and learn Swahili, these parents largely shunned the fad. Their families didn't need to explicitly teach African pride and heritage; they lived it every day. Some, like Mr. Maldonado's grandparents, wore African clothing, practiced African religions (ritualistically reciting the few cherished words remembered from long-forgotten African languages), and followed specific traditional food customs. Mrs. Santos mentioned that these practices had occasionally embarrassed her as a child, especially when her grandparents practiced their "weird" religion in front of her friends. But now, of course, as parents themselves, Mr. Maldonado and Mrs. Santos appreciate these cultural traditions and the historical legacy they represent.

But talking about racial pride, often in vague, undifferentiated terms, is not the same thing as mastering the specific strategies that pride can lead to. For our parents racial pride meant rooting for and feeling good about Joe Louis, Jackie Robinson, Jesse Owens, Marian Anderson, Paul Robeson, Phillip Randolph—blacks whose achievements were receiving worldwide attention, not just in the pages of *Ebony* but in *Life* and *Look* magazines, newspapers, and TV. The accomplishments of these blacks, and the national recognition they received in the media, provided a much-needed dose of self-dignity to the black community.

On the other hand, some parents I talked to acknowledged that they were aware as children that other black people harbored ill-will against their own. "Niggers ain't worth shit," "They can't do nothin' right," and similar phrases of self-contempt were most often saved as direct shots against "those foul-mouthed, good-for-nothin', bad-actin', low-lifes that are dragging us all down." Parents who grew up hearing such deprecating language say they were able to resist internalizing these attitudes because they had received thoughtful countermessages from trusted adults. That need hasn't changed for black children today, who, like their parents, need to hear messages from trusted adults, the decent, proud, and self-respecting people that most of us are.

Many of us black baby boomers learned lessons of racial pride in our homes, sometimes through admiration of the few black superstars allowed to break through to the public consciousness in pre-civil-rights America. Others of us received huge doses of racial pride in the 1960s during the very public actions of the black power movement. Today, when racelessness is falsely valued and promoted, it is far harder to teach our children un-abashedly about racial pride. But there is no such thing as a color-blind so-ciety. And to suggest that there is no value in racial connections disconnects us from the energy and strength of our legacy of resistance. These are truths our children need to hear from us, clearly and often.

WHITE PEOPLE AND POWER

The fear that drove my aunt to send her daughter Karen north to live with us was genuine. For our parents the focus was on surviving whites, not just getting along with them. The skills they taught their children were critical and difficult to convey. They taught the importance of adopting a submis-sive posture, of silence and capitulation, as a tool for survival. And they taught the peril of a misstep, which, especially in the Jim Crow South, could lead to death.

Today we must orient our children to the world of power dynamics in a different way. We no longer feel the need to teach them to adopt a sub-missive demeanor, or to fear a misstep so powerfully. Now we must teach them to recognize racism in its many guises, which requires that we help them cultivate a sense of caution and distrust. And we must attune them to racism without turning them into racists.

African Americans of our parents' generation conveyed a lot of mistrust about whites, a sense that you shouldn't deal with them any more than you had to. Many of us grew up knowing how much our parents disliked white people. The writer Toni Morrison has said that her dad, a man of fierce racial pride, held feelings about white people that were so strong he wouldn't let them into his house. Often there weren't many opportunities to socialize, but even so, we didn't want them socializing in our homes. Parents warned children not to say things in front of whites because it could come back to haunt them, because of fear of retribution. To deal with this we black children were taught the value of "doublespeak"—ways of talking about whites behind their back.

For southern rural families, lessons about how to deal with white peo-ple were taught firsthand, within the context of their parents' employment, primarily as sharecroppers, domestics, and day laborers, often cheated out of their wages and forced to work long hours for too little pay. Joanne Ta-mor, 46, now a secretary in North Carolina, said her parents and grandpar-ents had instructed her to:

generally do what they say . . . mostly in their presence. But when they were not around you could use your initiative. In order to get [certain positions] you were to present that front in front of them. You kind of played it low-key. That got the results you could live with. And sometimes you would feel guilty about it, because it was dishonest. You didn't like doing it, but you had to. But even though it was dishonest, there was a line you didn't cross.

In order to adapt and survive, we learned to wear what the poet Paul Laurence Dunbar referred to as the "mask"—the pretense of submission. In the words of the old blues tune, "Got one mind for white folks to see, 'nother for what I know is me." Back when we were little, our parents taught us to wear the mask, and in so doing they took on the daunting task of teaching us a spirit of discernment, of playing by admittedly unfair, dehumanizing rules created by whites to maintain authority. Our parents' job was to help us understand that to adopt a submissive posture was to wield a tool for survival within the white power structure. They had to make certain that we knew which circumstances required the mask, and which did not. Most important, they had to teach us that when we wore the mask we had to maintain a vigilant consciousness—for wearing the mask *was* a strategy and no more—lest it stick to our faces.

Howard Vaughn, a North Carolina native who vividly remembered the fear he and other, usually older, young black male friends and cousins lived under, recalled that his parents' conservatism was born out of the profound fear they felt about the things that could happen to their children. In particular he remembered them talking about the awful things that could happen if a black boy or man were to talk to a white woman. The death of Emmett Till in 1955 and scores of others before him robbed his childhood of its innocence. "My mother only showed me the fear of white folks. She didn't know anything about how to operate inside their game." "White is right" was the message reinforced daily.

Leon Morrison, a Philadelphia bus driver and father of two, told me he was taught you had to defer to whites and be twice as good if you expected to compete. His father emphasized a strong work ethic, partially because he felt it would enhance his son's relationship with whites. The focus, his dad believed, was not on getting along with whites, but on *surviving* white people.

Liza Stone, who was raised in Arkansas, spoke about her slow but steady indoctrination into the world of dealing with whites:

When I was four years old, I didn't know there were any people other than black people. And as I got older, all I was told was that white people had everything, and that you have to kind of set your standards aside in order to work with them. It was not *with* them; it was *for* them.

My grandmother raised me. [I'd] come home upset because the white lady at that store was being snappy to me, and I hadn't even done anything to her. And the bottom line . . . [my grandmother] would tell me that all of us have eight and two. I'd say, "What is that?" Eight and two is that you've got eight fingers and two thumbs and she used to refer to the fanny a lot, too. She'd say, "That means their ass is cold when the weather comes just like anybody else's. So it doesn't matter that they're trying to make you feel you're less. We're all the same.

Even though as children they were taught to be silent and to capitulate to whites in order to survive them, black people still had standards about how to behave in the face of being degraded. Leola Corbin, who told me her stepfather never spoke about race, said that her mother hated the way he wouldn't stand up to whites. His was a family that grew up in the South, where black men couldn't speak up. The father later moved north, which is where he met and married Leola's mother, and he brought his silence and deference with him. "Though she understood it, Mother hated it," Leola said. "She called her husband a punk for running behind those whites. This ain't Georgia!" Now that his social context had changed, Leola's mother expected her husband's behavior to change as well, and she berated his inability to stand up for himself. Like many blacks of his time, this man concealed his own sense of self-worth as a survival tactic. As conditions changed, lots of us, like Leola Corbin's mom, began to allow ourselves expressions of worthiness. Slowly, cautiously, we held the expectation that we should and must resist our dehumanization.

THE CONTINUING THEME OF RESISTANCE

Just under the surface of these African Americans' life stores is a sense of active resistance, a fighting back. We hear it most often when parents talk about explaining racial reality to children—that this is not about us; it is about them. This kind of talk was an attempt to tell kids the real deal.

Not all of our experiences of oppression were negative and depressing. Blacks have not always been passive victims. We exhibited models of courage and bravery, especially as it related to our children. Mrs. Young told me a story of being slapped away from a water fountain by a white man. As she put it,

> I remember when I was in Charlotte, North Carolina, and I think this might have been in '52 or '53. I was in Woolworth's with my mother and my aunts. They had the Colored and the White fountains. I ran over to the White fountain, and I made the mistake of trying to drink out of it and was smacked away from there by a white man. My aunt and my mother proceeded to kick his ass royally. So that was my first lesson on race. Okay? They got locked up. My father had to come and bail them out. They're lucky that . . . the city was progressive enough at that time not to even consider lynchings. Plus, my great-aunt was an established person in the community.

Similarly, another mom raised in the segregated South in a strong black family that was well known and respected by both blacks and whites said she was raised to think of herself as "somebody." Her family made the conscious effort to build her sense of worthiness, of what we now call "self-esteem." The stories she heard growing up motivated and prepared her to get ready to deal with whites.

The most arresting stories black baby-boomer parents remember from their childhoods are the ones in which we blacks are fighting back, standing up to, psyching out, or in some other way cleverly and defiantly resisting. These stories carry a power that lasts throughout adulthood, just as the stories of our own resistance that are witnessed by our children today will stay alive and meaningful for them as they grow older.

A mother from New Jersey talked about her family's specific strategies aimed at increasing their children's racial esteem. Ms. Bourne fondly recalled going with her Garveyite dad on Sundays to Newark to hear Malcolm X. She remembers the speeches Malcolm delivered and the strong sense of racial pride, purpose, and direction they imparted. Malcolm X was the next in a long line of black men willing to put their lives on the line for their own beliefs about racial advancement. By exposing his daughter to Malcolm's radical ideas, Ms. Bourne's father empowered her to think beyond the limits and to learn to identify and appreciate liberation ideologies.

A generational consciousness evolved from the social influences acting on these black baby-boomer parents at the time they were raised. We learned our place in the social hierarchy, and we learned to defer to and distrust whites generally. We learned to wear the mask and to use religion to help us cope with everyday life under Jim Crow as well as covert racial oppression. Our own parents worked hard to balance messages of deference and avoidance with messages of self-worth and racial pride.

What most of us children of the era didn't get was much preparation in how to navigate living in the world where blacks are equal to whites. There were few cultural road maps to the new racial reality that was to come. Would white people really change? Would they give up power or share it? Would they change their attitudes, think differently about black people, or about themselves? Would they accept us as equals, or would racial dominance prevail? Many of us were justifiably ambivalent about integration. Skeptical, we worried about whether whites would or could really change. As the civil rights movement caught on, with photos of white resistance broadcast into our living rooms daily on the evening news, blacks were left to wonder: How long would white people stand in armed revolt against government demands for change? The anger in the eyes of white resisters was vehement. Just what would integration truly look like? Assimilation or annihilation?

THE RUBBER HITS THE ROAD: REVOLUTION

By the early 1960s, historic social changes were becoming obvious to all—blacks and whites, rural and urban—all over America. The Woolworth's lunchroom sit-in and other displays of nonviolent social protest (wade-ins, read-ins, and pray-ins, where students prayed as a form of protest) brought with them an undeniable sense that things weren't *about* to change; they were changing, right now, before our eyes. When Bull Connors turned fire hoses and attack dogs on civil rights demonstrators led by Martin Luther King in Birmingham, when four little girls were killed by a bomb in a church in the same city, the news shook the world. And much of the world responded, with embarrassment, outrage, and—finally—legal action.

Jim Crow laws were repealed in many areas, followed by desegregation of public accommodations. By 1963, the centennial of the Emancipation Proclamation, nineteen million Negro U.S. citizens forced the nation to take stock of itself, mounting the historic March on Washington in August of

that year and filling television and newspaper news for days in the late summer months. With President Kennedy's support, a federal civil rights bill
was proposed and passed.

Medgar Evers, executive secretary of the Mississippi NAACP, was
slaughtered in that state in 1963. Soon afterward, riots broke out over calls
to integrate housing and public school systems in the North.

Public schools and colleges became visible settings for the most fundamental change, as the movement set out—in the wake of *Brown v. Board of
Education*—to realize the promise of integration and better education for
blacks. Bold and determined black children and youth held high the hope of
equal opportunity.

Although segregation was outlawed by the mid-1960s, the slow pace of
southern school integration ensured that only a few of the youngest baby
boomers attended integrated high schools. Black schools were dilapidated,
with outdated, hand-me-down books, few supplies, and little or no money
to pay overworked staffs. Teachers were caring and hardworking people
who did the best with what they had, who taught with authority, understanding, and dedication. Some black teachers instilled racial pride, but as
Toni Ellis, who was raised in the South, remarked, teachers in her racially
segregated school said that if a child didn't hear about race and racism at
home, they shouldn't expect to find the answers at school. As Mrs. Ellis said,

> [My dad] was not an educated person; he was a sharecropper. He did
> what the white man told him. We didn't ask any questions. Even in
> high school, in a black school, we didn't talk about race. We went to
> school for the purpose of getting an education. We didn't have any
> racial problems because we were so far away from the white kids.
> [When we asked him why we had to go through the back door] he
> said, "Well, that's just the way it is." But he would never explain.
> Then, of course, you would go to your teacher if your parents hadn't
> explained something to you, [but] they certainly weren't going to ex-
> pose themselves to getting in trouble. It was like, if you didn't get it
> from home first, don't come and ask me.

She went on to describe the reactions of teachers when pictures of civil
rights protests first appeared on TV and local demonstrations began: "We
were not allowed to go. It was off limits. [They'd say things like] 'You'd better not go down there; *I'll* kill you first.'" These teachers were in a survival

mode. They believed that to be silent was the best way to protect vulnerable black children.

Even though change was surely coming, there was tremendous fear among both blacks and whites. The brutal 1964 murders in Philadelphia, Mississippi, of three civil rights workers, Andrew Goodman, Michael Schwerner, and James Chaney—and others who had laid their bodies on the line to secure voter registration in the Deep South—fueled fears of retaliation against protesters, and put everyone, blacks and whites, on guard.

Pete Allport laughingly remembered going into a White Tower restaurant in the South during this time. When he stopped a waitress and innocently asked, "Excuse me, can we get served?" whites in the restaurant panicked, fearing they were about to be in the middle of a civil rights demonstration.

And white folks were on edge, all over America. Social change was definitely in the air; ways of thinking and being were shifting. The movement angered, frightened, and confused white people who were seeing their way of life come to an end and could only guess what was to come.

For those parents who were bending over backward to shield their children from racial reality, the civil rights movement of the sixties posed a serious threat to their authority. A generation of parents (and therefore their children) found themselves quite unprepared for the backlash that accompanied the race revolution. Black parents were afraid for their children as they were moved to the formerly white-only schools; images of the school integration in Little Rock, where black children were spat on and pelted with eggs, filled newspapers and televisions across the country.

School integration brought blacks and whites together in unprecedented numbers. Black children were moving out of their communities, confronting white ideologies about race earlier in their lives than before. And often they navigated this on their own. For many, school integration meant parents were no longer close by. It meant loss of attachments to neighborhood and community, a loss of the structure that reinforced shared values, codes of proper behavior, and communal expectations. And many kids had to make sense of it alone.

This increased exposure to whites brought about a new socialization context and agenda. Growing up for these children was not just about identity development; it was about surviving attacks, being a token, living out others' agendas. As Mr. Creighton said, "Growing up was not a matter of finding myself. It was a matter of surviving. Race wasn't a big issue growing up in the segregated South. Most of my learning about race was self-taught when I entered an integrated school."

By the end of the 1960s, scenes of civil unrest were routinely broadcast on the TV news. From Vietnam War protesters burning draft cards to long-haired hippies with their rebellious clothing, loud music, and countercultural lifestyle, and feminist bra-burnings, gay-rights marchers, and Gray Panthers, formerly disenfranchised groups were rejecting the established order, projecting a vision of a moral, just, and inclusive society, all the while competing for their Warholian fifteen minutes of fame. One mother talked about sneaking out of the house to attend protest rallies. She had questions, yet her parents maintained their silence, maybe simply out of fear. Her mother was totally against her child's involvement in the movement and warned her to stay away from "the radicals."

Mr. Lane told me that his parents were constantly trying to encourage him to develop wider perspectives, to imagine a future for himself that was larger than what was scripted by his racial status. But these messages, he says, over time caused him to slam head first into his racial reality:

> I was beginning to think there must be something wrong with me, because I didn't seem to see where I could fit in any of this. Then came the sixties and in the sixties it became clear—the conflict wasn't with me, it was from without. And that something had to be done. And of course, I got into the streets with everybody else. And we turned it around. And I marched off with a brand-new, "Hey, we're on our way." And for a while, it worked.

The 1960s was a watershed decade in the lives of most young blacks. Just when the nation was going through the process of self-questioning (much of it the result of the country's increased military presence in Southeast Asia), black people, particularly young blacks, were going through their own individual and collective processes of questioning their allegiance to majority values. No longer passively accepting their subordinate position, black Americans became energized and incrementally more defiant with each successful advance in civil rights legislation. But political participation and protest were not without costs, and the violent opposition of whites to change, in both the North and the South, created a climate of racial suspicion. White hostility to civil rights enforcement was met with black bitterness and despair. Tired of seeing white justice dispensed in half-hearted, paternalistic, and begrudging ways, many young blacks began to question racial integration as the ideal. Their challenge, as a collective rejection of the burdensome weight of internalized self-hatred and submissive inferiority, expressed itself in many ways. Young blacks across the nation proudly embraced the signifying tenets of a new black referent as the primary source of validation and emulation. The bravado of the Black Panther Party, from its in-your-face rhetoric of black nationalism and nation-building, to its kid-leather gloves, dark sunglasses, slick leather jackets, and how-high-can-you-go 'fros, began to change our consciousness of ourselves and our status in society. African clothes, like dashikis and headwraps, African jewelry, Afros, cornrows, and other natural hairstyles became the norm.

More than one parent mentioned the influence of handsome, strong, and oh-so-full-of-himself Muhammad Ali (formerly Cassius Clay), who captured the tenor of the time when, in 1967, at the height of his career, he refused induction, saying, "No Vietcong ever called me a nigger," thereby sacrificing his heavyweight title, career, and the money that went with them. Here was, we believed, a new model of black manhood: a young, bold, and brave figure, willing to stand on principle and assert his black identity.

As the black nationalist movement swelled, so did our emotions, and the country reeled from the assassinations of John F. Kennedy, Malcolm X, Dr. Martin Luther King Jr., and Robert F. Kennedy, all within five years. Vietnam was rapidly becoming a war fought primarily by the sons and husbands of minorities and the poor. And some of us took to the streets. In the 1965 Watts riots, 34 died, and the city suffered $40 million in losses; in the 1967 Detroit riots, there were 41 deaths, 3,800 arrests, and 5,000 black residents were left homeless. *Time* magazine called it "an ugly mood of nihilism and anarchy."

Suddenly many young blacks looked different, talked different, and behaved different from what our parents expected, and boy, were they ever shocked. One parent I talked with said her mom cried when she came home with an Afro, not because of the way it looked, but out of a sense of fear that her daughter wouldn't fit in, that she'd lost all chance of succeeding in the economic mainstream.

Even attitudes previously entrenched in assimilationist blacks were shifting in response to emerging political consciousness and heightened racial awareness. Black colleges previously mired in tradition were caught up in actively challenging the old ways of business as usual. At the time, most of us lucky enough to attend college went to black colleges, and in many of these institutions colorism remained alive and well. A mother in Boston told me a story from her college years about skin-color prejudice in the black sorority to which she belonged.

> In the past, only really light-skinned women won the position of homecoming queen. So we went out and campaigned for a dark-skinned woman and she won the Queen contest, which was a big thing. As promised, the president did not show up to crown the Queen. That was a real awakening for me. To find out that your own people were discriminating against you. We had to remind the light-skinned females on campus that they were black just like we are. "Just because your skin is a little bit lighter than ours, you think you are superior to me?" The entire four years that we were there, there was always a dark-skinned Queen. We made sure of that!

Just as Muhammad Ali and Malcolm X freed our brothers to reexamine who they are and what they believe, we sisters had our own battles to wage. Black women had to take on our demons of the past, those "if you're light, you're all right; if you're brown, stick around; but if you're black, get back" mindless attitudes of skin-color preference that destroyed many a black girl's self-esteem. The reemergence of racial pride, with its emphasis on creating and embracing a new black aesthetic, helped to loosen the psychological control of a generation of black women. And young sisters coast to coast began their own journeys to reclaim and recover our Black Beauty ideal.

By the mid-sixties, the media began to recognize and respond to the growing black consumer market hungry for our history presented in our own terms, and for narratives and portrayals of a confident, productive black community. James Brown's *Say It Loud, I'm Black and I'm Proud*, became a number one hit and an anthem of black youth from Boston to Los Angeles. Blacks no longer had to rely only on the white power base for representations of themselves; now we became the record producers, book publishers, and journalists. Black students' demands for African American studies programs fueled an industry of black historians, social scientists, writers, and literary critics. Our newly aroused appetites for self-knowledge turned to cravings for more, and there was plenty to be had. There was a collective exhilaration at the correction—at long last—of intellectual, social, and expressive disenfranchisement.

Although social mobility had never been a sure thing for African Americans, the prosperity of post–World War II, coupled with the increased opportunities that accompanied the civil rights years, led us black baby boomers to cautiously assume we would lead lives much like, and even better than, our own parents'. After all, we had more schooling than any earlier generation of blacks. Having come of age in the turbulence and excitement of the civil rights and black protest movements, we joined the workforce and began raising families in the 1970s, just as the nation's unemployment rate began to soar. Our high expectations for social and economic mobility ran headlong into a crippled and crippling economy. High interest rates and inflation, "the cold realities of rising housing prices, flattening job pyramids, and low wages, cut into standards of living and into the capacity of many young blacks to provide for their children." With plant shutdowns and economic relocations, blue-collar jobs were rapidly disappearing, and blue-collar wages steadily fell.

As the Reagan-Bush presidencies took hold, young black families across the nation came face-to-face with the cold realization that Martin and Malcolm were dead, and the Panthers, whose fiery rhetoric far outstripped their capabilities, were either killed off, locked up, or victims of personal disintegration. More disenfranchised ghettoes with black families barely surviving on government AFDC, the Attica-inspired awareness of swelling populations of black men behind bars, and lingering distrust of whites' motives in dealing with problems of racism and economic oppression left us increasingly uncertain about the future, for ourselves, our children, and our race.

THE POST-CIVIL-RIGHTS ERA: RAISING FAMILIES WITHOUT A MAP

The civil rights revolution brought about tremendous social and economic gains for black parents, as it did for all Americans. Expanding education and economic opportunities, coupled with an increased participation in political and civic life, helped to establish a solid and sizable black middle class. Black cultural awareness movements of the 1970s, emerging black consciousness, and heightened racial identity bolstered a collective (and unprecedented) sense of racial pride, esteem, and purpose. The movements also brought about a collective questioning of authority—the development of a pervasive "says who?" attitude.

Ultimately, when they entered the 1970s and 1980s, young black adults were left with many questions. What does it mean to be a black person in the post-civil-rights era? Those of us as young parents starting our own families during those decades found ourselves entering a new social order with few cultural roadmaps to draw on, embarking on a search for a black identity that could be successfully defended and sustained.

The backdrop against which black families raise children today provides compelling evidence that, in general, black American youth in the 1980s and 1990s are growing up during much harsher times. Common indicators of societal distress—increasing poverty, teen pregnancy, juvenile crime, and school failure rates—indicate that African American children and youth continue to suffer disproportionately. In the post-civil-rights era we African Americans find ourselves facing diminishing opportunities, and as we ride the current wave of government cutbacks, we struggle as a community to raise our children, with too many fragile families on the brink of despair. Within this climate, black parents must figure out how to impart the knowledge and skills our youth will need to build their capacity for economic independence, personal fulfillment, and responsible adulthood as black women and men in the future. Yesterday's battle, the social and political civil rights revolution, is over. In the present climate of economic instability and destabilized communities, African Americans now believe that the battle today is psychological and calls for a resistance of the psyche, a strengthening of the spirit, a resolution of the soul.

2

PARENTING BLACK
CHILDREN TODAY

A friend of mine told me about something she'd seen at her son's school that set her thinking hard about what black boys face today that they didn't have to contend with a generation ago. At dismissal time a teacher pulled aside a seventh-grader who was wearing a sweatshirt with a hood. "Think about what you're wearing," she said to him. "To you it might just seem like warm clothes, but you'll create fear in some of the people out on that sidewalk." My friend was right to find the incident thought-provoking. When we were growing up our clothes annoyed some people and maybe shocked them occasionally, but they never provoked the kind of fear that a black teenager, or even a preteenager, provokes when he wears a dark, hooded sweatshirt.

In many ways, being a parent today means what it has always meant. It means working to raise a child to become a physically and mentally healthy adult who is a contributing member of society. It also means providing guidance, setting limits, and nurturing. The kind of parent a person will be is influenced—and always has been—by many different factors, including the parent's personal history and psychological resources, the child's individual characteristics, the stresses the family faces, and the supports that are available to it. These factors aren't static; parents' personal histories, life events, and psychological changes unfold throughout their adulthood.

Ellen Galinsky, in her description of the stages of parenting, says that when children are preschool age through the teen years, parents are in the "interpretive stage." Their job is to interpret the outside world of authorities—teachers, other family members—to their children. They must help their children understand who they are and where they fit in. They must teach values and morals, guide their children's attitudes and behavior, and help them understand how to negotiate people who may not share similar values. After this stage comes the "interdependent stage," when knowledge and power are shared.

Black parents, like all parents, must take on the jobs that Galinsky describes. But black parents have additional work to do. For blacks, race defines the parenting process in ways whites could never imagine. Race is inextricably tied to a sense of self as a parent. Black parents are acutely aware that their children link the past and the future. Through children a family passes on its values and traits; children also provide their parents with a sense of meaning and purpose. We know that our children's issues are our own, and race issues affect both generations. Most important, knowing that we must raise our children in a world where racism not only continues, but continues in increasingly subtle guises, keeps alive the distressing question, How long will this madness persist?

HIGH EXPECTATIONS VS. THE NEW REALITY: ADDRESSING THE DISCONNECT

> My personal problem with what is called "the sixties," roughly that period between the Brown decision of the Supreme Court (1954) and the election of Richard Nixon (1968), is that I think we won.
>
> —NIKKI GIOVANNI

Many parents I talk to echo Nikki Giovanni's words as they remember the high expectations and anticipation that they brought to their adulthood. Some, still charged from the experience of the civil rights era, say the calls for "black power" and "nation building" still strike a chord in their hearts. When the doors opened, those of us who could wasted no time availing ourselves of the expanding opportunities, higher education, and job advancement. We entered into parenthood with the highest of hopes, planning to do well for our families and our communities. Many of us were the "first to's" in our families: the first to finish high school, go to college, work in a major white corporation, move away from home without a marriage license and a husband, move away from the community and into a white neighborhood, send our children to predominately white schools, or cultivate a white friend.

Many baby-boomer parents reaching midlife begin to reflect on the meaning of the psychological and social upheaval of the civil rights revolution. It is a time of reappraisal—of who we are, as black adults and as black parents, and what we stand for. For us, the civil rights revolution is seen as a successful, purposeful struggle. It has meant genuine social changes, like integration, the legal prohibitions against race and gender discrimination, and increased opportunities for education and financial advancement.

As Mr. Nickerson, a grandfather raising his grandchildren, said,

It's always been an uphill battle for the black man. When we came along, it was rough. Then—I got married in 1952—things started getting a little better slowly. Then we hit the sixties. Boom! Those who were able to get their foot in the door in the sixties are doing quite well now. But I think things have peaked and now they're leveling off . . .

Today we hear cynical reflections on the sixties: the Summer of Love, tuning out and turning on. But many parents believe it was a positive time to be black in America, and I agree. It was a time of reaffirmation for the black race—of our authority, strength, and self-determination. As one father, Bobby McGill, said as he reflected on how these social and political events shaped his formative years, "I got my strength from my black experience."

Psychologists tell us that the transitional years of middle adulthood, when we hit our forties and fifties, are a period of introspection, of questioning the purpose of life and the values that guide work, happiness, and the functioning of social institutions. The developmental tasks of these years also include reappraisals of earlier commitments to people; to social, political and economic systems; and of personal identity. In the case of black adults, this can also mean reappraisal of the meaning of one's blackness. Middle-aged blacks have lived the struggle, and some of us—beaten, arrested, and jailed during the movement—have paid a high price. We entered adulthood faced with new opportunities scarcely imagined even a generation before, opportunities that came about because the social and political system yielded under the pressure of our resistance. The balance of power slowly tipped in our favor, and that brief period of empowerment expanded our thinking about race, self, society, and the future. We black baby boomers brought into adulthood and parenting the idea that we don't have to raise children the way we used to. We could let go of the fear, the submission, the pressure to teach our children to settle and make do. We believed that we had changed, that relations between the races had changed, that society had changed. But had it really?

"I remember a time when I was a kid and all the kids in the area used to play in this old abandoned-tire trash heap," Ralph Hall, an intake worker and part-time basketball coach at a youth center in North Carolina, told me.

> This old white man owned it and he never would bother the kids about playing *except* when he saw us. Then he'd get crazy and start yelling, "Get those little nigga kids outta my yard!" That man was mean. He hated black kids and he had no problem telling you how he felt.
>
> Today, we tell black kids what we think of them in sneaky ways. Like the county I work in has a community center right in the heart of the black neighborhood that hasn't been renovated in decades. Old shabby gym, leaky ceiling, warped floor boards. The playground wouldn't know grass if it saw it. The county hasn't allocated funds to fix stuff up in the black neighborhood in years. They keep voting it down. Something else is always more important than our kids.

Black parents have a special, and difficult, responsibility: to orient our black children to a social system in which they are devalued. We must teach our children that they may be victimized by racism, yet we must also be careful not to allow our children to adopt a victim mentality. One father, Jim Harris in Albuquerque, said sadly, "There's still a conspiracy to wipe out our kids." He also said,

> I'm a product of all my experiences in America. I have a certain survival instinct within me that's been geared up and developed over the generations and passed down to me. I think we still face the same sort of things that we faced when we were younger, particularly around the racist aspect of the world today. The only thing is it's a bit more sophisticated than it was when I was younger. [Then] it was just wild and open . . .
>
> I feel that I'm still in the mode of survival like all black folks will be. But on the other hand, I feel very fortunate because I am somewhat secure professionally, and in terms of lifestyle, I'm very fortu-

nate versus a lot of my black counterparts. I grew up in the sixties
when we were going through the civil rights revolution, so I have
never forgotten that, and I often refer to that in terms of reality.
Racism—it's just shaped different. The same elements are existing
today.

Many parents that I talk to today express a similar strong belief that
racism is shaped differently now than it was when they were children. As Ed
Nobles, a divorced father of three who married at eighteen and is raising his
children alone, explained,

> I want my kids to know their heritage. I don't want them to be prej-
> udiced, but I do instill in them that we were done an injustice, and
> when I instill that in them, I don't know whether I'm doing it in a
> prejudiced sense or not, but I want them to know exactly what's go-
> ing on.

Or as one mother, Edna Vitale, put it, "I have to work along with my
husband to send our children out to survive in a world that is very different from what we grew up in."

Ralph Hall, Jim Harris, Ed Nobles, and Edna Vitale have a generational
identity that serves as a source of their social orientation and personal identity. Over the decades of the seventies and eighties this cohort became parents. Their children were toddlers, preschoolers, and school age during the
"me" decade of the eighties—a time when blacks' economic development
was marked by unevenness. Some blacks were successful; many others
weren't. Jobs disappeared in center cities. The crime rate escalated, especially for crimes associated with the drug trade. Downswings in the nation's
economy led to massive layoffs and unemployment across the board. In the
1990s, organized white resistance to desegregation, residential integration,
and, more recently, affirmative action derailed the revolution.

The psychologist Barbara Okun describes the lives of today's middle-
aged parents as "marked by the shifting perspectives they have on their own
identities, their world, their expectations and their timetable for those expectations." We are building our lives and rearing our children in a world
that is dramatically different from the one we grew up in—a world acceler-
ated by technology and made smaller by a global economy, a world where
racism and expanded opportunities for blacks live in the same space.

Parents are hopeful, yet angry. We want our own children to know exactly what's going on. A complex task for any parent. Mr. Ellis explains that black kids must be protected, encouraged, and shielded from, but also educated about, racism:

> You want to give the message that if you work hard you will achieve. And you want to give the message they can trust, but be careful not to be taken advantage of, be left out, or isolated because of their skin color. [You want to] be careful, don't get them so paranoid they think every white is out to get them. Yet be careful how they interact with whites. [You want them to] know how whites react to them and know there are racists.

Like many black baby boomers, his experience in the sixties—his knowledge that things can be different and that much about the black community is positive, valuable, and shouldn't be lost—informs his parenting. He hopes to pass on a sense of *spirituality,* strength, and resistance.

PREPARING TODAY'S BLACK CHILDREN FOR THE NEW RACISM

Over the past thirty years, things have changed, including the experiences of black children. Most black children today have never been directly called a nigger, or been forced to drink from a colored-only water fountain or been legally prevented from exercising their rights as American citizens. Yet overt signs of racism still exist, often disguised in the daily course of conduct. In the past, we knew what to expect. We were prepared (well, as prepared as we could be) for racial attacks; we could anticipate—even predict—when they would happen. We had a clearer understanding about who would be held responsible, who was to blame. Today there is a climate of denial about racism. White people are suspicious of those who claim it exists. Black parents know racial attacks will happen, but we don't know when or how, and often this uncertainty brings with it a state of hypervigilance, a kind of cultural paranoia. We perceive a need to prepare our children in order to protect them from the increased vulnerability suffered by children wounded by racism.

The sociologists tell us that black baby boomers, like our white counterparts, have less extended family than earlier generations, which for us means there are fewer of us participating in the communal parenting practices that had long been part of our cultural legacy. Today we feel less free (and even less obligated) to parent other people's children, and we feel less social and emotional support for our own. Our siblings, friends, and sometimes even our own parents are in the workforce, with fewer hours to spend on family matters. It's difficult to find and rely on common values and mores, especially when we must compete with the influence of the electronic media and its mainstream values, which holds the attention of our children for so many hours each day.

Many of us have a profound sense that we have won the battle but lost the war. For although we've have gained access to higher education, or are employed in mainstream corporate positions, many of us report often-crippling alienation in white institutions. And although affirmative action may open doors, they aren't open wide enough; most poor blacks have been locked out. Those of us who experienced the psychological liberation that arose from heightened racial consciousness brought about by the reawakening of racial identity and a sense of black power are now confronting the reality of diminishing expectations and the reality that, once again, black folks get the short end of the deal.

TALKING ABOUT RACE WITH CHILDREN: HOW TODAY'S CONVERSATIONS DIFFER FROM YESTERDAY'S

Across the life cycle of any given black family, the developmental aspects of parenting shift, particularly as they relate to the task of socializing black children to their racial environment. Shifting contexts—changes in the social structure, the economy, the community—require changes in parenting roles.

I wondered about the basic motivations and preparation today's black parents are bringing to their child rearing, and whether they thought their racial socialization role was less necessary than their own parents had thought it to be. I asked parents whether their messages to their children were different from the messages they had received as children, and, if they were, I wanted to find out why.

Mr. Bailey, a teacher in North Carolina who grew up in a tight-knit, black, working-class community in the South, explained,

My parents were very conservative. My mom was protective. She only showed me the fear of white folks, but other than that, she didn't know anything about how to operate inside their game. Mom came from a position of fear, Dad from a position of anguish because he couldn't do a whole lot. He knew what the consequences were.

Although times have changed, and more blacks have joined the ranks of the middle class, parents tell me that the messages they pass on to their children are essentially the same messages they themselves received as children. Echoing their parents' lessons, blacks parenting children today continue to address "life issues," stressing the importance of achievement and hard work, with particular focus on education. They also say they want their children to grow up to become "good" people, and often this emphasis on moral character has, as it did when we were coming up, a religious base. Finally, many parents of black teenagers today talk about racial pride, which they connect to self-esteem. Once again, those "I'm black and I'm proud" messages that shaped a generation of black boomers seem important enough to us now as parents to pass on to our children.

In her study of racial socialization in black families, Marie Peters, working in the California Bay area in the mid-1980s, found that black mothers were acutely aware of racism in their own lives and that they shared their personal experiences of discrimination with their children. The parents in Peters's study felt they had a responsibility to tell their children the truth about the sociopolitical situation, and to teach them that they would probably face discrimination in their lifetime and must be prepared. This preparation includes presenting alternatives, instilling racial pride and self-respect, and offering the assurance of love as a protective buffer against the negative images a black child might encounter.

Michael Thornton and his colleagues at the University of Michigan's study suggest that older, married parents (most often the mother) who live in racially mixed neighborhoods are more likely to talk to their children about race. Their study results suggested that black parents in the Northeast are more likely to discuss racial matters with their children, perhaps due to the parents' increased contact with whites. Although a surprising 30 to 35 percent of black parents in this study didn't pass along racial socialization messages to their children, those who did, most often stressed racial pride, positive self-image, the importance of a good education, individual achievement, spirituality, and a solid moral foundation.

More recent research finds that parents teach in both tacit and explicit ways the importance of racial pride, black history, and cultural traditions.

Phillip Bowman and Cleopatra Howard at the University of Michigan found that such racial socialization messages tend to cover four categories: (a) racial pride, (b) self-development, (c) racial barriers, and (d) humanitarian values. In this study, parents who make it a point to talk to their children about blocked opportunities due to racism seemed to have a sense of themselves as better able to achieve what they set out to achieve. Black children who were conscious of race barriers also reported higher grades than did those who were not.

In other studies, the psychologist Margaret Beale Spencer at the University of Pennsylvania found that black youth resilience is associated with child-rearing practices in which black parents teach their children about black history, social discrimination, the importance of personal strength, and racial acceptance. These same factors were found to support intellectual competence in black children as well.

To me, a successful racial socialization is one that prepares black children psychologically to resist their racial subordination by learning how to identify racism and knowing when, where, and how to develop the strategies they will need to withstand and overcome the unpredictability of today's manifestations of racial oppression. The lessons learned, adapted, and passed down in black families inform this process. They also prepare our youth to meet the goals of adult social and civic life.

These messages about race and place not only shape a black child's identity but also initiate black children and youths in the current race game, helping them to understand which "moves" they can make toward their intellectual, academic, and financial success as well as to understand which "moves" can be made against them. Generally, these messages—direct or indirect—are passed down not only by parents but also by teachers, friends, extended family, and other people black children regularly encounter. Racial socialization serves to forewarn children about the nature of their racial reality, teaching them what to expect and how to develop adaptive techniques to resist the negative forces of racial devaluation. In essence, it buffers racism by fostering resistance, and this resistance is a protective factor that further buffers the effects of stress associated with racism.

This theme of resistance rose above all others when parents spoke about what they consciously hoped to transmit to their children about being black. Time and again they described a strategy of forewarning their children about the reality of racism and of strengthening them to resist its insidious effects on their social and psychological development.

If there was value in the message of the past, then it makes sense to us to repeat it today, passing on to our children the best of what we were told by our own parents. And when it comes to matters of race, today's parents tell me two things: First, they say, we've got to talk. Second, they say we've got to change what we tell our kids. I hear this from parents who grew up talking about race and from parents who were raised in families where little or nothing about race was shared ("Folks said just do the best you can") or only a qualified silence was passed along. I also hear it from parents who can only remember an older generation downplaying talk about racial conflict, opting instead to stress humanist values, such as focusing on the person and not the color.

A few parents—some of whom are not black or native born—say they try hard to deemphasize race when dealing with their teenagers. For them, this deemphasis is a strategy calculated to achieve another goal. They say that if we really believe that race doesn't matter, then we need to train our children to believe and act as though race doesn't matter. But even these parents are quick to add that if something race-related comes up—especially if their child is victimized—as discomforting as such conversations may be, and as unprepared as the adults may feel they are, they will talk. They, too, recognize that there are times when you must prepare children for a world in which race clearly does make a difference.

Gary Johnson of Philadelphia grew up in the same neighborhood where he is now raising his three sons. He explains that his strategy of child rearing concerning racial matters is a clear and necessary break with the past and is, given the climate today, the right thing to do. As a dad in Philadelphia said,

> My parents would have said, "Hold your peace"—more or less. Or, "Just keep doing what you know is right and sooner or later they'll come around and you'll be rewarded"—what I perceive as a very Christian mindset. My attitude with my kids is, "Be good, and then when you hit this situation, decide whether you want to play it or not, decide whether you want to fight it, or decide whether you want to step back."

Black parents like Gary Johnson say that in order to orient their children to the existing social and political environment, they must be up front about their racial reality. As a mother in North Carolina said to me, "We know what reality is." It is our responsibility to pass that knowledge on to our children in ways that are honest, forthright, and meaningful, and that serve as guidance for effective resistance.

Resistance as a goal rose repeatedly in my conversations with black parents. So did its four major subthemes: truth-telling (the importance of forewarning children about racial reality); helping children understand the dynamics of power that operate within a system of oppression; preparing for psychological assaults; and maintaining racial connection, all of which serve as guideposts on the road to successful resistance.

As the writer Adrienne Rich has so eloquently put it, "Lying is done with words, but also with silence," a fact of which black parents are deeply aware. We don't need to look far to find black people's lives misrepresented and distorted in the larger society, whether through overt lies perpetuated to serve the interests of others, or through lies concealed by silence that marginalizes African Americans. In either case, black parents see the misrepresentation and distortion as undermining blacks' efforts to gain self-determination and to achieve personal and racial affirmation.

Black parents also know that silence is often the voice of complicity. The black individual who is unwilling to stand up in her own defense is vulnerable to cultural and psychological anxiety and confusion. In my study, black parents break the silence with political knowledge and self-knowledge. As one parent said, "I don't teach it's an even playing field, all men are created equal, do what's right and you will be received fairly."

Has black people's style of racial socialization changed since the days of the baby boomers' parents? Mr. Evans, a high school history teacher who lives in a suburb outside of Boston, said,

> It's not much different, [because] my parents always gave me the message that you're as good as anyone else, and that you had to work hard in order to achieve—and that's the message I've passed on. They probably taught me to be more cautious with white people than I'm teaching my children to be. In that it's a little different. But I think that this whole thing about your being able to compete with whites successfully because you're as smart and as bright as they are—that I've passed on. And for the most part, I think they've gotten the message.

Shifts between grandparents and parents were most evident in the parents who placed importance on consciously preparing their children for racism and discrimination. At first glance, their observations of racial in-equities seem consistent with the older generation's. But today's parents say that racism is more subtle now, and that this accounts for the differences in what they emphasize and why.

Mrs. Evans put it this way:

My mother works as a domestic. She lives in the homes of white peo-ple. When I first started wearing my hair natural, my mother looked at me and cried. Okay? To her it just didn't fit. She didn't say, "Don't trust them." She really didn't. And she never talked overtly against them. Whereas I think I do with my daughter. It's not talking against [them]. It's saying, given a chance, the group will try to put you off in a category to eliminate you from the American way of life. You know, the home, the house in the suburbs, the travel, the education, the affluence. I really think that they [as a] group will do it.

I guess I'm sort of giving double signals. Because at the same time I'm saying personally, we can't [attribute] this to all whites, be-cause of the friendships we've had and because of my experience with white individuals. But, it's like there's this white blur out there—that's one thing. And then there's my white individual friends, that's another.

These parents feel it is necessary to help their children identify and an-alyze issues of power and authority embedded in relations between blacks and nonblacks. They expect that their children, as they grow older, will find themselves competing with whites, who will have little desire to give up their power and privilege. These parents are disillusioned with the slow pace of racial progress, especially in the face of the promise of the sixties.

We also feel a loss of white allies who, in the 1960s and 1970s, claimed to be committed to the cause of social justice—whites who, like us, ap-peared to believe that racism permeated all American institutions, and that it must be rooted out and destroyed. Frequently, black parents say that white midlifers today tend to acknowledge only begrudgingly, if at all, that preju-dice exists, and, they claim, whatever prejudice does exist is minimal. To them, race relations in general are improving. They feel no urgency to dis-cuss racial matters with our children or their own.

Today's black parents worry that with earlier and more exposure to whites and the white sense of superiority, our children will internalize inferiority before they acquire tools to combat it. This increased contact, which is occurring for our children at an earlier age than it did for us, lends an urgency to our task. We also worry that our children's friendships with whites may cause them to let their guards down and make them vulnerable to being hurt. We want our children to understand more about the institution of power, its systems and dynamics. We want them to think about power not in terms of a fear of power, but as a tool for them to master and to use as they prepare for the adult world.

Mr. Fireman, a bricklayer, having learned from his own father in Asheville, North Carolina, years ago, described himself, even though he was recently divorced when we spoke, as very involved in the lives of his two children.

I tell my kids you must understand white folks. You can't play the game if you don't know the rules. And blacks gotta have an education just to play the game. My parents always said, "Ain't no white in the world better than I am . . ." I came up in the era [of the sixties where I developed the attitude] of "Hey, the hell with this. Just try me!" I am crazy; I demand things. I want my children to be able to stand up.

A mother in Raleigh, Mrs. Douglas, remembered,

I didn't have to compete with whites as these children do. My mom and dad were farmers in South Carolina. They worked somebody else's farm and I used to hear [them] tell me stories about working so hard for twenty-five cents a day. And how important it was for Daddy to leave South Carolina and come to Virginia and get a job and bring his family out of being subservient to the white man. The stories they always used to tell. . . . I used to get the message that if you work hard—and we can prepare you to be a hard worker, and give you the tools you need—you won't have to deal with white people in the way we did. [You won't have to] be under them the way we were under them, be dependent on them for your livelihood in the sense that we were.

Now Daddy and Mama didn't say those words exactly, but [we got the messages] through the stories they used to tell and how they used to deal with people when I was growing up.

Many black parents struggle with contradictory attitudes about whites. While on the one hand we relate religious and humanist values of love for all, we are not confident of the honesty, integrity, or reliability of white people as a group. Although blacks must interact daily with whites, our survival, both individually and as a race, is often tied directly to the ability to "survive white people." It is hard enough for an adult to make sense of the fact that while many of us have intimate white friends, we also harbor tremendous apprehension about white group behavior. How can a child possibly grasp this complexity? How do we parents discuss this ambiguity with our children, and teach our children to discern who is trustworthy?

Mr. Foley, the father of several children, contrasted his parents' attitudes with his own:

They [my parents] took for granted, in an ordinary way, that they were black and that this is what happens to black people. I don't take it for granted in an ordinary way. I'm somewhat mad at some of the pain we have to experience and some of the suffering that we have to experience. I don't like it. I don't like some of the things I've seen happen in the places I've worked, and the expectation that you should take a second-class position, you shouldn't rise to the top and the like.

My mother and my grandparents were much more tolerant of race than I am. They were much more able to cope with the pains of race. I'm much more intolerant and impatient than they are. I'm much more conscious in trying to interject race in a real way, in a deliberate way into the lives of my children. My parents did it in an ordinary, gradual way, because it was all around them.

His parents, like many black people of their generation, used a coping strategy rooted in the idea of individual effort—a strategy of yanking yourself up by the bootstraps—even if you have to make them yourselves. As he put it,

They kind of blamed themselves and bought into the business about you stand and fall on your own wits and resources. They underestimated the role of deliberate exclusion and prejudice, and because they were all right in the sense that they had food on the table and were never starving and destitute, they were more grateful for reasonable lower-middle-class survival.

"Just do the best you can, boy"; this is what one father heard over and over growing up. And as Mr. Foley's story demonstrated, a strong will and faith that things would some day be better seemed to propel many of the older generation forward and helped them to resist dehumanization. While the parents shared many stories of heroic or even foolhardy resistance (risking death to protect family members, passing for white to secure special favors for those at home), for the most part the messages these parents had received as children were summed up in the following phrase: "Hold your peace, do the right thing, and someday you'll be rewarded."

Black parents today are far more active in their resistance than their own parents were. They tell me that they are designing and promoting strategies that attack racist ideology at the root—in the psyches of their black children.

As Ms. Robinson in Raleigh-Durham explains,

> When I started out, every now and then we would have little talks [with my parents and grandparents], and we'd go and ask questions, but they didn't purposely set aside times to build your esteem about race, you know. It was just day-to-day living, and if something occurred, and you asked, then you were given an explanation. But if you didn't ask, then you weren't told. [My husband and I] take time and we purposely purchase things. My folks never did that.

When I asked her why she was doing things differently, she replied, "Because I know I've got to start early, because there are better ways to destroy your self-worth now, more sophisticated ways."

The purchases Mrs. Robinson and other parents talked about included things like books by black authors, black dolls, video documentaries about black history, and works by black artists. Surrounding their children with objects that educate them about black history and achievement is yet another means of teaching resistance, by fortifying self-worth and racial pride.

I've learned from talking to African American parents that to build strong black children and youth we must talk about race with them to prepare them for the reality they will meet, every single day of their lives. We must orient them to their minority status and to institutional and societal power issues, prejudice, and discrimination. By teaching our children that they are not only *in* the group but *of* the group, by helping them learn the mechanisms of collective self-understandings and meaning making, we are providing them with the knowledge, critical-thinking skills, and self-confidence—an entire belief system—they will need to become healthy resisters.

The fact that white folks *can* avoid orienting their children to race matters while black folks *can't* is an important difference in the child-rearing agendas of black and white middle-class families. As Mrs. Adkins put it,

> When you're white and growing up, it's very easy for you to ignore the rest of the world. Your parents can effectively shut you off from any kind of interaction with other people who are different, and you can grow up with this idea that black people are on the periphery of life, and that's where they belong, and it's something you don't have to deal with if you don't want to. I think that if you're black, you are forced to deal with whites, and that's a different situation. And if you're not comfortable for a black person, if you're not comfortable being black, you're going to have some problems.

As black children confront their racial reality, they can't afford to ignore or discount the effect of the disparity on their lives. This is why prior preparation, including strategies to cope and overcome, is so important. Mrs. Adkins continued:

> I used to talk about historical things, like why things are the way they are. And she [my daughter] never really seemed very interested. It was almost as if she [were thinking] things were always like this. Like, there were these civil rights laws [passed] and then, okay. She never had to go to public school and be bussed, so she never had to deal with that direct confrontation with whites who didn't want you in there. Once she got into the school she's in, the white environment was very nurturing. [They said,] "Oh yes, just come on in." I still wanted her to be clear that that doesn't mean everything's okay. It doesn't mean those whites aren't racist. The same sorts of things can still go on. And a lot of it is veiled racism that, to me, is worse than the person throwing the rock at the bus. At least you know how to duck.

Ted Burns, a computer analyst in Raleigh, talked about socialization in terms of resisting the domination of the worldview and perspectives that marginalize black experiences:

When I think about myself and my family and my kids, and how I reared them, I try to make us the norm. So that when I'm talking about my family, you will have to understand that I'm talking about black, and if you want to know something about the juxtaposition with being white, you'll have to ask me specifically, because I do not include them in the equation. I have learned, and am continuing to try to cultivate the mindset that we are [at the center]. Anything else has to be defined, not us be defined. I'm trying to cultivate a perspective that probably would be viewed as racist or narrow-minded or whatever, but I am actually trying to cultivate a perspective that somehow the world's perspective is our perspective. Then if I want to talk about another perspective, I have to identify it. Because I grew up in a world where the perspective was a white perspective and any time you wanted to give your perspective, you had to identify it as being black. And I'm sure I still fight with my thinking that way.

Mr. Burns's words echo the ideas of Mr. Foley, who told me that he is trying to live within the cultural values and understandings of black people. Both men are referring to a particular knowledge and perspective that provides the foundation upon which healthy resistance is built.

During one interview, a teenage daughter came home from school, dropped her backpack on the kitchen table, and fixed a snack—all within earshot of the dining room where her father and I were talking. He invited her to join us, and, as always, I was happy to meet the child I had heard so much about during our conversation. When she entered the dining room, he turned to her and said,

This is a case where I know you can't fully understand what I'm talking about. . . . Right now you can't see far enough to understand some of the tomorrow situations that you have to be prepared for today. But somewhere down the road, something will happen and you will finally understand why [and] how and you'll say, "Now I know what I know." That's part of the responsibility of being a parent.

"Knowing what you know" speaks to the idea of a black folks' wisdom, a kind of survival knowledge, a concept that I and many black parents run into again and again during conversations about raising kids. "Knowing what you know" is an important tool of resistance, a "way of knowing" that black parents and children create together, in a fluid, dynamic, living process that responds to the racial reality faced by each generation.

By this I don't mean knowledge that's passed down unquestioned and undiscussed as absolute truths. I mean a form of knowledge that's fluid and dynamic and built by the generations together, improvised and constructed as we live. Some of this wisdom, like the fact that racism exists, is constant and seldom changes. And some of it, like what racism looks like from generation to generation, changes with time. This kind of knowledge—this collective self-understanding—is what a black child needs to know.

THE BRICKS AND MORTAR OF BUILDING STRONG CHILDREN

Crafting a Strategy of Resistance

Your child does not belong to you, and you must prepare your child to pick up the burden of his life long before the moment when you lay your burden down.

—JAMES BALDWIN

When I was growing up in the early sixties, I had a piano teacher who never missed a chance to admonish me when I missed a note or forgot my fingering. Mrs. Evans was what we call a "race woman," and in her frustration with my foolishness she'd remind me of a time not long before when black pianists weren't allowed to perform in the finest concert halls of this nation. Since things were different now, she warned me, when and if I ever got to one of those concert halls, I'd better know what I was doing and I'd better do it right for those behind me.

Mrs. Evans was using her story to prepare me for my racial reality, and to teach about racism, racial segregation, and racial connection as well. She wasn't preaching revolution so much as she was sowing the seeds of long-term resistance. And at the end of a turbulent century and the beginning of a new one, Mrs. Evans's message still rings strong: it is clear that nothing can be more important for black Americans than continued resistance, and teaching our children the skills they need to resist effectively.

As I've walked through high school hallways across the country, I've thought about the lessons I've learned about race from my own baby-boomer childhood. There are no easy answers as to why legions of black students don't do much and wind up tracked into low-level courses with watered-down curricula and teachers who don't expect much. How do we prepare black children for a racism that is nameless, shameless, and blameless?

As the psychologist Adelbert Jenkins has said, "Blacks come to the world with the mental equipment oriented toward conceptually organizing experiences, not just accepting what is given." Growth results from new ways of responding to experience and organizing it. The stress of racism disorganizes and undermines this growth. As parents, we must help our children interpret their social world, seek alternative meanings, and imagine a sense of self far greater than anyone's disbelief—to free themselves from the inside out so they will be fortified and ready to resist the new racism. To make this happen, we need to instill a degree of psychological health sufficient to withstand adversity and allow our children to grow despite the reality of racism. As part of this process, we must turn to the base of knowledge that has nurtured and sustained blacks for generations.

I fear that in the current climate, where racism is subtle and more carefully disguised, too many members of the "opportunity generation" (black parents of today's teenagers) have forgotten what worked in the past: the body of knowledge and folk wisdom born of the black experience that was always there for our ancestors. We've failed to pass down the tools that will help all black children oppose low expectations and resist self-imposed constraints.

BLACK FOLKS' TRUTH: THE CHANNELS THROUGH WHICH RACIAL WISDOM FLOWS

Mrs. Evans represented a generation of black folks who, though they knew the ways of white folks, still believed in the promise of civil rights and racial integration. While she prepared us to be citizens in an era marked by equality and justice, she operated from a "black folks' truth": a fundamental understanding that power is everything, that those who have it use it to maintain their power, that people don't like to give up what power they have, and that power in America is, and always has been, white.

Mrs. Evans drew on the truths of the time. But times have changed. In the post-civil-rights era of integrated schools and work sites, baby-boomer parents argue that the struggle is not over. Wary of our nation's lack of commitment to color blindness and individual merit, we teach our children that race still matters in life-defining ways. With the benefit of hindsight, history, and midlife review, we are modifying and refining what we say and believe about being black in America, and about finding a place in society that culturally feels like a good fit.

I am not saying that black folks had no voice or experiences of resistance before the sixties. African Americans have been standing up and resisting for centuries; most people I know have the family stories to prove it. But these early voices of resistance were muted and their attitudes constrained before the civil rights era. The 1960s released that voice, vibrant with moral force and a claim to more than our parents ever had or dared to want. And in the process, psychological resistance grew—in men and women; rich, working class, and working poor; and in every city and hamlet across the country. This liberation of voice was so extensive and so profound that it ultimately transformed the fabric of black adult lives. Now, when we black adults experience racism, we adopt the oppositional stance forged in the sixties, a stance that stands contrary to the prevailing political thought, and we pass down that stance to our children as well. As another parent put it, "If you want your children to be able to survive in this society, they'd better understand what reality is, you know, and you can never forget who you are."

Parents, in teaching resistance to their children, are continuing to evolve black folks' truth: a unique perspective that has evolved over time from blacks' social position, the historical legacy of victimization and subordination, and traditional values. This kind of perspective, created by black people to sustain and guide black people, interprets dominant mainstream knowledge claims and challenges them, too. Black folks' truth embraces the values and whole history of black people in America, from which African Americans must act in ordering their lives and in helping their children learn to resist. It is informed by the strength, power, and clarity gained from knowing what the truth is. "Knowing" comes from being told the truth and learning how to interpret one's own experience, how to remember and to trust your own voice and perspective, even if it means swimming against the prevailing current of thought. It comes from mining for the real and the essential in matters of race, being responsive to and responsible for the knowledge that will sustain and support the voice in the wilderness.

There is power in black folks' truth, and blacks believe they can wield it to foster power in their boys and girls, who are stigmatized many times over across the social class system—all by race, many by poverty, and, in complex and problematic ways for black men, by the interaction of race and gender. Drawing on the strength of black folks' truth, black parents bring to their lessons of resistance authority and experience forged in a common history of moral and political indignation at oppression. They thus empower their children to take a stand for those things that are affirming to themselves as individuals and to all African Americans.

RESISTANCE: LEARNING TO WITHSTAND AND TAKE A STAND

Resistance is to black people as apple pie is to America. Stories of resistance are our sustenance, from childhood to old age. From mammies to militants, blacks, who have been situated in the most marginal of positions in American society, have crafted a rich and gripping history of resistance. Drawing on black folks' truth to empower our children to stand up for what is right is a critical component. So is building our children's psychological health by helping them to continue to grow despite the reality of racism, to bounce back in the face of it, to have ready access to strategies that allow them to recognize and name racism and oppose it in healthy ways, and to replace it with something effective and affirming.

Children who haven't been provided with the skills and strength to resist the new racism are at tremendous risk. One example is Kira, a 15-year-old from Albuquerque. From the time her family moved to New Mexico when she was a toddler until ninth grade, she never attended a school where there were more than three black children in her grade. Throughout elementary school she socialized with white children, who liked her and still do. But once she reached junior high, when cliques began to form, things changed. "She seemed shaky," her mom told me. "She told me she felt like the girls were pulling away from her somehow—like she didn't belong and she didn't know why."

Once high school started, things took a dramatic turn for the worse. Her white girlfriends became interested in dating and capturing boys' attention. Although the high school had a larger group of black kids, Kira didn't know any of them and didn't understand how to relate to a black peer group. Although the white girls continued to like her and socialize with her, the white boys weren't asking her out. She became the target of a few black kids, who teased her about her taste in clothes and music, which had been formed for the most part in her white social circle. Kira began to feel a profound sense of isolation and sadness. No, she told me, she hadn't brought these issues up with her mom. Since they hadn't talked about racial issues in the past, she said, she figured that it was something that shouldn't be discussed at all. Without guidance about how to understand her feelings, or how to interpret the behavior of her white and black peers, she was unprepared to withstand the exclusion and ostracism, powerless to resist and grow, and vulnerable to depression and despair.

Just as vulnerable are black teenagers who think that all their problems (and the world's) are race related. Without the skills to recognize what is and isn't racism, the opportunity to name it, and strategies for healthy resistance—all taught by trusted, interested adults—teenagers like these can easily fall prey to violence and self-destructive behavior. One 17-year-old, Dion, told me he was angry all the time, an anger that was reflected in the raging lyrics of the songs he listened to, the clothes he wore, the way he walked, and the way he treated his family. Teenagers like Dion feel they are entitled to a nonracist life, which of course they are. But because he sees racism everywhere and in everything, he opposes it irrationally and thoughtlessly, refusing to trust or interact in a meaningful way with nonblacks and denouncing those who don't share his views, a stance that can't be sustained or defended over time.

The tensed black teenage boy we see in our schools and on our sidewalks—creative, angry, sexualized, and fighting back—has, like Dion, internalized our legacy of resistance. He is our creation. This is how we have taught him to be, and his unhealthy strategies of resistance are a direct reaction to the sociopolitical environment that has shaped him. It is our responsibility to channel his energy into effective resistance: to define for him the war, the enemy, and the stakes. Parents need to teach what they were taught, which includes lessons aimed at developing character, morals, and values, as well as lessons in caution, suspicion, and at timess the judicious use of self-silencing to control race-related emotions like anger, frustration, and fear.

Black baby boomers, beneficiaries of the increased opportunities available since the sixties, are in a paradoxical situation. Our increased exposure to whites, combined with our increasingly sophisticated understanding of the culture of power, is in part responsible for our growing disaffection with white-controlled systems like schools, courts, and social welfare institutions. And we understand the nature of our complicity in maintaining the political, economic, and racial systemic inequities that continue to limit opportunities for so many of us.

The parents I interviewed socialize their children based on cultural and political interpretations and assumptions about the social world derived from their attempts to live rich and meaningful lives in "the skin we're in." From their perspective, black children and families are under attack in many ways, but most egregious of all is the psychological warfare against which they must do battle. These parents understand that the battle has moved inward, and that now the psychological survival of a black child largely depends on the ability of black families to perform a complex juggling feat: they must negotiate conflicting and multiple role demands while at the same time enduring and overcoming the unpredictability of contemporary manifestations of racial and often economic discrimination.

As parents, we are judiciously selecting from the messages we received in childhood that helped us build our own strong self-concept and develop our racial identity, and we are passing these messages on. We are also incorporating previously denied or neglected aspects of the self that we now value and feel necessary to cultivate in our next generation. We are teaching a particular kind of resistance, one that fuses knowledge gained from historical analyses and personal reflection, a resistance born not from hate and anger but from love and purpose, racial pride, and connection.

Parents offer a variety of strategies for instilling the kind of psychological health in their children that will help them withstand adversity. When I asked one father, Mr. Drucker, what he thought were the most important things that he says to his children about race, he responded,

> Be good. Be excellent. Achieve in such a fashion that you never have to question yourself. That's the goal that I charge them with. There is no such thing as an excuse because you didn't achieve, or you didn't do something because you are black. This may sound contradictory, but we talk about this all the time. We talk about how being black puts you at a disadvantage, but at the same token, when I flip it, I don't let them use it as an excuse.

He went on to describe his task in terms of providing his children with emotional survival tactics:

The survival that they have to worry about is psychic, I think. People messing with your mind, trying to convince you that you're not as good as you are, or trying to convince you somehow that you don't deserve what you've gotten.

The message I hear from parents is clear: resistance is a family value, one that can be taught most effectively in the home. A home space is the greenhouse of resistance. It's where we pass on the knowledge necessary for resistance, where we construct identity, and self-create. It is where we—and our children—develop an oppositional gaze, and develop our unique cultural and political perspectives. It's where we learn when, where, and how to resist or adapt to oppression.

Resistance doesn't just mean finding a voice; it also involves, for some, an internal reformulation of self, an effort in adulthood to define the self in one's own terms. It means grappling with questions about who we are as an African people, and where we are headed. Although this is an intensively private developmental process, I heard it expressed aloud by more than one parent. They conveyed a genuine sense of trying to cultivate a different mindset, a perspective that centers the black experience, making blacks the subject rather than the object. These parents are actively working to define themselves, their values and perspectives, and the parameters of culture. They are refusing to accept external kinds of definition. They are consciously fostering resistance as a tool of psychological warfare against widespread silence about the malevolent reality of white racism, the dissemination of misinformation about black people, and denial of lived experiences of racial injustice and inequality.

It is clear from what parents say that this notion of teaching resistance emerges from the generational consciousness held by black baby boomers. It was forged in the crucible of the sixties, which endowed those of us parenting today with a sense of psychic protest and purpose, and it was strengthened by our disillusionment and frustration over the unfinished agenda of the civil rights movement. It is fueled by a strong sense of racial pride and race consciousness, feelings of impatience that we haven't come further as a nation, and anger that blacks as well as whites have dropped the ball. It reflects black people's feelings of frustration and alienation that arise from a loss of community, and the shift from extended family to nuclear child rearing that makes many of us feel as though we are raising our children all alone. Parents fear that too many blacks have lost the ability to resist effectively and are succumbing to some of the worst of America's values and practices.

Finally, listening to histories of parents' lives has brought me to the conclusion that for this generation, the idea of teaching resistance is born from a sense of survival through hard times—including our own struggles with integration—and out of a sense of hope, of activism, and of purpose. It arises from the challenge of sending children to integrated schools where you are not sure if the teachers have high expectations or even know or care about your child, from living in an economy that makes it hard for blacks to get and hold jobs, and from listening to the rhetoric of color-blind meritocracy that flies in the face of persistent racism.

Within this resistance is a recovery of the sources that sustain our sense of self-worth: a belief in our own humanity and the strength to keep on going, lessons that are critical to personal and to group integrity. By teaching resistance, we parents are also sending a message having to do with the moral content of racial identity: We want our children to become people who can appropriately and effectively rise above racial devaluation.

4

TEACHING STRATEGIES FOR HEALTHY RESISTANCE

As African Americans, we have a history of resistance that is long, strong, and extraordinary. Slaves resisted their dehumanization in a host of ways as they imagined a reality different from the harsh one in which they lived. Some ran away; others tried to escape with their faith, hope, and dreams. After emancipation, African Americans worked tirelessly to form mutual aid networks to support one another and to take care of their own when no one else would. We have relied on extended family for sustenance and on the black church for community and the kind of deep inner faith that sustains our personal and collective resistance and provides us with a moral compass by which to guide our daily lives. All along we have struggled to maintain hope, ward off internalizing our conferred inferior status, maintain a sense of self, and build upon our individual and collective strength.

We have created as many ways to resist as there are contexts to resist in. We are used to resisting; we expect to resist. In the decades since we tasted success in the civil rights movement we have felt entitled to justice and our piece of the American dream. But now—in a time of what seems like unlimited economic prosperity for whites and disheartening challenges to affirmative action—many of us are angry and frustrated by what we see as a dream deferred.

Black teenagers are standing at the threshold of adulthood, taking their measure of the social world into which they must take their place. Many feel angry and combative, but, because they are uncertain where the war is or who or what they should be fighting against, their tactics are often mindless, their efforts to resist dehumanization incomplete and ultimately ineffective. The problem is, not all resistance strategies that we've developed are healthy. Here's an example:

Rasheed and John, both 11th graders, were offered summer jobs in the mayor's summer youth program for teenagers across the large metropolitan area. Rasheed, who is black, and a few other black teenagers from his neighborhood were assigned to a kitchen maintenance work crew at the state hospital. John, who is white and lives on the other side of town, was assigned to the X-ray department as a helper in the lab. Each day the kitchen crew prepares and serves breakfast and lunch to the employees who work at the hospital, including the other high-school workers.

Two weeks into the job Tony, another member of the kitchen crew, pulled Rasheed aside, saying, "Hey man. Have you noticed that all the white kids in the summer jobs program are working upstairs while we're down here in the kitchen?" At first Rasheed dismissed Tony's concern, but as the days wore on, Rasheed started to notice what his friend had observed. Sure enough, although there were one or two white kids in the kitchen with them, most of the maintenance crew was black, while most of the white teenagers had jobs scattered throughout the hospital.

After a while Tony decided he'd had it. "Man, I ain't doing this no more," he told Rasheed, "and you shouldn't either. Some of the other guys have quit already. Maybe you should too." Rasheed noticed that over the past few days several of the kitchen crew had called in sick, come in late, or didn't seem to want to work when they were there. The boys who stayed seemed mad or just didn't seem to care anymore. At the end of the summer, Rasheed overheard his supervisor complaining to the mayor's office that next year he didn't want to accept kids from the black neighborhood, citing their bad attitude and poor work ethic.

Tony and his buddies recognized an injustice: differential job assignments based on neighborhood and probably race. Outraged, they decided to take action and resist the unfair treatment. However, the actions they chose—to quit, to slack off, or to behave indifferently toward the job responsibilities—were ineffective.

I call these defensive strategies "resistance for survival" strategies. The young men used them because they felt psychologically under attack. They perceived that they were being mistreated, discriminated against, devalued, controlled, and they chose to cope with and survive the onslaught of negation by simply disengaging.

There may have been good reasons that the work sites were so racially imbalanced and the black and white teens received different work assignments. But Tony and his friends did not ask for an explanation, nor did they ask their counselors to review the situation. Perhaps it didn't occur to them, or maybe it did but they were afraid their concerns would fall on deaf ears. Their strategy, to sullenly withdraw, emotionally and physically, was ineffective. It didn't change the situation; the boys were still employed in positions they found demeaning. They didn't effectively challenge the system of job distribution; the white kids still had a wider variety of jobs to be placed in and learn from. And their actions were ultimately self-destructive: the boys received poor work evaluations that could hamper their chances for future employment.

Tony and Rasheed's strategy (resistance for survival) can be appealing in the short run, yet ineffective in the long run. These unhealthy resistance strategies

- are self-destructive, which means they impair people psychologically by diminishing self-esteem, undermining self-efficacy, and distorting a sense of self. They can lead people to behave in ways that cause injury to themselves, and may also create negative reactions in others.

- are short term and nearsighted. They focus on the immediate (How does this affect me today?) rather than on the larger picture (How can this make lasting improvements for the entire community?).

- fail to provide tools that transfer to future crises in effective ways.

- fail to provide real control over a damaging situation. Instead, they leave the teenagers disempowered, ineffective, and unable to make the changes that could bring them the respect and value they seek.

In resistance for survival, survival itself is seen as victory. The boys on the work crew thought that quitting their jobs or slacking off would hurt the boss, not themselves. They felt they had been done an injustice and this was their way of evening the score. Of course, they never voiced their concerns except to one another, and failed to share their plight with other adults who might have been able to help. Like many teenagers, they thought their actions would speak for them. They were doing what they believed they had to in order to survive the situation with their self-respect and dignity intact.

Unfortunately, they only hurt themselves and their friends: their actions led to poor evaluations and jeopardized the youth jobs program for their neighborhood the following summer.

Tony, Rasheed, and other black teens urgently need to know how to respond effectively to these and other situations of perceived racism. They need to thoughtfully design, assess, and control their resistance strategies, and involve responsible adults in what they're doing.

The truth is, unhealthy resistance strategies are hard to change. This is partly because the strategies are often initially seen as effective. Tony and his friends, for example, probably felt a sense of triumph when they decided to slack off on their job responsibilities. Because of this initial success, teenagers like these often become invested in continuing their tactics. And because they are trying to fulfill a deep psychological or urgent social need, and feel that an enormous amount is at stake (including their own and the group's integrity), they can be blinded by emotions, making decisions that are more reflexive than thoughtful.

To nurture psychologically strong and socially smart African American teens, we need to help them cultivate healthy resistance strategies, to fortify them from within. Healthy resistance strategies teach teenagers

- to be aware of the sociopolitical context of race in America and the role that racism, sexism, and social class bias continue to play in shaping attitudes, beliefs, values, and behaviors of Americans of all colors.

- to develop the ability to accurately assess the threat to themselves or African Americans as a group and determine the most appropriate way to respond.

- to *withstand* negative social influences and *take a stand* for those things that promote positive self-validation and group affirmation.

- to seek solutions that empower them through both a positive sense of self and the strengthening of connections to the broader African American community.

- to design effective and self-affirming offensive and defensive strategies that have their long-term interests at heart.

- to identify and reject unhealthy resistance when they see it in others or in themselves.

The Four-Step Model: Read It; Name It; Oppose It; Replace It

When an incident of discrimination or a racially charged situation arises, teenagers like Rasheed and Tony need to know that they should turn to a trusted parent or other adult for help, and we must be ready to help them, by asking and answering questions, fielding comments, making connections, and acting responsibly.

In the following pages I will describe ways to design effective and responsible resistance strategies that will help teenagers address the vast range of racial issues they face today. Working together, parents and teenagers can learn to resist racism by learning and applying the following model:

1. Read it.
2. Name it.
3. Oppose it.
4. Replace it.

The goal of the model is simple: to encourage teenagers to think critically about who they are and their place in the world, and to help parents carry out their paramount responsibility of helping their children know and respond appropriately to their racial reality. For teenagers, this means understanding and acknowledging that racism exists and that as an African American you may become its victim. It also means understanding how racial dynamics operate within any given setting, particularly the subtle racism that is infused in our social institutions, like schools and the workplace.

The model allows parents to think of every conflict as an opportunity to talk with their children about race and empowerment in a meaningful way. It provides teenagers with a way of thinking about how to react to conflict in their social environment. It also helps them understand where their power resides. Children who are victimized feel powerless; the analysis that the model encourages helps them realize that they still have power to psychologically resist, to refuse to buy into the reality being thrust upon them, or to do things differently.

This model can be applied to the two kinds of situations that teenagers tell me they most frequently encounter. The first are racial conflicts—situations in which teenagers feel they have to make a decision, and that race somehow plays an important role in the situation, but they aren't sure of the right thing to do. These can be tough, high-stakes situations where important issues are at risk (their self-esteem, sense of pride, racial identity, moral values, self-concept, and the like). The second are general, everyday situations teens face, which, although they may not be as highly charged as those in which the participants are in dispute, nevertheless call for teenagers to make what may turn out to be important decisions, and to factor race appropriately into the calculus. These include dealing with issues such as what friends to hang out with, whom to date, how to make and spend money, how to act in public, or how to get through school.

The model can help across a variety of race-linked situations, and with black teenagers from many backgrounds. When you think about the model, it's important to keep in mind that social class interacts with race in unique ways. In some situations, for example, middle-class status may mediate or obscure the impact of a situation. And racism plays out differently by gender as well. All teens—middle class, working class, low income, rural, urban, suburban, young, and older—need to possess problem-solving skills that allow them to examine their social world critically from multiple perspectives, make connections, generate alternatives, and determine significance. A teenager who can use the model—Read it; Name it; Oppose it; Replace it—is well on the way to possessing a repertoire of healthy and responsible resistance strategies.

Using the model involves thinking, feeling, and acting, as well as organizing, interpreting, and critically analyzing complicated experiences. It also helps teenagers come up with strategies that will assist them in identifying and coping with the intense emotions aroused by racial matters.

The model assumes two things: first, that racism is a pervasive force operating at several levels—interpersonal, cultural, and institutional—simultaneously; and second, that racism can be hard for children to make sense of because it is so frequently denied in the post-civil-rights era in which we live.

APPLYING THE MODEL

Read It

Knowing how to "read" a situation—the most complex step in the process of creating a healthy resistance strategy—is also the most important. When teenagers perceive that they have been wronged, particularly when they perceive racism, emotions can run high and words can be spoken that cause reactions that our children may never have dreamed of and aren't prepared to handle.

We can use the model to help teenagers understand how to read a situation for racism by breaking it down, examining its parts, and figuring out how the parts fit together. This requires looking at both the immediate context in which the event took place and the larger sociopolitical forces that affect it.

Reading involves paying close attention to the teenager's feelings, attitude, and conduct related to the situation, and to the feelings, attitude, and conduct of everyone else affected. It also means exploring the situation with questions—about evidence, the different perspectives involved, connections, and patterns—and about the significance of what's been drawn out.

Here's how an adult might have helped Rasheed read the situation that existed at the summer youth program, probing and guiding with questions:

PARENT: What's the problem?

RASHEED: The summer job program treats the black kids different from the white kids.

PARENT: What's your evidence? How do you know?

RASHEED: I see the black kids working in maintenance and in the kitchen all summer while the white kids get to work in all kinds of jobs all over the hospital. And that's unfair.

PARENT: Why do you think this happened?

RASHEED: Maybe they think the white kids are smarter, or better than us. . . . I don't know. So the hell with them.

PARENT: And that makes you mad, right?

RASHEED: Yeah it makes me mad. They're stereotyping—they just think we're dumb and lazy. They don't care about us.

PARENT: And you probably feel cheated, devalued—like your work isn't worth as much as the white kids' work. Like you don't deserve a higher level of work experience.

RASHEED: Yeah. So I stopped working.

PARENT: I know. You got mad and you stopped working.

RASHEED: Yeah, that's right. I ain't no chump.

PARENT: Did you talk to your supervisor about this? Did you ask him to explain why the white kids seem to have different jobs than you black kids? Did you tell him you were mad and had some questions about what was going on?

RASHEED: Nope. What's talking to him gonna do?

PARENT: So you didn't talk to him; you just stopped working. And what do you think your supervisor thought then? Rasheed, put yourself in your supervisor's shoes. What does your refusal to work look like from his perspective?

RASHEED: I don't know. I guess it looks like we're lazy and don't want to work. But we aren't.

PARENT: That's right. But how's he gonna know that? And who gets hurt when you refuse to work?

RASHEED: I don't know. Me, I guess.

PARENT: You got that right. Man, I understand you were angry, you felt your supervisor was stereotyping you. You got frustrated, but then what did you do? You stopped working. You said, that boss treated me wrong, I'm gonna do wrong. And Rasheed, you know that ain't right. You gotta know that what you did made it bad for you and your buddies. It just fed right into any racist ideas that man might have had. Think about it. What else could you have done?

RASHEED: I don't know.

PARENT: All right. Well then, let's take a minute and try and figure out what would have been better for you to have done.

Rasheed's father focused on helping Rasheed understand how to avoid getting caught up in reacting. He helped Rasheed read the situation, analyzing each action step by step. Rasheed's father asked him to think about what his feelings were, where they came from, and how they were connected to the way he acted. He required Rasheed to think carefully about his evidence; about how and why certain attitudes, feelings, and behaviors are linked; and to view the situation from multiple perspectives, analyzing the feelings, attitudes, and behavior of everyone involved. He asked Rasheed to think about the significance and consequences of his behavior. Rasheed's father asked him to consider these questions carefully in order to prepare him to move on to the steps of naming what had happened, opposing it appropriately (when need be), and replacing what in this case might have been a knee-jerk response with a thoughtful, effective one.

Name It

PARENT: And that makes you mad, right?

RASHEED: Yeah it makes me mad. They're stereotyping—they just think we're dumb and lazy. They don't care about us.

PARENT: And you probably feel cheated, devalued—like your work isn't
worth as much as the white kids' work. Like you don't deserve a
higher level of work experience.

RASHEED: Yeah. So I stopped working.

PARENT: I know. You got mad and you stopped working.

"Naming it" means acknowledging the presence of racism—or sexism,
or class bias—and bringing its reality into full consciousness, however
painful it may be. For someone who feels like the victim of a discriminatory
decision, attitude, or attack, naming is a powerful experience. In the current
political climate, where racism is so often denied, it is likely to be interpreted
as a subversive act. But naming is essential, because only through naming
can a teenager actively confront the issue. Ignoring, discounting, and wishing it weren't so are not at all helpful in the face of bias and discrimination.
But acting may have serious consequences. So it's critical to help teenagers
know how important it is to be very clear about assessing the evidence and
to be exceedingly thoughtful about deciding the best way to resist.

Naming it doesn't necessarily mean saying it out loud. One can con-
clude that racism is at the heart of a situation ("know what you know") yet
keep silent about this knowledge until safety is reached. This is particularly
true for children and teenagers who are alone when they come into conflict
with adults. Children should learn that it's best to hold their tongues in
cases like this, then to come home (or to a trusted adult elsewhere) for support, clarification, and help with determining if one is correct or if one is
misnaming the situation. Then the child and adult together—or the adult
alone—should confront the individuals involved.

Silence doesn't always imply a failure to name. However failure to name
can carry emotional costs. People who don't name might internalize self-
blame, shame, and powerlessness. The act of naming provides a sense of
agency and a sense of strength that comes from knowing that you can accurately apply your knowledge to a stressful situation.

Acknowledging racism, admitting that it brings up feelings of fear, fury,
and powerlessness, is extremely tough for many of us, especially children
and teenagers. Naming it takes courage and fortitude. It also requires, of
course, that you know how to call it when you see it. We must teach our children that just because a situation may have racial overtones this time, it may
not necessarily be about race next time.

Then, too, some teenagers are hypersensitive and too eager to label a situation racist, assigning blame to others and relieving themselves of personal responsibility. And some adults, in an attempt to support or curry favor with their teeenagers, may act irresponsibly, choosing to play the race card a little too freely. These teenagers in particular need our guidance. They have to learn how to better interpret events and attribute meaning to them in appropriate ways, and they need to learn how to take responsibility for their own behavior if that has contributed to the problem. It may help to offer them alternative understandings that they can bring to a given event—other ways to make sense of what's going on—so that they have options other than racism on which to attribute their negative assessments and feelings.

In this case, Rasheed clearly had a strong sense that race-based attitudes were at work, attitudes that made him feel angry, indignant, and justified in opposing unequal treatment. In the safety of his own home, and after reflection, he could attribute the situation to racism (here in the form of stereotyping) and be free to think about and weigh the most effective course of action.

Oppose It

PARENT: I know. You got mad and you stopped working.

RASHEED: Yeah, that's right. I ain't no chump.

PARENT: Did you talk to your supervisor about this? Did you ask him to explain why the white kids seem to have different jobs than you black kids? Did you tell him you were mad and had some questions about what was going on?

RASHEED: Nope. What's talking to him gonna do?

PARENT: So you didn't talk to him; you just stopped working. And what do you think your supervisor thought then? Rasheed, put yourself in your supervisor's shoes. What does your refusal to work look like from his perspective?

RASHEED: I don't know. I guess it looks like we're lazy and don't want to work. But we aren't.

PARENT: That's right. But who's gonna know that? And who gets hurt when you refuse to work?

RASHEED: I don't know. Me, I guess.

PARENT: You got that right. Man, I understand you were angry, you felt your supervisor was stereotyping you. You got frustrated, but then what did you do? You stopped working. You said, that boss treated me wrong, I'm gonna do wrong. And Rasheed, you know that ain't right. You gotta know that what you did made it bad for you and your buddies. It just fed right into any racist ideas that man mightta had. Think about it. What else could you have done?

RASHEED: I don't know.

"Opposing it" means engaging in action that avoids or defies or circumvents a negative force—such as racism. Today's African American teenagers must oppose a lengthy list of behaviors and attitudes that, if unopposed, will prevent them from growing into psychologically healthy, socially smart adults. They include feelings and attitudes that others have about blacks, and that blacks sometimes have about themselves, such as internalized self-hatred and contempt, despair, hopelessness, anger, complacency, worthlessness, and self-destructive behavior. And they include conduct that can arise in reaction to a racially charged situation.

Before Rasheed could oppose the racism he had named, he had to go through the difficult process of understanding that the form of opposition he had chosen—the slacking off—was inappropriate and ineffective. With his father's help, he came to realize that although his desire to oppose his devaluation was a reasonable response to his strong feelings, his resistance strategy was shortsighted. It failed to factor in how Rasheed's actions would be seen by those with the power to make decisions about his (or his neighborhood friends') employment status, and was ultimately self-destructive. Rasheed's father helped him assess the reflexive strategy he had come up with and see how his feelings, attitude, and actions were connected. And Rasheed learned an important lesson: that in life there is a path that will lead him toward what is in his best interests, just as there is a path that will lead him toward what is not in his best interests, and that it is his responsibility to find the good path and follow it.

All teenagers need to feel safe and in control of their lives and to know the feelings of pride and accountability that come with mastering their social environment. However, black teens in particular must learn there's a difference between opposition that is constructive and opposition that is destructive. Responsible resistance should be tied to a healthy and positive sense of oneself and one's moral values and to a sense of where one wants to be in the future. Parents who help their teens critique and construct healthy resistance strategies, like Rasheed's father, do well to teach them to constantly ask themselves: What's at stake? Who is benefiting by my acts of resistance? Who is getting hurt?

Replace It

PARENT: All right. Well then, let's take a minute and try and figure out what would have been better for you to have done.

Just as there is active opposition, there is internal opposition, or what some people refer to as "double consciousness": holding fast to a belief, value, or sense of reality that is different from the one that's being promoted. "Replacing it" can be seen as a form of internal opposition. It is the act of putting something new in the place of the feeling, attitude, or behavior that is being opposed. It helps the person who is resisting racism to take a stand for fairness and justice, reinforce personal integrity, and instill the confidence and power that result from taking effective, positive action.

These kinds of replacements include self-protective attitudes and ways of acting that build self-confidence and self-respect. For example, a black teenager who finds herself in a classroom where a teacher holds low expectations for black students may resist internalizing this attitude by replacing it with her own positive assessment of her—and the other students'—ability and self worth.

At this point in the conversation, Rasheed and his father were ready together to come up with alternative ways for Rasheed to communicate his displeasure with the job assignments, ways that would have shown that Rasheed took the job seriously and felt he should be treated fairly and with respect. The goal would be an attitude and course of action more proactive than reactive and would tap into Rasheed's own sense of self-worth. Writing a letter to the program administrator outlining the problem and asking for a meeting to talk about it might be one alternative. Setting up a meeting among Rasheed, his dad, and the other black teenagers involved might be another.

After following the model with his father's support, Rasheed was better able to critique his own resistance strategy and its effectiveness. He could evaluate it against his own developing maturity in social judgment and self-concept, and his personal moral code of behavior. And he was better prepared to handle any future situations that he felt were race linked.

THE QUESTIONS

Throughout the conversation, Rasheed's father persisted in asking questions: about evidence, multiple perspectives, connections and patterns, alternatives, and significance. With enough help and practice, teenagers can develop the habit of asking themselves these questions, becoming more confident each time about handling race-linked situations. Asking these questions can help parents, too, as they grow in understanding and learn how to support their children.

Depending on the situation, here are some questions that will stimulate and encourage clear thinking and analysis.

Evidence

- How do you know what you know? What is your evidence? Is your evidence credible? How do you assess the evidence of others?

Perspectives

- What does the situation look like from the other person's perspective?

- Whose perspective will be privileged, favored, or believed? Why?

- Whose perspective is being silenced, ignored, or lost? Why?

- What do you learn when you look at the situation from the other person's perspective?

- Does one of the perspectives appear to hold more power?

Connections

- How do the attitudes, feelings, and behaviors connect? Why are they connected? What is cause and what is effect? Where have we seen or heard this before?

Alternatives

- What if things were different? What would it be like if you were treated fairly, honestly? Imagine what would be the fair, just, caring way to be treated in this situation.

Relevance

- What does this matter? What difference does it make? Who cares? Why?

The chart shows how Rasheed's father carefully and intentionally framed his questions to support the model.

PARENT: What's the problem? RASHEED: The summer job program treats the black kids different from the white kids. PARENT: What's your evidence? How do you know?		***Read it***
RASHEED: I see the black kids working in maintenance and in the kitchen all summer while the white kids get to work in all kinds of jobs all over the hospital. And that's unfair.	**EVIDENCE** *How do you know what you know?*	
PARENT: Why do you think this is so? RASHEED: Maybe they think the white kids are smarter, or better than us . . . I don't know. So the hell with them.	**VIEWPOINT** *What do things look like from the other person's perspective?*	
PARENT: And that makes you mad, huh? RASHEED: Yeah it makes me mad. They're stereotyping—they just think we're dumb and lazy. They don't care about us.	**CONNECTIONS** *(helping teen to identify feelings)*	***Name it***
PARENT: And you probably feel cheated, devalued—like your work isn't worth as much as the white kids. Like you don't deserve a higher level of work experience. RASHEED: Yeah. So I stopped working.	*How are these ideas connected? Where have you heard these ideas before?*	

PARENT: You got mad and you stopped working. RASHEED: Yeah, that's right. I ain't no chump. PARENT: Did you talk to your supervisor about this? Did you ask him to explain why the white kids seem to have different jobs than you black kids? Did you tell him you were mad and had some questions about what was going on? RASHEED: Nope. What's talking to him gonna do?	*Establishing cause and effect: Do you see how your feelngs caused you to behave the way you did?* ALTERNATIVES *Were there other ways to handle your feelings?*	**Oppose it**
PARENT: So you didn't talk to him; you just stopped working. And what do you think your supervisor thought then? Rasheed, put yourself in your supervisor's shoes. What does your refusal to work look like from his perspective? RASHEED: I don't know. I guess it looks like we're lazy and don't wanna work. But we aren't. PARENT: That's right. But who's gonna know that? And who gets hurt when you refuse to work? RASHEED: I don't know. Me I guess.	PERSPECTIVE *What do you see when you look at your actions from his perspective?* *Whose point of view is silenced or will be ignored?* RELEVANCE/ SIGNIFICANCE *Why and how are your actions important? What does it matter that you quit working?*	**Assess strategy**

PARENT: You got that right. Man, I understand you were angry, you felt your supervisor was stereotyping you. You got frustrated, but then what did you do? You stopped working. You said, that boss treated me wrong, I'm gonna do wrong. And Rasheed, you know that ain't right.	CONNECTIONS *(helping teen to see how his feelings, attitude, and behaviors are connected)*
You gotta know your actions made it bad for you and your buddies. it just fed right into any racist ideas that man mightta had. What else could you have done? RASHEED: I don't know.	PERSPECTIVES *How do your behaviors contribute to other people's negative beliefs about racial differences?*

PARENT: All right. Well then, let's take a minute and try and figure out what would have been better for you to have done.	ALTERNATIVES *How could things be different? How would you act, think, feel if you were treated fairly?*	**Replace it**

THE IMPORTANCE OF TALKING ABOUT RACE

I came up with the four-step model while talking and listening to black teenagers and their parents discuss the ways they try to design resistance strategies in their lives. The teenagers recognized how valuable conversations with their parents about race are, especially as a connection between their current lives and future aspirations. According to parents and teenagers alike, these conversations are essential in helping black children to know their racial reality. It is because of conversations like these, the teenagers said, that they have learned to recognize that some things, like relationships with white individuals, have changed, and that others, like the prevalence of racism, have not.

When I asked them why they thought their parents were willing to share this information with them, their general response was, "Because they want me to know." Sandra, a 15-year-old in Boston, was more specific. She said that her mother wants her to be able to deal with the stresses associated with racism. Sandra's mom put it this way: "I want you to know what I went through, so you don't have to do it, too. If there's anything bad, I don't want you to go through that."

Studies have shown that not only are we black parents acutely aware of the reality of racism in our own lives, but many of us share our personal experiences of discrimination with our children. We do this because we believe it is our responsibility to tell our children the truth about the world around them, to teach them that they will probably face discrimination in their lifetime and that they must be prepared. Yes, we parents heard those same messages when we were growing up, but times are different now. According to black baby-boomer parents, the buck-up, grin-and-bear-it days we came of age in are over. Those aren't the messages we want to pass to our children.

One dad in Boston, his voice escalating as he emphatically pounded his fist on the table, told me, "I tell my boys don't let nobody walk all over you!" That proud and defiant self-respect has a greater urgency now that it is part of our parenting agenda. The difficult task is to communicate this will to resist to our children while at the same time teaching them to be ever mindful of where they are now and where they want to be, and the consequences of missteps.

We do this by talking with our children, even when we're tired, even when it's painful, even when we'd rather not. We do it by instilling racial pride and self-respect, and by helping our children to imagine other ways of being than those presented by the larger Eurocentric culture. Most important, within these intimate, sometimes difficult conversations, we shower them with love as a protective buffer against the negativity they encountered and will encounter again.

It's not enough to make time to talk. It's also critical that we learn how to talk about these matters in ways that will engage and help our youth. There are important differences between our own adolescence and our children's, and much we can learn from each other. Our teenagers know the particularities of the racial reality they must navigate, and we, as parents, have a greater understanding of how best to effectively resist. Working together, applying the model, asking thoughtful questions, we can engage in the process of co-constructing a knowledge base that allows our teenagers to draw meaning from experiences and fashion healthy, effective resistance.

Arlene, the 15-year-old daughter of a small-business owner, finds strength in the intergenerational perspectives offered by her parents to help her make sense of the sociopolitical world. She holds tight to her parents' wisdom. She told me,

> You know, my parents don't always come out and say, "You're black and you need to watch out" or things like that, but they always try and prepare me. My father, I know, has been through a lot to get where he is today. He's been cheated, taken advantage of, and he just had to work extra hard to get where he is. I can't say for sure, but if he was a white man, I think he would have gone up there much faster. And in instances where he was just as intelligent, if not more so than another person, in a job offer, because of his race, he wasn't given the same opportunity. I can't tell you how they did it, but they've instilled in me that I need to be prepared. I know I'm going to have to work a little bit harder to get ahead.

Audrey, 16 years old, said this about the value of conversations with her mother about race:

> A lot of times we learn together. My mom hasn't dealt with whites as much as I have. She grew up in the projects. She didn't have to deal with a lot of white people. She was always, like, in the black atmosphere. She went to work, she worked with them, then she came home. She didn't have to deal with them on a regular basis, like we do at school. I don't think she ever had to really deal with being around them as much as I have to deal with it now.
>
> I think that the things that she does tell me, it sinks in. Knowing that someone black is also sharing what they know with you.... If they share with me what they know and I share it with somebody else, and they share it with somebody, soon everybody should know.

George put it this way:

Me and my parents, we try to keep a close bond where it's like they're educated in what I'm doing. It's like we share knowledge. I'm sharing knowledge with them that I'm gaining, and they're sharing knowledge with me that they have. So, its like we're exchanging views.

And Karen described it like this:

As I get older, I take what my parents said to me and I take what I also believe, like what I see around me, and I kind of use that together and make my own justifications.

What Audrey, George, and Karen allude to is a collaboratively constructed knowledge base, wherein African American families—parents and teenagers together—participate in producing political perspectives and ideological truths that allow our children to become appropriately socialized to be in, and relate to, the many cultures they must navigate. As these youngsters attest, they are teaching their parents about their particular racial worlds, knowledge they've gained through interactions with people within and outside of the black community. This process provides a knowledge base from which black teenagers and their parents can build effective resistance strategies and invites our children into the community of resisters, transmitting across generations the truths they need to know to come to trust themselves as sources of knowledge now and in the future.

Many teenagers told me that their parents used conversations as an opportunity to instill racial pride and build self-esteem, the foundation upon which a healthy self-concept is built.

John, a 14-year-old, explained,

I see both of my parents as being successful and overcoming the odds. It's not hard for me to talk to them about some of the things I encounter because maybe somewhere down the line they've seen some of the same things, and of course, they got over them. Once you get out into the world, you're going to hear things that you have to have the pride to back you up. That's something I was given at a very early age. I was never told that "you can't do this because you're black," or even "you can't do this because you're too small." I was always allowed to try. My parents didn't refer to the black race in any derogatory ways. I think that helped me out a lot in my early age, not to hear those things. My parents still identify themselves with the black race. Knowing that, seeing them in the black community and in the black church, they set an example for me throughout the black community.

Over and over, the teenagers I talk to say that along with traditional mainstream values such as a strong work ethic, the value of educational achievement, and a solid moral foundation, their parents talk with them about feeling proud of their race, knowing their racial heritage of struggle to overcome the odds, and maintaining and drawing strength from their racial identity and connections.

When I asked Wakim, a 17-year-old, "Why is it important to talk about these things?" he said,

If something isn't told to you over and over again, you may forget it—and you don't really want to forget about the best part of your heritage. [It's also important to remember] how people have struggled to get to the point they are now—and to remember . . . the will to continue to succeed and to lift up the race instead of keeping it in the mud.

Sean, a young sophomore in a large public high school in Boston, Massachusetts, explained that his parents

tell me about racism, slavery, and how we got here—why we have racism, why some white people hate black people. They tell me about my history. Even though we got here through slavery, they tell me just to be proud of myself and be proud of who I am. That's what I've always been conscious of. The way I was raised, I wasn't taught black pride, black power. But I was taught the power of being black, you know. Learn about who you are and also learn about everybody else because we're not the only class who had to struggle. Like the Native Americans, they had to face many of the same problems we had. They always taught me what I needed to know to survive in the world, so that when I would encounter something, I'd be able to handle it, since I was taught to handle it.

As parents, we guide our children's moral behavior by our example and by what we say in our conversations with them about matters like racism and racial justice. But we can't limit these conversations to racism and victimization. We must help our children imagine the alternative, and free them to imagine how it would be if we as a people were treated and were to treat others fairly all the time, in a just and caring manner.

Psychologists who have studied resiliency—the capacity to bounce back after problems and trauma—say that teenagers who have caring adults who are actively engaged in their lives are more resilient. Caring for our teenagers and engaging in their lives by helping them create and adopt healthy resistance strategies will surely aid their resilience. Endowing our teenagers with these strategies gives them a sense of pride in their ability to handle the stresses of their racial reality, and a feeling of confidence and readiness to handle the next race-related stress that comes along.

The more we talk to our children about racial matters the better. In times of conflict, the more that we can encourage our children to carefully analyze their racial reality, and adopt a problem-solving model that asks them to read it, name it, oppose it, and replace it, the greater the chances that they will internalize these steps and eventually be able to wield these techniques on their own and teach them to others.

Jump-Starting Conversations about Racism

Conversations with our children about race are not always easy or comfortable. For some of us, the hardest part is getting the conversation started. Here are a number of guidelines, gathered from parents, for having effective talks about race with teenagers:

- *Above all, keep the lines of communication open.* This means be ready to talk about racial matters whenever they may come up, no matter how tired you are, or how inconvenient the setting. Maybe your teenager or your teenager's friends will initiate the conversation, or maybe you will have to raise the issues for them.

- *Be supportive of teens' developing capacity to understand, reason about, and evaluate moral issues like racism and sexism.*

- *Be honest about how painful the reality of racism truly is,* and about the difficult feelings that discussions of racism can arouse in both parents and teens. Be sure to address and validate these feelings in a sensitive way.

- *Emphasize the positive when you can do so truthfully.* Help teens acknowledge that there is something that they can do, that they are not powerless victims. They may need you to create and present alternatives.

- *When a particular situation arises, get as much information as you can about what has happened.* By asking your teenagers questions and soliciting their views and opinions, you not only gather the information you need to be able to create effective resistance strategies, but you also help your child to develop increasingly sophisticated analytical and moral reasoning skills.

- *Remember, while it seldom helps to overtly criticize teenagers for the way they think or behave, you may sometimes have to confront your child with his or her behavior.* Parents need to help their teenagers to understand how they may be rationalizing their actions. They may be working with an inaccurate theory, or with immature reasoning. If so, they need an adult to present them with new facts and help the teens absorb them. The goal is to help them gain the awareness they need to dispel their inaccurate or inappropriate beliefs.

- *Share your own stories of resistance and resilience with your teenagers,* particularly in times of crisis or when you are focusing on reading, naming, opposing, and replacing. Telling these stories of struggle and triumph can foster psychological and spiritual strength by instilling a sense of family and cultural pride. Sharing stories also demonstrates to our children that they, too, are connected to a long and rich legacy of powerful and resilient black people, a legacy that can help them stay rooted, focused, and self-assured. If you don't have these stories in your own life to share, watching television programs and movies about African Americans together with your children can provide a good starting point for conversation. Black literature is also a good source of examples of resistance and resilience that can serve as conversation starters for black teens and parents. You can use the resource list at the back of this book for suggestions.

- *Set limits around resistance,* through the example of your own behavior and by establishing guidelines for your family to follow. This means you must be willing to reflect upon and adjust your own behavior around issues of resistance. Ask yourself, What kind of model do I provide when my children watch me interacting with the world? Am I thoughtful, self-validating, culturally affirming, and standing firm against the negative cultural forces that shape our lives? Or am I engaged in self-destructive, defensive, self-loathing behaviors that may betray my own confusion and despair?

- *Assure your child of your love.* Research suggests that the assurance of love is an essential protective buffer that can mitigate the effect of the negative beliefs about blacks that our children encounter. We have to, as the cultural critic bell hooks says, "love one another to death." Along with building our children's self-esteem and self-confidence, we must teach them a self-love that purposefully promotes racial connection and instills racial pride and group esteem. We must always remember that we are on a social trajectory; and while it is true that may of us are still struggling with basic survival issues and that there is much more work to do, we must keep in mind that when we work together and stay headed in the right direction, we will achieve our goal. To that end, we must always be critical of the present yet optimistic about the future.

DEALING WITH HARD FEELINGS

Many parents and teenagers told me about conflicts and dilemmas that required them to deal with the difficult and painful emotions so often associated with racial discrimination and historical oppression. They talked about race-related anger and frustration often in the context of discussions about black youth crime, and viewed these emotions as a direct or indirect cause of interpersonal violence. Depression and despair were usually linked to the "quick fixes" of substance abuse and sexual irresponsibility, and fear was seen as limiting options and curtailing future plans. The sum of their thinking is, If we don't talk as families about our feelings regarding race, it increases the likelihood that our children may become overwhelmed by these feelings. It also increases the possibility that over time they may become tolerant of racism.

We want our teenagers to adopt a strategy of approaching these emotions directly—identifying and understanding their source. To counteract despair, we must teach them to develop and work toward goals.

Alvin, a 16-year-old from a large eastern city, told me a disturbing story about a time that adults failed to respond to an opportunity to help him deal with racism:

> We was going inside this gym, but it wasn't opened, and so we was waiting for the guy to come and open the door. We was outside playing, and then these two dudes walked up and told me to get off the court. I wouldn't move, and they just started throwing bottles at me. And then they hit me in the head, and I started bleeding. So some [white] lady came over and took me into the store and got me a towel. She kept asking me who done it to me, and I said, "some white guy." And she was like, "You shouldn't have been over there." But I said it was [a public] recreation center. So then she didn't say nothing because she was mad.

The situation didn't improve much when Alvin finally made it home. His mother was understandably upset, at his injuries and at his story. But, the boy told me, she wouldn't talk about the incident with him. Like the woman who had brought him the towel, she was too angry to form the words. Their anger had shut both women down. And although this was a sad but golden opportunity for learning about how to respond effectively to a racial attack, all Alvin learned was that life is often dangerous and that he shouldn't frequent a public gym on the white side of town.

Physical attacks cause many of us to fight back, or at least to want to, but some of us, like Alvin's mother, freeze in the face of conflict, missing the opportunity to teach. Subtle, nonviolent racism—like the seating arrangement in a classroom, or the distribution of awards based on a subjective system—is even harder to predict and decipher, or to battle appropriately or effectively. But like more blatant racism, it arouses anger and frustration. Children desperately need guidance about how to deal with race-related anger and frustration, from whatever source it arises.

Many parents suggest a "walk away" strategy, which helps their children understand the consequences of hate and the value of respecting others even when that respect is not returned. Hakim, a teenage boy in Albuquerque, told me how his parents presented this strategy to him:

My parents say, "Don't let every little thing bother you. They probably want you to argue with them, to get in a fight with them just to cause trouble. [They say] try to stay away from those kind of things. Don't stand there arguing with some bonehead. Don't bring yourself down to their level. Don't give in any more than you have to. Just walk away from it."

One North Carolina mother told me how hard it was for her teenage son to come to terms with his angry feelings about white people, and about her talks with him. "Ma," he told her, "they're stupid. I hate white people." That her son harbored feelings of hatred toward anyone was a troublesome matter for her, a Christian. She confessed that it was a struggle to get him to change his mind. "I talk to my son about race," she told me, "and he has told me more than once that white people are crazy and that he hates them. All of them. And I said, 'Son, you don't have to love them, but you've got to be on this earth with them, so it would be better for both of you if you got along.' I said, 'Nobody's asking you to love white people, but you've got to work with them, get along with them, respect them, and demand that they respect you. And that's all that's required.'"

Similarly, Randy, a 15-year-old, described the fury—or "flood of negatives," as he described it—that sometimes burdens him, and contrasted his own perspectives on racial matters with those held by his mother. "I don't look at things the same way as my mom," he said. "When I turn on the TV and hear about whites ganging up on one black guy and stuff like that, I get real mad. And I just want to take it out on anybody white. I just feel as though I should take it out on all of them. But my mother tells me I can't take it out on all white people. And I sometimes listen, and sometimes I don't."

Learning to handle emotions intelligently, especially the emotions of anger and frustration, are critical skills for teenagers. So is summoning the strength and self-control to walk away from a fight. The psychologist Martin Seligman, who has studied the effects of optimistic and pessimistic attitudes toward adversity, suggests that parents teach their children to counter pessimistic interpretations of situations with questions such as, What is the evidence for my belief? What are other, less destructive ways to look at this? What is the usefulness of this belief? As Seligman advises, it's important to "focus on the changeable, the specific, and the non-personal causes" of a situation. Then parents and children together can come up with alternative explanations and ways to handle problems in the future.

Talking about, interpreting, and converting anger into personal and social action defuses its destructiveness and channels the energy behind it into productivity rather than negativity. How to do it? First of all, it's important to listen to what your child has to say without passing judgment. After the problem is out on the table, anger and all, you can talk to and be with your teenager as he or she struggles to make sense of these powerful emotions. You can also help your teenagers see that they have choices about how to react to events. Helping teenagers "chill out" like this serves the critical purpose of reducing the immediate stress of anger and frustration, allowing them to replace their negative thoughts with positive, self-affirming ones that are focused on the future—searching for the doors that are open rather than wasting time on the ones that are closed.

As Mrs. Douglas told me, "We attempt to teach our children not to take ownership of somebody else's craziness." When we pass messages like these on to our teenagers, we help them sustain the desire to stay motivated, to keep on pushing, to bounce back and try again—and again. Most important, when we teach our teenagers not to hate, we help them to love themselves all the more.

When our teenagers turn to us for support or to discuss difficult or painful race-related situations, they need to feel safe and secure. It can be difficult, but it's best to try to remain calm during discussions like these. You will be able to think more clearly, and your demeanor will have a calming effect on your child. A word of caution: Sometimes teenagers may act as though they don't want to discuss these issues, but the reality may be that they are observing you to make sure that you are really listening and that you care. So listen carefully. And ask questions, not just to determine who is right or wrong in a situation, but to help you understand your teenager's thoughts on the issue, which may well be different from yours. Over time, and with practice and experience, your teenager will develop a repertoire of skills and a mastery of effective resistance.

DEVELOPMENTAL CONSIDERATIONS

When we talk with our teenagers, it's important to remember that at any given time, different teenagers are at different levels of racial consciousness. Some have little or no thoughtful, organized ideas about race; the subject is nowhere near their consciousness. Adolescents like these tend to be preteenagers or in their early teens—although they may be older—and have often led sheltered childhoods with few race-related conflicts. Not surprisingly, there has been little talk about race in their families. This may be because concrete and specific race-related issues directly affecting the child haven't yet come up. Or if they have, they've been dismissed. Regretably, adolescents with limited racial awareness may be more vulnerable to racism. When confronted with it they may use up valuable psychic energy denying what's around them.

Other teenagers have a greater, but still limited, sense of their racial reality. They know racism exists and may have a vague sense that they themselves have been treated unfairly, or know other black people who have been. These teens need help putting the pieces together. They need our guidance in naming what they see and considering what next steps are appropriate.

More fortunate are the teenagers who are consciously aware of their racial environment. These teenagers tend to be knowledgeable about racism. They know how to identify it and are willing to call it when they see it. These teens need our continued support and validation. These are the future adults who, if we train them well, will be the leaders of their peer groups. At some point, we hope, they will help other African Americans navigate their racial reality in positive, caring, and consistent ways.

We need to remember that children develop different capacities at different points in their lives, and that the information we give them about race should begin modestly and simply and grow more complex over time. Younger teens experience intense and volatile feelings, and constantly shift between feeling powerful and powerless. They often need considerable help recognizing and controlling their emotions. When we talk with them about our racial reality, we should expect strong, often painful, race-related emotions to surface. We need to teach them to cope with these emotions by refusing to allow them to equate their disappointments with psychological destruction.

It helps these younger teens if we break our messages into small pieces, decoding attitudes and behaviors in the context of real situations. We need to help them put situations in perspective, helping them understand how attitudes and behaviors of the past influence attitudes and behaviors today. We also have to teach them what we know, to give them a knowledge base about race that includes our history as well as the reality of our contemporary social and political conditions. We must help them develop their own understanding of what it means to be a black man or a black woman—a member of the group—and to comprehend the power issues that are related to our minority status. We must also help our younger teenagers understand how to carefully and accurately make connections among their attitudes, feelings, and behaviors.

Perspective taking, which requires recognition that someone else's point of view may be different from one's own, is also developmental, and a teenager's capacity to comprehend this grows in sophistication with the passage of time. In order to understand another perspective, a teenager needs to be able to analyze the factors that may account for these differences. Older teens are better able to appreciate the various roles, perceptions, and feelings of other people, but younger teens may need help putting themselves in another person's shoes and understanding their feelings and motivations around race. Again, adult supervision and guidance in building these skills are key.

As our teenagers grow older and gain experience decoding their racial world and establishing healthy resistance strategies, we can feel more confident that they are able to bring forth their successes and handle their failures on their own. But our task isn't done. They still need our encouragement and support, especially as they take on the work of evaluating their own skills and strategies. They need to know to ask themselves questions like these: Is my strategy merely self-serving, or is it something more than that? Is my analysis helping me feel powerful and in control of the situation? Do I know my options? Is my perception of reality clear and reasonable and am I comfortable with it?

An Anthem of Resistance

I carry with me a story that I treasure. Like an amulet, I keep it near, and touch it for strength and encouragement. It stands for all that I hope we as parents can instill in our children through the force of our example and the strength of our conversations.

Sharon, the 17-year-old woman who told me her story, was from Albuquerque. A few months earlier, she explained, she had auditioned to sing the national anthem at her school's largest sports event of the season. The school's athletic director had chosen her from a field of many others, and had been enthusiastic at her audition. Then the big day arrived. About ten minutes before Sharon was scheduled to sing, the same athletic director came down into the pit where she waited and said, "You'll do great. Have fun, but just try not to sing it too . . . you know."

"No. I don't know," I told him. "What are you talking about?" And
he said, "Just don't make it a jazz piece." And then he gets this very
condescending tone of voice and continues. "See, a couple of years
ago a black girl sang the national anthem, and she sang it to the
point where no one could even understand it. It was just a bunch of
frills and groans and grunts." I just looked at him. I couldn't believe
he was saying this. So he walks off, and then in a few minutes he re-
turns and asks, "Are you ready? Remember, you're going to sing it
right, aren't you?" I said, "I'm going to sing it my way." So he says,
"Well, we don't need you to sing it if you're going to sing it that way."
Now here I am stressing—I have thirty seconds before I have to get
out there and sing in front of a stadium full of people and I don't
know . . . if I sing this song "black" is he gonna come and take the
mike away from me?

I asked Sharon what was going through her mind during what she had
described as the longest half minute in her life. She told me that she prayed,
and then she asked herself:

Should I be black or should I be white? Not that I could be white
physically, but in terms of the song. So I got up there and I sang the
first two bars very white and then . . . then something just came over
me. It was worse than what I was going to do! I wasn't going to be
that black . . . and if he hadn't said that to me, it would have been fine.
But he did, and I . . .

I asked her if she thought she had done the right thing, and she explained. "I know I did, because it felt so good. Not only do I have the right
to sing my own way, but if that happens to be in the Afro-American heritage
that I've acquired, I'm just going to do it that way." And then Sharon lowered her voice and sat up straight in her chair and declared, "And I believe
that was a stand for being black."

Throughout our time together Sharon had spoken to me of stories told
and lessons learned in her family about racism, race relations, and racial
identity. Her parents, who were themselves strong and defiant role models
of resistance, appear to have successfully nurtured Sharon's psychological
growth, emotional maturity, and strong self-esteem. According to Sharon,
her parents neither sugar-coated nor avoided the truth about racism. They

are models of a parenting style that integrates a liberating truth-telling into their repertoire of racial socialization strategies.

As Sharon's parents knew, children's issues are our issues. Matters of race affect both parent and child. The act of reconciling racial expectations with racial reality, and developing strategies to make that happen, creates in both parents and teenagers a unity of purpose and resolve.

Most important, we must place faith in our history of resistance. Ours is a legacy of standing up, fighting back, speaking out, and asserting our moral authority in the face of continuing injustice, intolerance, and ignorance. It is a legacy we can never abandon. Our children face a new kind of racism, with far fewer of the community supports that once nurtured black youth into responsible adulthood. When we teach our children to understand racism; when we take the time to teach them to read it, name it, oppose it, and replace it; when we help them to have the psychological strength to be resilient in its face, to speak up, to build community in new ways, and to always remember to "know what we know," we sow the seeds of resistance. We arm them not only to survive in a racist reality, but also to flourish, make new gains, and create genuine, ineradicable change.

PART TWO

5

GROWING UP FEMALE

Teenagers spend much of their time in developmental turmoil. Everything is changing, from their bodies, to their relationships with their families, to their sense of right and wrong. They are making critical decisions in their lives, about education and career, who their friends are, and who they are themselves. They are questioning and shaping and reshaping themselves, finding out who they want to be, who they feel they should be, and who they will become.

With the onset of puberty—that hormonal explosion that seems to arrive with all the suddenness and chaotic force of a hurricane—biochemical and physical changes occur at breakneck speed. There's an often-staggering growth spurt, accompanied by a maturing of the reproductive system, followed by the struggle to feel comfortable in a newly acquired, often mysterious adult body.

Adolescents make tremendous cognitive leaps as well, which allow them to organize how they think and feel in dynamic new ways. Now they can think critically about the world around them and their place in it. Their new capacity for abstract thought lets them hold on to several varying and possibly contradictory points of view at the same time. For black teenagers this often means an increasing awareness of the hypocrisy inherent in a society that preaches justice while practicing discrimination, a society that calls for tolerance yet practices exclusion. I have found that attitudes held by black teens about their racial, gender, and social class identities are closely tied to their growing understanding of the political world.

And the world is indeed a difficult place for most black teenagers and their families today. In 1994, a survey of over 1,000 black adults and 421

black children from 11 to17 found that 80 percent of parents and 64 percent of black youth believed that times for them are tough. Seventy-seven
percent of black adults and over half of black youth worry that they or a
family member will be a victim of violence. And a full quarter of the children surveyed are not optimistic that they can achieve the future they desire, even if they do work hard. To compound problems for today's black
teens, there is a persistent narrative of crisis that pathologizes them. The
transgressive, rebellious, risk-taking "problem" teen is defined as the norm,
and admirable traits of ordinary black adolescents are ignored or given little attention.

But families that are making concerted efforts to prepare their children
well to stay confident, be productive, and make change in a racist world do
exist. During my interviews I began to understand how some teenagers are
able to rise above social pressures and expectations to make their own decisions about what is or isn't the right or wrong way to be black. For the
black teenagers with whom I talked, adolescence is a period of renegotiation of social relationships and power dynamics. It is this renegotiation,
which often demands a redefinition of the self, that finally allows teenagers
to make independent and, we hope, healthy decisions about who they are
and what they believe. Parents can help their teenagers navigate this rocky
terrain.

In these chapters I explore what black parents of teenagers—and the
teenagers themselves—say are the skills necessary to grow up confident and
secure in one's identity as an African American, ready and able to resist externally imposed definitions of blackness. While there is overlap between
the information parents hope to impart to both teenage boys and girls
about gender-identity development, there are a host of issues that are gender specific.

Just as resistance is critical to the construction of personal and racial
identity, it is critical to the formation of gender identity as well. Effective
parenting helps young black women and men determine what to take a
stand for and what to resist. And although resistance plays a role in gender
identity whether you are male or female, the role is different for each. Much
of what I learned about the development of gender identity in girls came in
answer to my questions about what it means to be black and a woman, and
the kinds of messages parents and teenagers felt best prepared teenage girls
to be healthy black women. In subsequent chapters I turn to the specific
issues of young black males.

The Path Toward Womanhood

How many of us as little girls dancing at the edge of a circle of adult women were hushed by our mamas and aunties, shooed away and told to stop jumping into adult conversations, admonished for being "too womanish," a bit too grown for our own good? Surrounded by black women who spoke their minds, we wanted to speak ours, too. But we needed to learn that you earn your place in the community of strong, willful, and assertive black women.

The developmental task of younger school-age children—around the ages of 7 to 12—is to learn and master a host of social and physical skills. At this age our children interact with others more in schools, on sports teams, and in other extracurricular activities. Social comparison becomes key, with a focus on competencies: what they and their friends can or cannot do. They learn to observe each other, and are almost constantly assessing their abilities, appearance, and behavior—usually in relation to those around them. During this time they must develop an understanding of the masculine and feminine social roles they will soon acquire and internalize. They begin to develop attitudes toward social groups, including their own. They also develop an understanding of, and attitudes about, social institutions and their place in them. As children approach and undergo adolescence, these competencies and inquiries start to shift. Working to establish their separate identities and to become independent of their parents, their focus turns inward, to the classic self-absorption of adolescence.

What I wanted to know as I explored the terrain of black teenage girls across the country was, What does it mean to a girl at this time in her life to be a black woman?

Arlene is a 16-year-old daughter of a friend. She lives in a pretty, tree-lined section in the outskirts of Albuquerque. Although she was quiet when our conversation began, as she continued to talk about growing up black in racially isolated Albuquerque (only 2 percent of the 2,000 students in her school were African American), she grew animated and was clearly eager to share with me her newly developing sense of identity. She told me that to her, being a black woman meant "a lot of different things. My mother instilled the meaning of a fierce pride in being black and being who I am."

Arlene, like many other young black women interviewed by me and other researchers, was proud of the messages her mother, her aunts, and her mother's female friends had passed on to her about traditional African

American values such as cooperation, collective responsibility, interdependence, and group loyalty. As Arlene put it, talking with her elders about the necessity of being assertive, powerful, independent, and resilient filled her with pride in herself and in her racial group. That pride is directly related to the value black women place on developing strength—of knowing that things will be tough, but that the woman, mother, or family that survives will be the one with sufficient inner resources not only to withstand the adversities, but also to create the conditions under which women and their families can flourish.

Establishing this prized sense of identity is a critical task of adolescence. Without it, a teenager runs the risk of confusion about the adult role she will adopt, and may even shy away from taking on an adult role at all. Black teenagers need to anticipate the multiple roles they will have to embrace in the near and distant future, as student, spouse, parent, and worker. Instead of fearing these roles, they need to feel competent to assume the roles and their related tasks successfully. Moreover, they need to be able to resist self-doubt and simply be themselves, and to know how to affiliate, to be in communion with others rather than isolated and alone.

As one mother, Mrs. Young, told me,

> I think it's important that black girls know that they don't need to get their verification from men. Whatever is going to make them happy has to make them happy by themselves. Whatever they do in life, that has to be their choice, and they must know that they do have choices. So it has to be that they're doing it because they love themselves that much, to be doing it.

She went on to explain that she uses this notion of self-love to motivate her children as well as to castigate them when they do wrong.

> I see it as a positive message, and I use it when I punish my kids. I say, "What's going on here? You know, you don't love yourself enough. You wouldn't be riding around, out in the street doing what you were doing, if you loved yourself. What's going on?" And it worked. Oh yes, it worked.

Adolescence is truly a period of self-creation. When I think about this process, I'm reminded of the time, while I waited for a meeting with a high-school guidance counselor, I watched a small group of black girls descend the staircase. One of them, a dark-skinned teenager with large eyes, bright red lipstick, and long, braided, platinum-blonde extensions, brushed past me. The counselor, softly giggling as she read my face, whispered in my ear, "The blonde? That's Roshanda. We never know what she's gonna look like. Next week that hair might be blue." I quickly entered her office, stifling my own chuckles as I reminded myself that adolescence is truly a time of making and remaking the self; a time of precariously balancing restraint against excesses, of constantly trying to respond to the "who am I?" each day.

For black girls especially, it is also a time to recognize, explore, and integrate the multiple identities of race, class, and gender. To do this they look to us, their mothers, grandmothers, aunts, and other grown women for help in shaping the personal fortitude—the independence, inner strength, and perseverance—they will need to undertake the struggle.

Research studies bear out that black teenage girls are especially equipped to withstand the struggles toward identity and self-respect that come with adolescence. The American Association of University Women's study of girls' self-esteem found that although American girls overall suffer a drop in self-esteem during adolescence, the drop is not nearly as pronounced in black girls. Similarly, the September 1997 Commonwealth Fund Survey of Adolescent Girls, a survey of a nationally representative classroom sample of over 3,500 girls in grades 5 through 12, found that black girls showed signs of strong mental health, with more than half of them indicating high self-confidence and 83 percent exhibiting few or no depressive symptoms. According to these findings, many black girls feel confident, competent, and ready to take on the challenges of adulthood, despite their devalued racial and gender status.

Marva, a 17-year-old I talked to in Raleigh, finds that being a black woman is exciting as well as a source of pride:

> It really is, because I listened to what my mom would tell me about what life was like when she was 17 years old, and I think of all the different opportunities that I have, and all the different chances and things that I have that she never had, and the things that I can do that she couldn't do, and you know, the things that are accepted now that weren't accepted then. And it's—it feels great, because I think about it and it's like, if I were ever to have kids, they're going to have so much more than I have, especially the girls, I mean, because . . . first

of all, being black, and then being a woman, is a big setback to begin with, and there are so many intelligent black women out there today that are role models, that it's—it just makes you feel good, because you stand out, especially when you do something good.

She attributes much of her positive attitude and strength of identity to the examples set by other women in her family:

Every year, we have a family reunion on my mom's side and this past year was the big one. I went back and I saw my family, and I saw everything that they were doing, and—especially the females in my family, how strong they were—and I realized, and I said, "Hey, I'm just like them." I mean, I can do just exactly what they're doing. They're so independent. They are going out and doing exactly what they need to do. And they are in control of their lives, and nobody can tell them otherwise, and that was the big turning point. And it made me say, "Hey, when I want to do something, I can do it," and there's nobody out there who should be able to stop me.

I asked Felicia, another 17-year-old, to tell me what being black meant to her.

It means that I have to work harder to succeed in what I want to succeed in, and it means that I have to—because basically it's hard being a black woman because of all the racism and everything, so I have to work very hard to do the things that I want.

Felicia, like other girls her age, is aware of the ways in which the social systems in which she lives disempower her. She uses that social knowledge to calculate her strengths and weaknesses to deal with the limitations she faces. Girls who shared with me this awareness of double jeopardy—the effects of gender *and* race—seem to have a heightened level of introspection and self-examination. They, more than others, have made sense of this knowledge in ways that suggest that it has become part of their identity.

"If I had a daughter," one 16-year-old told me, "the first thing I would tell her is that it's hard enough being black. It's hard enough being a woman, and what's going to make it worse is if you don't have an education. I definitely—I would definitely stress education." She wasn't alone with this observation. Nearly all of the black girls I talk to cite education as crucial to preparing them to successfully navigate through adulthood and to helping cultivate healthy resistance attitudes and behaviors.

African American women of the baby boom generation tend to reject the traditional notions of womanhood that are equated with dependency, submissiveness, obedience, and conformity. And we pass this resistance down to our daughters as we prepare them for the multiple roles they must assume. We tell our daughters not to assume that their husbands and male friends will be solely responsible for providing and protecting. Indeed, young black girls today say they are being socialized toward both traditional (care and nurturing wife and mother) and nontraditional roles (worker and employee). We parents clearly recognize that our daughters will be at least partially, if not wholly, responsible for the financial survival of their families. We black women have always found it necessary to redefine womanhood to more accurately reflect our racial reality, and it is this knowledge that compels us to orient our daughters to the dual roles of mother and worker, and to place a high value on black women's strength and perseverance.

The sociologist K. Sue Jewell says that black women who are at the bottom of the social ladder are more likely to experience the effects of various forms of discrimination, and that these injustices are more likely to "occur simultaneously as their effects are interactive rather than interdependent." And while we know that we must help our daughters understand how gender, race, and class influence each other and how they affect the individual lives of black women, men, families, communities, we are also keenly aware that they must know and avoid unintended consequences associated with underplaying or overplaying the prevalence of racism. It's a tough job to help teens develop a consciousness of social and political context and know the constraints they are operating under, all the while staying positive enough to take calculated risks to meet their goals.

"I want them to know that they have as much of an opportunity as anyone, if they want to pursue it," Mrs. Davis told me.

I want them to know that barriers can be overcome with help. As black women they need to focus themselves, focus on what they want. Prioritize their goals. Stay involved with their family if their family is supportive, and if not, seek whatever support there is out there to help them get what they want. Never feel that they can't pursue something just because I'm black. Or that this road is blocked to me just because I'm black. Never give up. Never feel hopeless. But at the same time, you can't just put out there [the message] "You can do it" without helping show a way to do it.

Mrs. Davis's point is well taken. For a number of reasons too many black girls live in circumstances where they may not know anyone who can help them find a way out. Their families may not be available to them, or they may be in a difficult relationship with their parents, or they may be parentified teenagers, shouldering too much of the family responsibility. That's why it's important, as Mrs. Davis reminds us, for black women across social classes and geographic regions to stay connected to the community and to help one another—especially young women—reach their goals.

In healthy black families, parents nurture resistance by supporting their children's expressions of individuality, their emerging confidence, and their evolving competence. We can do this for example by encouraging our children to attend a new and unfamiliar after-school activity, or try a sport they ordinarily wouldn't (like swimming or tennis), or take a risk and socialize with kids they wouldn't ordinarily hang out with. We do this because we want our children ultimately to be able to stand on their own and negotiate the racialized world without us.

Fathers teach different kinds of lessons to their daughters. One father in North Carolina, self-described as middle class, told me that in raising his two daughters he feels he needs to socialize them to the professional world. His oldest daughter has already been elected class president, and, as most fathers would, he has high hopes for her future success. It's a world that he wants his daughters to prepare for and eventually be successful in, and he talks with them often about it, especially about the reality that it's a world dominated by competitive, usually white men.

Sometimes with my girls I try to tell them they can't respond the same way in different situations. In other words, right or wrong, I think there are a certain set of emotions that are okay in general, but if you are in a public arena, like in school or in professional meetings of some kind, I would probably not promote being emotional. I would promote being very thoughtful and reflective and calculating even.

He told me a story about being in a meeting once where several men, who were not happy with the direction the woman manager was taking the group, reacted by insulting her and undermining her authority. The woman was so rattled she had to leave the room. Mr. Grady came right home and shared the story with his daughter.

> I told my daughter, "You've got to take that." I know for a fact that when men get mad, angry or whatever, they will do that. But I tell my daughter, "You've got to learn how to deal with that, keep it inside, always look professional. No matter how wrong the man is, know that the people sitting around the table are still taking away something from the meeting about how that woman responded to the situation. And even though they can say things like, "Well, he shouldn't have said what he said; that would have made me cry too," you better know that there's something else that's being taken away. [They're thinking] "She wasn't tough enough. She couldn't handle it." So I'm trying to teach my children that race and gender are real phenomena. That you have to acknowledge it in practically all of your dealings and that you have to be sensitive to the nuances. Know how to take life situations and play it to your advantage, whatever you think those advantages might be.

Mr. Grady teaches us that building an identity is a lifelong process that doesn't begin and end in the teen years. He has learned important lessons about the meaning of being black, including the processes of repudiation and affirmation that must continue throughout life, from his personal experiences in the work world. And he is passing these lessons on to his daughters, providing them with the psychological resources to be successfully resistant in the future.

Some messages parents pass on to their daughters are intended to help them identify and tap, when necessary, internal supports—strength, knowledge, and fortitude—as well as external supports—parents, teachers, and other trusted adults who will listen to them, encourage them, and remind them that they have the strength to keep on keeping on. These are the supports parents have found indispensable for helping black children mediate stress, cope effectively, and stay resilient. For example, Mr. Michaels told me he wants his daughter to find her strength from within, and he tells her,

"Realize your heritage. Realize where you came from and don't try to be like everybody else. You've got something deeper and stronger in you. Don't expect things to be too easy for you. Don't expect the recognition. But when it does come, take it in a humble way. Take the applause and everything but remember that someday, further down the line you will have to fight. Your tough time is going to come and you have to be strong enough to take the bitter with the sweet."

At the same time that black baby-boomer parents are assessing and reflecting on their lives and choices, they find themselves steering their own children through the process of adolescent identity formation. It is fascinating to see how each process influences the other, and to hear how the resistance strategies boomer parents teach their children today combine the parents' reflection on their own experiences with an understanding of how the racial world is shaped differently now.

After walking away from an abusive relationship that she had endured for too many years, Mrs. Bell described how life had been difficult for her and her daughter. She had scrimped, saved, planned, sacrificed, prayed, and eventually educated herself while keeping her young daughter on the straight and narrow. Finally, after seven years, she worked her way out of the projects. When I met her she was employed as an office assistant at a large downtown firm. She told me that she wants her daughter to focus on the doors that are open rather than the blocked opportunities she will inevitably encounter.

When I first had my daughter, that gave me a totally different perspective on life, because it meant now that every decision I made or what I did not only affected me but [her, too]. [T]he main thing was that if I had a major failure or something, like if I lost my job . . . I had to regroup and I had to bounce back very fast—fast enough for her to know that you can get knocked down, and it's your choice if you want to lay there and suffer. And know that the best thing to do is to get back up and keep on, no matter how many times you get knocked down.

She also told me how hard she worked to avoid burdening her daughter unnecessarily with adults' concerns while trying to make sure that she understood the reality of the adult challenges she would one day face.

As it is with many women, Mrs. Bell's development coincided with the birth of a child. She is aware that her daughter is scrutinizing her, that she is observing the social world and how her mother navigates through it. She knows that resilience is a critical survival skill, especially if you're young, female, and poor. Her legacy to her daughter will be the ability to bounce back, maybe even stronger than before, despite the unfair sucker punches of life.

Mrs. Bell has a deeply felt understanding of what young black women, like her daughter, need. To be psychologically strong, they must develop the ability to withstand adversity, hold on to hope, keep the faith, be creative, and learn from their mistakes. To be socially smart, they must understand the sociopolitical context in which they will do battle. They need the ability to recognize opportunities and, when possible, to take advantage of them. They must also be able to understand and detect the obstacles that derail poor black women and keep them disenfranchised. She can bring her lessons of personal strength, fortitude, and resilience home to her daughter with urgency and truth; they burn through a lens that collects from three vantage points: her race, class, and gender identities. She has learned them, lived them, and believes them.

Arlene, Marva, and Felicia find strength in the intergenerational perspective. They hold tight to their parents' experiences, which they perceive as being firmly rooted in the reality they too must endure. They believe that their parents' lives exemplify survival, growth, and resilience. Girls with competent mothers and fathers feel proud to identify with parents with such desirable characteristics. And knowledge of these characteristics has helped them discern their own personal and cultural strengths.

Just as critical to a young black woman's developing sense of self and empowerment is the ability to understand and find strength in the history of African American experiences, and to see themselves as part of an upward social swing. As 17-year-old Cara told me, "Black women are improving. They're showing that they can do something in this world, and that they're more equal and they can do just as much as a guy."

Her thought was a commonly expressed one: that black people, especially black women, were on a positive social trajectory, that opportunities were opening up and black women were stepping in and taking advantage. She told me that education about black history was largely responsible for her understanding.

When I was little, I didn't think about it that much. I mean, I was just like one of the other kids, you know, either black, white, Spanish, or mulatto, and I was just one of the kids. But now, it's like—since I've been learning the history of blacks in the U.S., it was a real shock to me, because I didn't know that the history had been so bad, you know, and we suffered that much. And I think I've been learning a lot lately.

One mother's story demonstrated clearly how becoming and being black is a process that never really stops, but runs across the life cycle. And as our identities evolve, so does our understanding of resistance and what we must teach our children. Mrs. Patterson, in her late fifties, told me a story with two parts, the first about herself in the past, facing a racially charged episode with uncertainty, and the second about her life today and how she takes pride and pleasure in asserting her racial identity. She started by talking about a time when her children invited white children from an extracurricular program they attended to a birthday party at their house, which was in a black neighborhood. She described her fears for her children at the time:

> I had no problem with the inviting, but I didn't want them to be disappointed because the white kids wouldn't come. If I invited the white children and these white kids didn't show up, it could be a message that somehow they [her black children] were not worthy of them coming. That's the way they would interpret it.

She also said she had worried about how she would handle the situation, since then she'd have to confront the situation and talk about *it* (meaning racism and racial exclusion) with her children, and she wasn't sure if she or her youngsters were up for it. As she said, "I was always being protective, you know; it was a protective measure so they wouldn't be hurt." She resolved the conflict by agreeing to invite the white children, who surprised her by showing up and having a great time.

But without missing a beat, Mrs. Patterson dispensed with her recollection of insecurity and self-doubt. Sitting up straight on the sofa, her fist balled up in determination, she suddenly shifted gears into a description from more recent times that served as a vivid testimonial of her personal growth and empowerment.

> I'll tell you something. Over the past ten to fifteen years, there were little things I may have equivocated about. I don't do it anymore. Now

it's definite. When I walk into my job and say, "OK folks—we're hiring a black [employee]"—that's it. I'm the strong, black bitch in that office, so don't mess with me. That's who I am and I deliver on it.

In an instant, the lack of confidence that had framed the earlier part of her story was replaced by an image of self that was strong and unequivocal, racially decisive and proud. Choosing to tell me a story of her life in which she, as a black woman and mother, began in one place (unsure and equivocating) and landed in another (strong and defiant) is as important as the actual transformation itself. She used her racial identity as a central organizing theme for both her personal life choices and her professional work. When I talked to her she was working in the school system as an advocate for minority students. She sees that as her purpose, a calling for which she will not be guilt-tripped: "I'm there for the black kids because the whites are there for the white kids. I know damned well what I want and I don't equivocate about issues of race."

These mothers describe midlife selves that are sure of their identities. They describe themselves as tested and confident, more self-assertive, self-accepting, and kinder to themselves than they were as younger women. They understand the value of paying attention to their own needs—what they like and don't like, and what does and doesn't give them pleasure. They have firm ideas of what is important and what is not. They have learned the value of speaking up, of recovering the ability to speak within a power relationship, and the power of resilience. Above all, they understand the importance of inculcating these same skills in their children and of helping them to grow strong and certain in their identities, as individuals and as members of the community.

Resistance Strategies

Unhealthy (Short-Term, Survival-Oriented) Strategies

- Internalizing devalued racial and gender status

- Buying into definitions of womanhood that do not accurately reflect black women's racial reality

- Succumbing to self-doubt, pessimism, lack of faith, or lack of pride

- Feeling confused and fearful about assuming multiple adult roles

- Inability to bounce back after adversity

- Refusal or inability to seek support or guidance from strong and positive adult women

- Resisting by talking tough and bullying

Healthy (Long-Term, Liberating) Strategies

- Teaching children (both girls and boys) to define, know, respect, and learn to stand up for a strong, internally defined self

- Stressing racial pride

- Encouraging our daughters to be independent, connected, and resilient, and to develop skills that allow them to act effectively in a variety of settings, including predominantly white and professional settings

- Teaching our children to move to the voice that is within them, not outside of them

- Teaching our children to recognize that it's not that there is something wrong with you because you're black, but that there is something wrong with a system that systematically devalues people who are black

- Helping our daughters understand that they don't need to get their verification or sense of identity from men

- Making sure our daughters have the opportunity to spend time with strong, independent black women

- Teaching our children the history of the African American experience

- Teaching our children to love themselves

- Helping our daughters develop independence, inner strength, and perseverance

Psychologically Strong, Socially Smart

A psychologically strong, socially smart black daughter knows how to withstand adversity ("take the bitter with the sweet"), hold on to hope, keep the faith, be creative, and learn from her mistakes. She understands the sociopolitical context in which she will do battle. She is able to recognize opportunities and take advantage of them, as well as to understand and detect the obstacles designed to oppress and disenfranchise black women.

THE CHALLENGE OF LOVING YOUR LOOKS

In the early 1960s, when I was seven or eight years old, I came home from school one afternoon to discover that my mother had replaced all of my white baby dolls with black ones. No warning, no discussion—just curly-haired, pink-lipped, brown-skinned babies in the cradles where my beloved white dolls had been, like changelings in a folktale.

My mother wasn't a child psychologist; a domestic worker at the time she seldom, I think, paid much attention to things like the effects that toys manufactured for white children might have on her own colored child. But by the mid-1960s, Negro children had gained the attention of American society as never before, and my mother, like many other Negro mothers, took action. *Brown v. Board of Education* was the law of the land. Newspapers and magazines focused on the plight of the Negro child—his deplorable education and inadequate socialization. Theories about low self-esteem, cultural deprivation, and pitiable self-hatred fueled an avalanche of social science research, teacher-training programs, early-childhood projects. Public-policy initiatives like Head Start and the War on Poverty grabbed the public imagination and pocketbook. Everyone jumped on the bandwagon of the self-contempt hypothesis; pitying these poor pathetic black children became all the rage.

On the one hand, the new focus on black children was pejorative. On the other, it was illuminating: black children were finally seen—by everyone, including toy manufacturers. Negroes suddenly joined mainstream America. We were a consumer demographic, a force to be reckoned with, analyzed, sold to. Toy makers rushed to market dolls created specifically for black children, and women like my mother rushed to buy them. The ones I remember most vividly were the black Chatty Kathy and her little sister, Chatty Baby. Neither of them worked well. When you pulled the string between their shoulder blades they produced garbled, wordlike sounds—that is, until the string jammed, which it always seemed to do, and then they lost the power of speech altogether. But that didn't matter. These pretty little Negro dolls were *me*.

Over a very short course of time I acquired quite a brood of colored babies. I loved those dolls, and carried them everywhere. Unlike my vanished white dolls, whose hair I was always combing or washing or cutting (until I finally learned that it didn't grow back), my black babies had—to my mind—perfect hair. I didn't dare experiment with my new babies' beauty; I simply marveled at it. Of course, black dolls from this time looked exactly like white dolls dipped in brown paint. Their lips and noses, hair length and texture were pretty much identical to those of white dolls. The hair color was different, though. The manufacturer would start with the yellow hue and then add a little brown to it, resulting in the bizarre peanut-butter tone that Tina Turner's hairdresser would later make famous.

Despite their lack of realistic black features, I somehow saw myself in all my new baby dolls, and they made me content in a different, fuller way than the white babies ever had. I believed she could be anything I wanted her to be, and I hoped she believed the same of me.

As members of American society, a women develops her self-concept, in part, from observing and internalizing what others think about her and where they place her in the scheme of power. Consequently, the attributes society assigns to the "attractive" and "unattractive" black female have profound implications for her psychological development. As Maya, who as we spoke was flipping through a fashion magazine, scrutinizing the models, said with a deep sigh,

> I think that you hear a lot about . . . you know, if you don't have hazel
> eyes, or your hair isn't straight, or if it's not long and pretty then you
> are an ugly duck, you know. And I think that we all are pretty. You can
> have coarse hair, you can have long hair, and you're still pretty. I think
> it's all within you.

Once in a kindergarten classroom that I visited I overheard a little white girl say to her black girlfriend, "You'd be so much prettier if you were white." The implications of this message were huge—for both girls. Clearly, the white child had already internalized white standards of beauty as the sole standard by which all girls must be judged. These are the standards promoted through television, movies, advertisements, pictures in magazines and mail-order catalogues: narrow, primarily Eurocentric conceptions of beauty. The black girl—even if her parents took pains to help her understand her own beauty—received an unforgettable blow. According to everything she knew, her look was far from valued and desired. In fact, she was incapable of being pretty. Like many African American girls, she would need to struggle to accept her own dark skin and naturally kinky hair as beautiful, to resist "light, long, and lean" as the mean of beauty.

One of my undergraduates students wrote in her journal that as a young teenager she had received a scholarship to attend a predominantly white private secondary school. She was well liked and socially accepted there. But among her group of white friends she was never seen as a "girl." It wasn't that she was considered unattractive. To them she was a black woman, loads of fun to be around but completely outside of the realm of what her white peers would consider attractive *or* unattractive. She was a different "thing" altogether. She wasn't, she wrote, an "exotic," since that implies beauty, although it may be different from the reigning standard. This black girl's appearance wasn't even up for evaluation; it simply wasn't relevant because she could not be beautiful according to mainstream ideals. At parties the white girls and boys would often talk about who among their friends looked good and why, which couple looked good together, and who should go out with whom. My student was invisible in these conversations, she said. Engaging a black girl in conversations about these matters just wasn't done.

Adolescents are often conscious, constant, and hypersensitive observers of their own physical growth. Heightened self-consciousness and concerns about being personally attractive and more appealing to others are common as dating begins. For black girls, while issues of self-image and physical attractiveness arise long before the teen years, the emergence of sexuality adds a new dimension to the significance some blacks place on the length and texture of their hair, the shading of their skin, and the shape of their bodies. In addition, for many black teens, the political dimensions of hairstyling suddenly become important, because their new abstract-thinking skills provide them with complex ways to organize and understand themselves and their experiences.

In American culture, beauty is generally based on a particular combination of hair texture and color, skin color, facial features, and body size and shape. And while appearance is important to most of us, personal beauty is frequently considered the most important virtue that a woman can possess. Among women and teenage girls, beauty is a status characteristic that affects both their behavior and their understanding.

A common struggle for black girls involves their feelings about their appearance—Am I pretty enough? What black woman hasn't struggled with the process of accepting how she looks, especially when the prevalent media and popular culture notion of "rightness" seldom includes our wide noses, broad hips, kinky hair, and dark skin.

The tyranny of these beauty myths is relentless: the unachievable bouncing, well-behaved hair, Barbie-doll bodies, shiny thin-lipped smiles. The identification of beauty as defined by white America has always been an assault on the personhood of black women.

What is physically attractive according to the dominant culture is, by definition, good. And according to the dominant culture, the prevailing standard is something to be achieved by any means imaginable and at any cost: coloring, permanents, hair straighteners, dietary aids for losing or gaining weight, pads for the appearance of fullness, Wonderbras to defy gravity. Then, of course, there's the scalpel. But when the ideal is white, and the reference point is the envied and revered white woman, femininity is out of reach for the black female, damaging her self-concept and relegating her to the social role of ugly duckling.

For black girls and women (as for most girls and women), hair, skin color, and weight are common preoccupations. Moreover, much like clothing and makeup, these are common qualities that we rely on for social comparison. Whenever I am with a group of black adolescent women, inevitably the double-talk begins. We say we're all beautiful, we say looks don't matter. But too many of us behave otherwise. Girls can't escape the cultural message that a woman's worth is to be judged by her appearance.

Once I was invited to observe a Saturday morning enrichment class for black girls in Boston. The program matched young adult women, usually college students, with young girls in the inner city. In the class I attended, the college student had assembled a group of six girls in a circle and began a conversation about music videos. Every single child in the group knew the words and the tune to a large number of top ten hits. The children giggled with glee whenever someone would recall a favorite verse. They jumped out of their seats, gyrating in rhythm, imitating the dance moves they had seen at home on their TV screens. It wasn't easy to interrupt the excitement, but finally the college student caught their attention enough to ask them a question. "What do you think about the images of women in these videos?" The girls slowly quieted down and shot her confused looks. "You know—the way the girls are dressed, how they look. How come they all have light skin and long straight hair?" "Because they picked the pretty ones," braved one little girl. "Cuz they look good," offered another. Soon afterward, the girls returned to their raucous singing and dancing and the college student was forced to abandon her attempts at media critique. "I really wish they'd get it," she told me after the class had disbanded. "I really wish they knew how these videos are teaching them to love certain looks and discount . . . their own."

A few years later, in a workshop on skin color issues in the black community that I conducted in a public high school in Boston, I shared this story with a group of 10th-grade boys and girls. The girls nodded in agreement, many offering their own observations and criticism of black music videos. Many of these girls were aware that the music videos teach powerful lessons about relationships between women and men, all through the lens of gender and racial stereotypes. I heard one girl talk about how many videos feature male artists who are unmistakably black fawning over women who are racially ambiguous—who are either white or look white, or if they are brown or dark-skinned, they usually have long, straight, Caucasian-like hair. As Sonja Peterson-Lewis and Shirley Chennault determined, "They suggest that black women of a particular [look] are more suitable romantic partners than others."

While the girls in this group seemed savvy, I fear that many black girls feel excluded by the white cultural ideal that black men have been socialized to value. They feel that black boys pass them by because they have been taught that their hair is too kinky, and their dark skin is unattractive.

Skin Color

We can be very cruel to one another when it comes to color consciousness in childhood and adolescence. We comment on and make wild assumptions about people based on skin color and features. Judging each other by a false standard of beauty, black teens—particularly black girls—can create a climate in which they or their friends end up internalizing these negative feelings about their looks.

The way teenagers develop and act can often prompt a parent's crisis or stimulate a parent's growth. Watching our teenage children struggle to make their way in the world, we parents often remember and rework our own feelings and conflicts left over from earlier years. We find ourselves forced to confront new questions in relation to ourselves, our children, and our own identity, which sometimes require us to think about being black in new and different ways. Mrs. Ashmore, for example, found that as her daughter grew older, she had to confront her own family's socialization around skin-color prejudice. In doing so, she was able to rework conflicts from her own past and discover new possibilities.

She talked with me about the skin-color issues she had grown up with as a child and her conscious decision to raise her own daughter to take pride in her dark skin color and to counter, with confidence, any effort to devalue her beauty. As a child Mrs. Ashmore felt she had been favored by her parents and was, as a result, resented by her darker brothers and sisters. Aware of the wounds that this skin-color prejudice had inflicted on her entire family, she is teaching her own dark-skinned daughter to resist colorism. She wants her daughter to learn at a young age the lessons she herself didn't learn until much later. As she describes it,

[I]n my daughter's case . . . I didn't want her to grow up feeling slighted. And so, when she was very little, I made her a tough guy. Like all the things that it took all these years for me to work myself up to, I . . . brought them to her at a young age. And she's like a really confident, self-assured person. She will not bite her tongue; she's very outspoken. She's very proud of her blackness. If you call her a black so and so, she'll say, "The blacker the berry, the sweeter the juice; what's your excuse?" She will not let you downplay her because she's dark. She will not let you call her ugly. She knows she's cute and bright.

As Mrs. Ashmore reminds us, it is within the family, where a variety of skin colors may be represented among individual family members, that many black children first learn the values attributed to the differences in skin color, and where the early seeds of color envy or dislike are often sown.

Parents who are teaching resistance have two important tasks that relate to notions of beauty. First, we must help our children challenge the belief that personal beauty is the most important virtue a woman can possess. Second, in order to overcome the deep-rooted skin-color prejudices formed so long ago in our own psyches and reinforced daily by white mainstream values, we must help our children to "name it"—that is, to consciously confront the notion that whiteness is rightness and that only what is white is good and beautiful. When we as black women turn against our lighter black sisters, is it any more than acting out the frustration and envy we subconsciously hold toward a racist and sexist society that assigns status and power to one's race and gender? By hating our array of skin colors, we are buying into the notion that beauty and femininity are a black woman's most important quality, thus relinquishing the power to define ourselves. Healthy resisters are able to oppose colorism by resisting the devaluation of those who don't possess a desired physical trait. They are able to name it for what it is, and they can replace such self-contempt with an appreciation of physical beauty in all its skin colors and hues.

Hair

An important developmental task of adolescence is to learn to feel comfortable with a rapidly changing body, and the change in others' response to those changes. Often teenagers want to try on different looks, experimenting with the way they've always presented themselves to the world. Some change their hairstyles, their makeup, their entire wardrobe, but it's the hair issue that most often confounds black parents.

Sherileen Forester, a friend of mine who lives in the suburbs, called me in a panic one day. Her 12-year-old daughter, Rochelle, had worn her hair in braids and other natural looks for years. But suddenly, out of the blue, it seemed, she demanded to be allowed to straighten it. Rochelle wouldn't let go of the idea, and the family was in an uproar. From Sherileen's perspective, the request was counterprogressive. She came of age in the 1960s, and for her, like for so many of us baby-boomer blacks, nappy hair was and still is a political issue, charged with symbolic power. To compound matters, she worried about the safety of the hair-straightening chemicals her daughter wanted to slather on her head. What in the world, she asked, is my daughter thinking? And how can I be sure she's simply trying to look her best and isn't trying to look white?

Today, black girls can adopt a wide array of hairstyle fashions. They can—and nearly 75 percent of black women already do—straighten their hair with hot combs or chemicals. If they want to wear their hair in a natural style, they can braid, plait, or cornrow it, with or without extensions and weaves. They can let it grow out in an Afro, or wild and free in a dreadlocks style. What we do with it, and even more important, how black girls feel about their hair, can also get hung up with the need for peer group acceptance and fear of rejection.

Straightened hair is often the standard for respectability. And sometimes black girls, particularly those in predominately white communities, feeling the pressure to fit in, may feel compelled to change their hairstyles, their dress, and their makeup in order to approximate the norm and increase their chances for peer acceptance.

Black women have long lived with the pain of seeing their beauty assaulted by society's devaluation of how they look. Many black mothers, like my friend, get nervous when their daughters ask to straighten their hair. Does a teenager want to straighten her hair to "fit in"? If she does, then who is she trying to fit in with? Whites? Other blacks? A teenager thinking about straightening her hair might, like many people faced with hard issues, simply be looking for an easy way out. Rochelle, like many suburban blacks, finds the pressures and struggle to assimilate exhausting. Relaxing her hair may feel like a way of lowering the pressure, thus relaxing herself as well, and she may not understand the fine line between tactics like these and cultural capitulation.

Rochelle, and other black girls, need to understand that adopting a hairstyle is a choice, not a requirement. As she must when making other choices, she needs to have a clear understanding of why she is making her particular choice. And when it comes to making choices like these, they shouldn't be made out of hate, self-contempt, or envy, but out of a love of beauty—in oneself and others.

One mother, Lillian, described for me how she transformed a routine as simple as brushing her daughter's hair into a loving lesson in the beauty of blackness and a powerful nurturing of resistance:

> When my daughter Patsy was 4, I would sit her down between my legs and every morning as I combed and braided her hair I would have her reach up and run her hands through it. "Look," I'd say, "look at how pretty your hair is. Feel how tight and curly it feels. Look at how pretty it can be when you style it up with ribbons, beads, and bows, or when you just let it be. Look at how different it is from your little white friends and how special that is.

Lillian, like countless African American parents before her, created a unique strategy for resistance. Her own awareness of what her daughter would soon encounter—the inevitable attacks upon her self-esteem by those who measure black beauty against a white standard, and devaluation of her blackness and self-worth—led to her invention of this loving, powerful ritual: braiding an extra strand of resistance into her daughter's hair, helping her develop into a competent, confident black woman.

Weight

As I traveled from home to home interviewing families, I learned powerful, encouraging lessons in the beauty of African Americans, in the rich shadings of skin color and the endless variety of features and figures. I'd be invited in, I'd set up my tape recorder and arrange my notes, and within minutes I'd be offered something to eat. Brought up too well to refuse, I often said yes. The delicious smells of sweet potato pies, baked chicken casseroles, fresh greens, and macaroni and cheese were too much for me to turn down. These black women—and quite a few times black men—could *cook*. And I enjoyed eating their food.

Apparently many of us enjoy eating our own food. We enjoy it so much, in fact, that obesity rates in our community are rising at an alarming rate. Black women and girls are particularly at risk. Researchers analyzing national data on obesity have discovered a 54 percent increase in obesity among white teenage girls and a 96 percent increase among black girls within a 15-year period. Our tendency toward obesity is brought on, experts think, by the high fat and high calorie content of the traditional African American diet, combined with lack of exercise. Interestingly, research suggests that black teenage girls report greater satisfaction with their physical appearance compared to white girls, and that black women are less likely to adhere to negative social pressure about being overweight. Ironically, this attitude may limit the extent to which weight-loss efforts, when undertaken, are sustained.

Obesity among black girls may be a quick-fix coping strategy to deal with the pressures and frustrations of daily existence. It can be all too easy to succumb to junk food after a long, hard day. To compound the problem, black girls in poor urban neighborhoods often have few safe, open spaces to play and be active in. Many are also limited in the grocery choices by local stores that stock few fresh fruits or vegetables, but instead offer high-calorie, high-fat packaged foods.

Some research suggests that black girls are more content with their bodies and less concerned about achieving a perfect body type than white girls are. Moreover, many of our girls describe the perfect size in terms of what they often see in their own communities: full hips, thick thighs, full breasts. According to some, looking good is less about size than it is about "having the right attitude."

Nevertheless, although black girls have in the past tended to use other black women's figures as their reference points, this may be changing. And psychologists speculate that for women of color, there may be a relationship between increasing opportunities for social mobility and increased vulnerability to disordered eating. One study shows black women college students binge at rates equal to white rates, and unpublished findings of ninth-grade black girls in a large urban high school recently found them bingeing and purging at rates equal to their white counterparts.

Unfortunately, evidence exists that younger black girls may now be succumbing to eating disorders and that they may be as obsessed with their bodies as some white girls are. Developmentally, these younger adolescent girls tend to be more self-conscious, their self-esteem is less secure, and they are far more sensitive to the perceptions and feelings of their peer group. Many of these younger black teen girls feel enormous pressure to look perfect and to match the European ideal portrayed on TV and in the print media. Perhaps older black girls are better able to resist the messages about dieting that fill the pages of girls' and women's magazines. The challenge to black adults is to get our messages of health and resistance through to our black daughters at even earlier ages, teaching them about the importance of good nutrition and focusing on what a body does and how well it works— on its strength, flexibility, and grace—rather than on how it looks. We must give black girls the tools to take care of their beautiful black bodies.

Black girls who live in or attend school in predominately white settings sometimes find that their beauty may not be acknowledged at all. For them, this means an incompleteness, a sense that a certain part of their being simply doesn't exist. To counter these messages (that your beauty can be erased, negated, and denigrated), black girls need messages from home assuring them that their beauty is cherished, and helping them to honor the beauty in themselves and in their black sisters. A black girl can be psychologically strong only when she knows and believes true beauty is from the inside, not the outside, and that she, too, is beautiful, especially when she appreciates the beauty in all.

But ensuring that our daughters know they are beautiful isn't enough. We must also teach them to understand the roles that racism and sexism play in shaping attitudes about skin color and hair; we must teach them to be "socially smart." They must know when survival dictates a trade-off (when succumbing to hair-straightening means a promotion that increases the family's income, for example), and when a trade-off is merely the easier response. At the same time, we must teach them to avoid allowing their identities to be compromised.

The first step is to create powerful and positive identities for ourselves. As parents, we must continue to learn, aspiring to gain a genuine sense of appreciation and love of our diversity, in all of our colors.

Ysaye Maria Barnwell, one of the members of the singing group Sweet Honey in the Rock, has said that she wrote the song "No Mirrors" in 1969 after a friend told her that because the house she grew up in had no mirrors, every day her mother or grandmother would describe to her in detail each of her features, cherishing her, letting her know how truly beautiful she was:

> There are no mirrors in my Nana's house,
> No mirrors in my Nana's house.
> And the beauty that I saw in everything,
> The beauty in everything was in her eyes.
> So I never knew that my skin was too black,
> I never knew that my nose was too flat,
> I never knew that my clothes didn't fit,
> And I never knew there were things that I missed.
> And the beauty in everything was in her eyes.
> Child, look deep into my eyes.

RESISTANCE STRATEGIES

Unhealthy (Short-Term, Survival-Oriented) Strategies

- Self-loathing due to comparing one's looks to a Eurocentric standard of beauty and hating oneself for coming up short

- Adopting hairstyles for the sole purpose of looking white

- Prejudging, preferring, and discriminating on the basis of skin color

- Engaging in unhealthy eating behavior (bingeing and purging, overeating)

Healthy (Long-Term, Liberating) Strategies

- Teaching our daughters to love their bodies for their strength, flexibility, and grace, not just for how they look

- Offering our daughters things to think about other than their looks

- Teaching our daughters to appreciate the diversity of beauty found in all women, particularly black women

- Teaching our daughters to exercise regularly and to use food for nourishment only

Psychologically Strong, Socially Smart

A psychologically strong, socially smart black daughter can resist succumbing to narrowly defined notions of beauty. She understands that this knowledge will have positive and enduring payoffs for her entire life. She knows that being healthy is not only good for her individually, but it will also benefit her into the future, as a mother, employee, and active community member.

OBSTACLES TO CREATING A POSITIVE IDENTITY

THE IMPORTANCE OF A POSITIVE RACIAL IDENTITY

Over the adolescent years, as teenagers make cognitive advances and increase their social skills, their racial identity unfolds as well. Slowly, important and complex understandings of race and racial identity emerge. And as these understandings of racial identity are formed, black teenagers must grapple with the task of integrating their individual personal identity with their racial identity. A stable concept of this dual identity, according to psychologists, is essential to the healthy growth and development of the black self.

Bev Patterson, a youth counselor at a local multiservice agency, once invited me to speak to a group of students in the after-school homework program at her agency. Since the eighth graders' social studies class was studying history through the lens of popular culture, I offered to talk about the 1960s from a black perspective. The students had read about the sixties in their textbooks, where reproduced *Life* magazine photos of counterculture characters—long-haired hippies and wild musicians—appeared alongside an exposé on the excesses of sex, drugs, and rock and roll. The text stopped briefly to offer a quick, sanitized version of the civil rights movement that primarily highlighted the superstars: Rosa Parks, Martin Luther King, Presidents Kennedy and Johnson, and major events like the March on Washington. In this textbook, the period was quickly summarized: on one page blacks didn't have their rights; then suddenly, on the next page, they did. I asked the eighth graders to tell me what they knew about the Black Panther Party—its philosophy of self-help and its efforts to instill black pride. Beyond what one student had heard in the lyrics of a few rap CDs, nobody ventured a guess.

Afterward, Bev Patterson and a few more of our friends and I went to dinner in a restaurant at a local suburban mall. Glancing around, we quickly realized that we were the only black faces in the crowd. Bev, the mother of a 17-year-old girl and a 13-year-old boy, joked, "Uh-oh. You know when they see more than two of us talking together they're sure we're planning a revolution."

Bev grew up in a college town in the 1960s, a hotbed of political activity and social protest. Black high-school students like herself, taking their cue from area college students who were actively demanding their rights, demanded that the local high school establish a black student union. "We called it," she told us, "the Black Room." I laughed out loud listening to Bev describe the room and its huge posters of Martin, Malcolm, Bobby Seale, and Chairman Mao. Long, loud wooden beads hung where the wooden door used to, making a racket whenever anyone entered the room. Wood carvings from Africa hung from the walls adding (the students had convinced themselves) an air of authenticity to their rap sessions. The black students talked endlessly about being black, about building a black nation, about saving up to visit the motherland. Bev remembered practicing Swahili phrases an East African exchange student taught them.

Sometimes, she said, they'd get outrageous. Feeling the need to assert their blackness, they'd get a rhythm going, first with their feet. Then they'd syncopate with the handclaps, whistles, and finally, a chant: *Uhhm, beep beep, Ungowha, Black Power; Uhhm, beep beep, Ungowha, Black Power!*

All of us sitting around the table could remember those days. We'd been into being black with a capital B: denouncing our woefully racially ignorant parents because they just didn't get it; cranking up the poetry of Gil Scott Heron and The Last Poets on the stereo—"*When the Revolution comes . . .*" We were BLACK teenagers and this was our way of figuring out who we were, as individuals and as members of a racial group slowly coming into its own. In black student unions across the country, black kids came together in droves. Sometimes black college students from neighboring campuses would come to the elementary and high schools to tutor and conduct workshops on African history, art, and music.

Bev explained,

See, back then when I was figuring out who I was as a black woman, so was everyone else. For a time there it seemed like everybody was into talking about being black. There was always someone or some-thing around—teachers, college students, books—that kept us thinking, kept us on our feet, helped us to challenge what we had grown up hearing and believing about who we were. That's when I first learned about the lost kingdom of Timbuktu and all those beau-tiful and powerful African kings and queens. Hell, I was almost an adult when I first heard about that stuff. Putting the pieces together, making connections between what's fact and what's a lie—Let me tell you, that was a powerful experience.

Bev Patterson, the other mothers, and I felt confident that things were different for us then than they are for today's teenagers. When it came to building a racial identity, we felt fortunate to have been able to forge our identities when we did. And although at the time we probably attributed far more blame to "The Man" than was fair or right, at least we talked, shared ideas, argued with one another over important political matters. Those loud, raucous debates in which we asked who is and who isn't black enough, who is or isn't a sellout, were where we worked through and determined the values we'd adopt, as well as those we'd let go of. We learned how to chal-lenge ideas and were given correctives to put in the place of those erroneous ideas we may have been exposed to.

Looking back on that time, I'm sure that to white folks we looked as if we were on the attack. But our attitudes and behavior were really more about protecting the fragile racial identities we were in the process of con-structing. No doubt our rejection of all things white was simply to shore up our newly formed, shaky sense of blackness.

But let's be real. Not all exclusive black groups are all good all the time. They weren't then, and they probably aren't now. Sometimes they do little more than provide a forum for reinforcing one another's insecurities. Sometimes they're more about keeping others out than about exploring what's within. But in the main, lots of important psychological work con-tinues to go on in those groupings that, at least for me, contributed to my positive sense of who I am as a black woman. And listening to black teenagers talk about the journeys they must take toward self-acceptance and group membership today, I'm sure there's a place these days for an ed-ucation that teaches black youth how to ask questions, search for evidence, make connections, and challenge conventional wisdom about race, leading and supporting them in their search for positive racial identity.

OBSTACLES TO CREATING A POSITIVE IDENTITY

At the end of Bev's story, she held up her hands in entreaty. "What do these kids have today?" she asked. "Who's helping them?" Bev's question lingered with me. And when I met Emma, a ninth grader, it took on special significance.

I was involved in a project at her school where other researchers and I interviewed more than a hundred girls, asking them to talk about how they felt to be growing up and taking on new responsibilities. My interview with Emma was the last one of the day. I was tired and Emma was, too. She sat in the large, worn, leather-bound armchair, her thick, unruly curls caressing her round, light-brown face. "I really think I need a haircut," she remarked more than once.

Adolescence calls for many adjustments. Emma's body was changing fast. "I changed my bra size three times last summer!" she giggled. And in addition she found herself paying closer attention to her social world.

Emma was biracial and had been raised in a white Pennsylvania suburb by her mother, a white European who knew little about American society, and even less about African Americans. Although Emma was the only non-white child in her entire elementary school from kindergarten through eighth grade, she was a sociable child and made many friends. There was, Emma assured me, no reason to think about racial matters while she was growing up, because, as she put it, there were no racial problems in her sleepy one-culture town. She had endured in silence what she described as a few incidents of racial denigration that arose at school. Race was simply never raised as a topic for discussion at home.

But once she began junior high she began to ask herself the classic adolescent questions: Where do I belong? Where do I fit in? Why don't I look like the others? Who are my people? However, with the taboo on racial discussion in place at home, she didn't dare ask them aloud. "In fact," she explained, "I don't think of myself as black. I mean I don't like to." Embarrassed at her confession to me, Emma continued, trying to make me understand the hard feelings that had been building in her over time and that tended to surface with a vengeance each time she encountered negative images of blacks on the evening news. As she told me,

> When I'm watching TV and stuff like that, I associate blacks with welfare and stuff like that. And it's really bad but, when we used to

drive through the bad parts of town or something, I would always see
blacks out there and [think] I can't be a part of that, that's not me.

It was heartbreaking to listen to Emma struggle to suppress and explain
away the deep feelings of shame she felt. Black people, particularly low-
income blacks, were offensive to her—their lives a mess, their communities
lawless and dangerous. With tears in her eyes, she muttered, her voice trail-
ing off, "I know I shouldn't feel like this, but . . ."

In her attempt to distance herself from "those blacks out there," Emma
showed her reluctance to identify with those she had been socialized to den-
igrate. Sadly, Emma's survival strategy—an attempt to maintain a positive
sense of herself amid an onslaught of attacks against African Americans and
her culture—places her healthy racial and individual identity development
at risk and leaves her vulnerable to the destructive effects of emotional isolation and self-alienation. In denying her connections to a collective culture,
she denies herself the collective strength such affiliation might provide. Had
she been fortunate enough to have contact with even one black adult like a
teacher or athletic coach, who could have helped her navigate her racial reality, Emma might well have taken life head on, engaged and psychologically
strong, instead of retreating.

The psychiatrist James Comer says that achieving a positive racial identity requires an integration of black culture and mainstream culture. To do
this requires that black children and teenagers be able to repudiate the negative perceptions and evaluations of others. Those who don't, like Emma,
often end up with diminished self-confidence and a distorted sense of self.

Professor Comer, whose studies and books on black children have inspired a generation of psychologists and educators, argues that there are
several problematic ways that black youth respond to the task of identity development, including rejecting their race and culture and attempting to exist as individuals (and remaining marginal in both black and white
cultures); rejecting their blackness and identifying with white culture only
(even accepting negative perceptions of blacks); or developing a strong,
pro-black posture with a rejection of all things white.

The task for African American adolescents is a large one: they must create and assert an identity that is self-defined while surrounded by other
people's competing efforts to impose on them their own definitions of
racial identity and status.

Many teenagers and parents told me about the difficulties they faced in developing—or helping their children develop—a positive sense of identity. Their stories illuminate the tensions that charge identity formation today: the peril of crossing over to the white side only to discover a conditional assimilation, where blacks are allowed to participate only on terms defined by whites; and the pressures they feel from many blacks, as well as the media, who pressure them to conform to a rigid standard of "blackness." Mrs. Allen, a 38-year-old mother, is pained by the discomfort she feels when she crosses over:

> I always know I'm black. It's an awareness that's constantly with me. A lot of it has to do with some of the environments I'm in. If I visit the museum, how many blacks do you see? When I go to my son's school, he's the only black child on the ice hockey team. So when I walk in, everybody knows whose mother I am. That kind of stuff can be a pain in the ass. There's no sort of anonymity, ever. I never feel as if I can really blend into a crowd. I always feel very black. I don't mind, but I'm just always aware.

Her exasperation is easy to understand. Even though American society is more integrated today than it ever has been, and many forms of segregation are, in fact, illegal, separation of the races continues in many arenas. Our neighborhoods, schools, and places of work persist as exclusively or primarily white or minority because of economic barriers, because of racism, and because of the comfort level it brings to many to avoid contact with the other races. It's also common to find situations where, although the numbers are there to support true integration, people choose not to cross the lines of race and social class. Parents don't associate or explore the other side, and children, always easily cued by their parents, don't either. And although there is a tremendous amount to be gained from exploring how others live, including, for blacks who dare venture over the line, opportunities for social advancement, few will take the step. To many blacks, crossing over feels treacherous.

For some of us, this feeling of peril permeates even mundane daily activities. One woman, who lives in a trailer park in a section of rural North Carolina that bordered Klan country, told me that her black friends were shocked when she told them she planned to go out to eat with some white coworkers. Even having white friends at work, let alone going out socially with them, was a huge step out of the ordinary as far as this woman's circle of black friends was concerned. People would be looking at her and talking about her, they warned. The friends' reaction—and the fact that this dinner outing seemed like such a monumental event to the woman who was going out—startled me. But constrictions such as these don't appear to be geographically based. In a magnet school that at least had the appearance of being multicultural (with almost equal percentages of black, Hispanic, and white teenagers), a teenage girl in Boston took me by surprise when she explained in a disturbingly matter-of-fact voice that although she went to school with whites, she didn't consider any of them her friends.

Although I should be used to it by now, I still take notice when I find myself the only black—or one of a very few—in a situation. This happens in both predominately white settings, where I would expect it, and in settings where I would have expected more black folks to be, like PTA meetings at racially integrated schools, at concerts, and, as Mrs. Allen mentioned, at libraries and museums. In these situations I glance around searching for my own, trying to acknowledge every other black at least with eye contact. I know how alienating and isolating being black in a sea of whiteness can feel.

The problem is that there's a tension between crossing over, which feels treacherous and unsafe, and a black insularity that limits self-exploration and community expansion. To resolve this tension, what teenagers need is to gain the psychic strength and social skills that will enable them to cross over while maintaining personal integrity, pride, and racial identity. What our black teenagers need and want are strategies that allow them to maintain their racial ties while honoring diversity within the race and working for group advancement and assimilation into mainstream American society on their terms.

Mrs. Ellis, in her mid-fifties, talked about her frustrations with what she perceived as a self-imposed fencing in, by many blacks, of their own communities, coupled with a failure to improve them. She fears that today's blackness is about exclusivity, not excellence. At midlife, she is learning who we as a people were, and have now become, by reflecting on what we have lost. Her sorrow was palpable:

> Today's blackness is a different kind of blackness than my grandmother instilled in me about being a person. I don't see the vying for excellence, the struggle to be a proud people and to own the land that God created and own it as ours. I see trash and debris and lack of services. There is this grouping of black people saying, "This is our com-

munity, and we're not going out there with the white folks," and I'm wondering why the exclusion, the separation.

Much like our teens, some of us black adults feel more comfortable in all-black settings that are familiar, where we can blend in and not have to be on guard all the time, where we aren't forced to represent the race but can relax and be individuals. But this closing down by some segments of the black community that Mrs. Ellis talked about—which I call "negative territoriality"—can easily dissolve into to an immature racial identity. As a defensive posture, it poses a genuine danger to black progress. If a significant body of blacks diverts its energy to protecting a deteriorated community instead of salvaging or replacing it with something better, our next generation is subject to intolerable risk. Moreover, fear of crossing over can lead to self-imposed limitation, exclusivity, isolation, and further marginalization of the black community. Some of us may become so hooked on the notion of conservation that we end up in denial, unable to see and respond to the decay, deterioration, and decadence. We focus not on striving for excellence, achievement, and improvement, but on conserving, resisting, and opposing change. Raising children to internalize the positive, productive values long abandoned by some of us will require an enormous effort, both by the parents who remain in the inner city, and by those who have fled.

TOO BLACK/NOT BLACK ENOUGH: WHO DECIDES?

Adolescence is a time to try on identities and to experiment with who you are and what you believe. But teenagers who allow others to do their thinking for them run into trouble.

Mrs. Avery, a 38-year-old woman, told me she was torn as she tried to decide whether to send her daughter to a predominately white private boarding school. "Should I really put my black child in this all-white environment?" She was especially concerned that her daughter didn't think certain issues concerning race were as important as she did. She was worried as well that her daughter would never develop a clear understanding of black culture and values. "I was afraid," she said,

> that she would sort of become this white kid with black skin. She would internalize so many white cultural patterns that I didn't think she should. Dating—I used to worry that she might get involved with

a white boy. And then I'd say [to myself], Well, you know, you put her in this environment, what do you think she's going to do? I worried about her perceptions of what's attractive. Was being white what she thought was attractive, or light-skinned blacks who looked white? I worried that she would try to change herself, sort of fit whatever the norm was, and that norm in this case was white.

She was also worried about her daughter's developing identity, both individual and racial:

A lot of this is adolescent stuff. Adolescents are going to have identity problems, and try to fit in with the group and that kind of thing. I think when you're black in that environment you feel pulled in two directions. Your white friends don't want to be with your black friends, your black friends don't want to be with your white friends, so you're on the spot. I think a lot of these issues she'll have to resolve for herself. But I do think that it's important for me to sort of provide some kind of base for her.

Mrs. Avery was right to be concerned for her daughter, and her concerns were precisely on target. She was worried that her daughter was uncritically internalizing white cultural patterns. Mrs. Avery knows that not everything white is right, not for them and certainly not for us. Her commonsensical experience is echoed by research showing that members of minority groups who have achieved an identity by adopting values from both their ethnic heritage and the dominant culture have a stronger sense of self-esteem, feel more competent, and have more positive relations with others. How can we help a black teenager learn to resist a definition of self that doesn't feel right, genuine, or fair? What does it take for a teenager to resist an externally assigned identity?

FIRST TO'S AND ONLY ONES

When I talked with Mrs. Jones, she was in a stunned, despairing state. Her 13-year-old son, Theo, she said, had been thrilled and proud at his father's participation in the Million Man March on Washington, D.C. But the next day, when Theo returned to his predominantly white school, his mood changed to fearful silence.

Theo worries, she told me, that his white friends will never understand the appeal of a national call for black empowerment and black self-help; he also worries that the same white friends, who believe Minister Farrakhan is racist and anti-Semitic, will assume the same of his father and the others who marched. He is under siege: his pride in his father and his race are countered by his fear of white rejection.

The Million Man March was what we educators call a teachable moment—a real-life incident that gave Mrs. Jones an opportunity to share, respond to, and assess her son's feelings while helping him to understand the origins of, and tolerance for, the conflicting thinking he will encounter in life. Mrs. Jones and other black mothers in similar situations can use times like these to help their children by gathering evidence, asking questions that explore the points of view of the black child and his white buddies, and identifying the attitudes and conflicting beliefs that may evolve from people's differing social positions and group histories. If we are to help black teens like Theo determine who they are (in Theo's case a black man connected to other black men, who have special needs, concerns, and interests, and who find strength in these connections) and what they believe in (for example, Farrakhan as a leader and authority with a valuable message and perspective that is racialized and runs counter to mainstream perspectives on race), we must teach them how to read situations like these and to make sense of the differences in racial perspectives. This process could have helped Theo put rejection by the white kids, whose friendship he valued, into context, and hold on to the positive feelings of pride he had initially felt about his dad's participation in the march.

Identity (knowing who you are) and ideology (knowing what you believe) are critical to developmental processes in adolescence. Teenagers are consumed with these issues. For black youth, moving beyond an internalization of racial subservience to racial pride begins first with a conscious confrontation with one's racial identity. Resolution of the so-called identity crisis of youth requires that all teenagers proclaim "I am not" as the first step to defining what "I am." At the threshold stage of the identity process, black teenagers like Theo, who are all too familiar with the demeaning stereotypes held about him and his racial group, must add, "I am not what you believe black people to be, *and I am black.*"

I remember sensing that I was hearing something important, something I should listen to very carefully, when John, a 15-year-old at a racially mixed school, tried to articulate his feelings about a dilemma he was in. The issue was whether to go on a weekend trip with his black friends or go on a school-sponsored trip with a group of all-white students. It was clear that he was trying to work this through. John went back and forth, starting a sentence about the pros and cons of one side, then he'd stop mid-sentence to consider the other. More than once I became as confused as he was, hesitantly vacillating in his deliberations. It was clear that he was reluctant to go on the school trip with the white students because he was afraid that he would feel uncomfortable alone with them.

When, in another interview in North Carolina, I heard a very similar concern voiced by another young man, I began to take notice. Not long before our time together, Michael had a choice of going to one of two summer camps: the first, an academically oriented camp attended by whites, and the second, a camp meant specifically for blacks. He described what happened:

> I chose to go to the more academic camp with the white people. Initially I think it was just the whiteness of it [that put me off] . . . I wasn't really looking at the outcome when I first thought about it. I learned that I shouldn't judge every book by its cover. What's best in the end, what's better for you. I probably would learn a lot of stuff that I don't learn at school. So I figured it might be better for me.

A third young man, David, told me about the difficulty he'd had when a white friend invited him to a party. He explained his dilemma this way:

> I'd be the only black invited. I debated whether I should go [whether I'd] feel out of place, awkward as the only black. I wondered . . . would people react to me being there, because I would stand out? [It's like a] black dot on a white sheet of paper. Color is the first thing they see. They usually don't wait to see how that person is. They think, Well, he's a black person, he's trouble. A black person—uh-oh. Something's going to happen.

In this case, David decided to go to the party, and he ended up having a really good time. Not only that but he learned something important from the experience: the best way to feel confident in a racially isolated setting is to enter knowing who you are. As he put it,

I have to stand up for me. I have to know who I am, and when I learn who I am then things will fall into place. If I hadn't known, I could've acted differently . . . said something or done something that I really had no reason to do, and I'd probably stand out even more if I did that.

The stories of John, Michael, and David bring home messages about identity vulnerability, and the fragile state that our teenagers are in as they negotiate their way through high school. Many feel compelled to respond to others' assumptions about who they are, while coping at the same time with myriad other demands of adolescence: fitting in, getting used to one's emerging sexuality, and changing relationships with friends and family.

Both Michael and David possess the skills needed to weather potential assaults on their identities; they both recognized the value of being open to new experiences, and both had developed the ability to make good choices in their own self-interest. Michael knew that he needed the confidence and self-knowledge to allow him to factor in his own needs and to decide that the intellectual development he'd experience at the white academic summer camp would be worth the initial discomfort he expected to feel. "My mom taught me that," Michael explained.

She always tells me to keep my eye on the big picture. Like, she's always saying that there's a whole lot in life that I'm not gonna like. Stuff that I should do that maybe don't feel so good cuz I'm black, you know. But see, I really want to go to college, a really good college. And I know that means I've gotta get really good grades. And I set that goal for myself. Me and my mom, we always talk about this. Stay focused on the goal. So when I was thinking about this situation, and it was the white academic camp on one side and the black regular camp on the other—I just thought about what my mom always says, and I knew what I had to do.

David's story went deeper into the origins of the discomfort black teenagers can feel in all-white settings, and, like Michael, his resolution of the conflict was the direct result of his ongoing conversations with the adults in his life. David's family taught him to anticipate, understand, and deal not only with his anxiety but also with the anticipated fears of the white party-goers. They helped him anticipate how he might be seen, and they helped him to name where such negative perceptions come from. "We talk about race all the time in my house," he said. "Especially about how a lot of whites believe what they say about us." David refused to allow a fear of the racial unknown to limit his choices. His thoughtful and courageous response to his situation sprang from a black folks' knowledge base—that is, that some non-black people who don't know a black male individually may react to him based on stereotypic assumptions, and that if any trouble were to happen it would be blamed on him. David had the knowledge to understand the depth of his dilemma, oppose the negative assumptions about who he was, and replace them with self-knowledge, self-confidence, and pride. These are the tools that allowed him to feel he could and should cross over racial boundaries, while maintaining the integrity of his identity.

Black teenagers face the daunting task of developing strong personal and racial identities and of combining the two while resisting a barrage of identities that others, even well-meaning family members, would impose on them. Jerry, a 19-year-old college freshman, faced the dilemma of deciding which of two colleges to attend: a historically black college or the predominately white university that he ultimately chose. Although his family had wanted him to accept the black school's offer, he chose the white school because, to his mind, being in a racially mixed setting would prepare him for the world he would inevitably enter on graduation. As he put it, "Blacks and whites don't know enough about the other. I'm helping to change that."

As Jerry explained it to me, he and his mother argued back and forth for a whole month over which school he should attend. Jerry's mother really wanted her son to attend a black college, and on the face of it, Jerry didn't seem to have a problem with that choice. But what was making him crazy was that his mother kept insisting that not only would he be unhappy in a white college, but even worse, said Jerry, "the white people there would try to turn me into what they want me to be."

Jerry's conflict, as well as the core of David's and Michael's dilemmas, arise from black people's fears that white people somehow have the ability to transform black people—to, as Jerry's mother put it, "turn us into what they want us to be." This is yet another incarnation of identity vulnerability: the sense that the culture in power can eradicate one's racial self. The black teens in these stories who fear what might happen when they cross over the racial divide sense that white people will search for, and make blacks adopt, characteristics that the white people find appealing, comfortable, and acceptable. The teenagers, in response, feeling both the desire to be accepted and the pressure to conform, may don inauthentic roles that mask their real selves. Some blacks in these situations may not have the power to resist. They may become submissive, deferential, and conflicted about their identity and their self-worth.

Fortunately, Jerry knows himself well and has faith in his ability to resist self-erasure within the white college setting. Confident of this, he saw no need to avoid the situation, the strategy proposed by his well-meaning but fearful mother, but chose instead to take a stand in support of the strong and courageous black man he imagined himself to be. Conflicts like these—which party to attend, which group to hang out with—sound at first like simple adolescent decisions. But they are actually far more profound and complex. The dilemmas these young men faced were about potential loss of self, about conformity, and about who decides what is black. They were about the courage and self-knowledge it takes to be the first or only one. They were about the willingness to risk discomfort for the opportunity to grow.

Malik, another 19-year-old, brought home for me the pain of bearing an identity assigned by whites. I had been talking with his parents for some time, and they told me that they talked often with their children about racial issues. They saw these discussions as an imperative, they said. As parents, they had a responsibility to guide and shape their children's thinking, to interpret the world for them, and to help them recognize problems and come up with solutions. Their two sons, Malik and his 15-year-old brother, were present for most of the interview. The younger one, a high-school freshman, participated in the discussion, offering his view or expanding a story. Malik, the tall, thin, and slightly self-conscious older brother, was quiet, even though it was clear to me that his mother, by sending him occasional disapproving glances, wanted him to join in.

When he finally spoke, it was with a gravity and consideration that made clear that he had been thinking hard about how to present his thoughts. He explained that he had a friend who was a white girl, and that the friendship was entirely platonic. Her parents were qute friendly with him; they appeared to like Malik and enjoy his company. The problem was this: the girl's boyfriend was black, and her parents refused to talk to him or for that matter even meet the young man..

He described his reaction to the parents' conduct this way:

This one white girl dates a black dude. Her parents don't want to meet this dude yet and still they will talk to me. So I said [to my friend], "What makes me different from him? What if he was my cousin?

Granted I don't know him, and I don't have to like him, but we're both black males and we might have some of the same characteristics." So I asked, "How does he talk? Does he talk like me, is that what it is?" And it dawned on me. She made me real upset, and she said, "Well, why don't *you* talk to my mom?" And I said, "Wait! I shouldn't have to talk to your mother, because I'm not the dude. She should want to meet him. But what separates me from this person? I'm just like he is."

At this point he was irritated at the recollection, but excited, too, at the discovery he had made. He went on:

It's good to have some white friends, but sometimes you've just got to let them know when they overstep the bounds. I know who I am. I mean, I'm not a white person, I'm a black person. And there are differences. They've lived such a sheltered life that [when they see] an articulate black person [they think], Let's give this man a quarter! You shouldn't be judged on the way you can talk, or your parents, or what car you may drive or something like that. I think they should meet this individual for who he is.

The mother, who had been nodding her head during Malik's recollection, finished up with a smile. "I knew he had a story in him!" she exclaimed.

Malik was understandably protesting the identity the white girl's parents had assigned him; refuting their assumption that he was acceptable because, in their eyes, he wasn't like other blacks, but like *them.* Empowered by many years of discussion with his parents about race, he asserted his identity on his own terms: "I'm not a white person; I am black. Whites have no monopoly on intelligence and articulateness."

Black middle-class adolescents in predominately white schools and communities (what one of my friends calls "trophy blacks") like Malik are particularly vulnerable to the pressure of "acceptable blackness." Some feel pressure to make whites comfortable by making them forget that they are black.

Malik's mother described her efforts to make sure her children weren't misled or confused by the identity assigned to them by some whites:

We've been blessed. We call our children "blue chips." They're high-profile children. They've been thrown into situations, as Malik said, where they are usually the only one, or one of a few in their classes or situation, and they've been fortunate to be blessed in terms of athletic and academic ability. We feel it's very important to teach them about race, so that they don't get confused . . . when people start swarming around them, and spotlighting them, and putting them up on a real high pedestal, and making them seem so very wonderful, that [they] don't get confused about why they're doing that . . . They're spotlighting you . . . while they'll ignore another black child in the same setting. We also have to [help] them know: do not think they love you because you are a black person. You are a *more acceptable* black person than some. [The white people] will say, "These are the best of the blacks because they're the smartest. They come from clean homes. Their mama and daddy are professionals and da-da-da." I don't want them to be confused as to why sometimes they're invited into white homes and places where some of their other quote/unquote "black" friends are not invited.

One of my undergraduates told me that when she was growing up she was labeled "the smart one." The teachers often invited her to special events, assigned her to special projects, and offered her opportunities that other black students never received. She was "the chosen one": chosen to enter the inner circle and mingle with whites. The other black students in her high school resented her status. Some were jealous and distrustful. Some thought she had sold out. "She's going somewhere," the teachers would proudly proclaim, which meant to her black friends that, by implication, they were not. My student grew to hate being the chosen, acceptable one—the one let in. She hated her white teachers for singling her out. She hated her friends for turning against her. Saddest was the devastating effect to her psyche and the many years she spent confused, alone, and hating herself.

Fran Robinson, a 45-year-old mother, shared a similar concern:

My kids have always played soccer. Soccer is not a black man's sport. The white kids expect [my kids] to talk white, dress white, and be that white role, where what I'm trying to say on this end is, "Hey, you're not a white kid, you're black, so your black heritage is that you dress black and that you be yourself, not white or black. *Be yourself!* Don't let people steer you in the direction they want you to be steered." I'm trying to get them back to their own self-image—that's the problem I'm dealing with.

She was especially troubled by the pressures on her children to bear one identity (a white one) during weekend soccer events, and the other (their own black identity) during school days. "My older son says, 'Hey, the hell with it. I'm going to be who I am; you're not going to change me,' you know. But it's more difficult with the younger one, because he's caught up into it more so than the older one."

As this mother points out, peer group influences, especially in the lives of preteens, are critical, since they provide the support and security these children so desperately need to negotiate the often rough transitions they face in the changing contexts of school, family, and friends. Older teens are more apt to use a black norm for reference and self-measurement, but younger children may need particular help with these issues.

Mrs. Robinson sees a continuing tactic of reinforcing her younger son's identity at home as a crucial counterweight:

> It's important to me because I know that once that game is over, he's
> going to come back home into a black family setting. His whole life
> is going to be steered with a black family. I want him to know his
> family origins, his heritage, and what we're all about.

Teenagers receive countless messages about peer pressure. We admonish them to avoid drugs, sex, and kids who might steer them toward these activities. Some of our children also receive similar messages, although not so explicitly, about avoiding white people. Like the "bad" teenagers who can so easily—almost magically, it seems—lead "good" teenagers down the path to drug addiction and promiscuity, white people, so the message goes, can make you lose who you are. What's behind this message is a concern about loss of racial identity that results from the effort to fit in and belong. Though not directly expressed in his interpersonal relationships, Mrs. Robinson worries that in a society that perceives black people as funamentally unacceptable, her son might feel pressured to change.

Such fear is provoked by the belief that the route is usually one way and has no outlet. It's always, teens tell me, the blacks alone who have to change, never whites. And transforming themselves this way does not guarantee acceptability; it means only that blacks can enter the *realm* of acceptability. The teenagers and parents I spoke with were reacting to that outlandish imbalance, the writing and enforcing of the rule that there's only one acceptable way to be: the white way.

Strong black families nourish teens with messages that negate the whitewashing message. As one 18-year-old told me, "I'm proud to be black. It means a lot. Acting white means you are not proud. It's okay to be friends with whites, but you should keep separate identities."

Black teens who are the first or only ones need to know that they are not alone, that other blacks have faced similar challenges. They benefit from being connected with other black teenagers who are in the same situation, a resistance strategy designed to ward off isolation and alienation and encourage the pursuit of dreams. I spoke to a mother whose child was the only black student on a swim team. The family didn't know any other black children (or young adults for that matter) who swam competitively. So they got on the phone and made calls—to schools inside and outside of their district, Y's, boys and girls clubs—until they found some like-minded friends for their son.

It is a paramount task of black parents to instill in their children the tools and attributes that allow them to resist those black teens who tell them they are acting white, or not being black enough. And we need to realize that the child who stands up to them and says, "No, I am not acting white," is acting in a moral domain. This child is making a statement about who he is and what he is willing to stand up for.

The black child who says, "I am going to stay on the swim team" (or in the chess club, or in the debating society), may in so doing show non-black students and teachers that black people enjoy swimming, and debating, and chess, and can be good at it. Not only that, their actions may show black students as well that they can be black and do these things, too. They are acting out of a moral responsibility to show the doubters of all colors that blacks are intellectual equals: motivated, strong, and courageous.

These decisions are in the moral domain in other ways as well. They offer teenagers the chance to stand on principle, to choose for themselves a right way to be black. They say, "I have a right to exercise my desire to be the type of person I want to be." They make me think about Tiger Woods, or Venus and Serena Williams, or Briana Scurry, the goalie on the U.S. women's soccer team that won the World Cup. All of these athletes are assets to black people. All are playing what are considered (in America) to be white people's games, and all are excelling. They are bright and articulate, and they challenge existing stereotypes about both male and female black athletes. Their visible success forces doubters to stop and think. When one black breaks into the white domain, it becomes a signal to other blacks that it's okay to participate in that activity; it's no longer "not black enough" any more. Now black parents are buying their children toy golf clubs. And their daughters are joining soccer teams, or, if they are on them, they're feeling more comfortable about being there.

Finally, we must tell our teens that they need to be the best they can be simply because you never know who you will be able to influence by your conduct and achievement. Every young black golf player, chess player, soccer player, and Merit Scholar needs to know she may still be the "first to" or the "only one." And because of this, other black people may be watching her and saying, "Because you did it, I can, too." It's morally right to do one's best and to set a good example.

That's the kind of black person I want my own son to become. I don't want him to be burdened by this mandate, but I do want him to believe and understand that unless things change rapidly and significantly for black people in this country, this is the way it's going to be for us. And nobody knows which black person will suddenly be in a position of influence. Who knows who will be the next Briana Scurry, who overnight evolved from anonymity into a national spokeswoman for Title 9, traveling the country to talk with black girls about the importance of athletic participation and setting one's goals sky high? I want my son to know that someday he may be in that position, and I want him to be prepared. We must try to raise our children to know that others will watch their conduct and choices, and govern themselves accordingly. They need to know that "it ain't just about you."

Black conservatives might argue that this is wrong, that I am asking my son and other black teens to carry the whole race on their backs. But I say that black people, especially the first or only ones, already do that, whether they like it or not. The burden is already there. And although there is a lot that is negative associated with this, it is, after all, reality, and I feel it is our responsibility as black parents to socialize our children to know that they still represent the race.

There are positive implications as well, including growing up as leaders and role models, and developing a strong moral sense. We want and need our children to have sound values and character and to be able to stand up for themselves, and, we would hope, for the downtrodden as well. I add to this that as a black parent, I want my child to stand up for other black people, but I also want him to understand which black people have his best interests in mind. I want him to know how to detect who is in the moral circle and who is outside of it.

Helping our children develop an unassailable sense of black identity is the most significant resistance strategy we have. By helping black children know who they are, both individually and as inheritors of a rich racial heritage, by guiding them in developing a value system that keeps them thinking about their futures rather than their immediate comfort (as the boy who chose the white academic camp over the black camp did), and by encouraging and affirming resolve and self-honesty, we are helping them to muster the determination and strength of character that allow them to take on the role of "first to" or "only one" with confidence, courage, and pride.

RESISTANCE STRATEGIES

Unhealthy (Short-Term, Survival-Oriented) Strategies

- Avoiding crossover behaviors caused by fear

- Retreating to cultural isolation out of fear of crossing over

- Behaving inappropriately in predominately white settings out of anxiety about being the first or the only one

- Buying into notions of individual achievement at the expense of the collective responsibility

Healthy (Long-Term, Liberating) Strategies

- Helping our children know who we are and what others may think we are (the identities others assign to us)

- Instilling in our children the strength to cross over when it will benefit their lives, even though it may mean temporary discomfort

- Finding ways to help youngsters who are the first or only ones understand how to ward off isolation, including searching for black peers with similar interests

- Helping children understand that they may be elevated to a position of influence at any time and that they must be prepared

• Making teenagers aware that issues related to racial identity are often moral ones, and that it is critical to do the right thing, even if it means taking a risk

Psychologically Strong, Socially Smart

A psychologically strong, socially smart black teenager is never politically complacent about how black people are viewed in the world. She is aware that racism can impact relationships, yet she refuses to allow it to lmit her options for self development. She can read a social situation and knows how to react when faced with subtle or direct pressure to conform to others' definitions and ideas about who she should be."

THE POWER OF BLACK PEER PRESSURE

Just as pressuring black adolescents to be "white like me" constrains the development of healthy and positive racial identity, so can the norms and pressures for conformity that exist among blacks themselves. For many, it's hard to imagine a successful outcome to their own lives when they haven't been entitled to the same things as the whites they see.

A graduate student of mine once complained to me that members of her family, confused about why she would leave a financially lucrative professional life to pursue her riskier dream of becoming a writer, criticized her decision as "wanting to be more than you are." This was not a comment on her talents; everyone knew she could write well. But to this woman's family, and too often to other blacks, wanting more—what my student thought of as fulfilling her dreams and getting her fair share—is seen as wanting to be like whites. What is lost with this kind of characterization (if you want more you are "inauthentic") is the simple idea that blacks are entitled to the same dreams whites have. As parents, we need to help our children resist other blacks who believe that there is only one way to be black, who want to denounce other paths and undermine dreams.

Karen, a 17-year-old high-school student, told me this story:

When I first hit high school . . . it was hard to be a so-called jock and then be black, especially with the sport that I played. It was soccer, and that's not a black sport. So when I would hang out with my jock friends, they were [white] soccer players. . . . [Some] black people, they were, "Oh, she's whitewashed." And it wasn't that. It was just that this was the sport that I played and those were the people I hung around with. And they thought I had to make a choice. Well they didn't realize that I didn't feel that I had to make a choice, that I thought I could fit in both places. And that was hard. . . . I should be able to be black and still have white friends as well as black friends. My mom said, "No matter what they say, you have to do what you think is right."

You have to admit, when blacks get around each other, it's a different situation than when whites get around each other, or when whites and blacks get around each other. . . . [I]n social relationships, blacks can understand a level that whites can't about themselves. I'd be with my black friends, having a good time, dancing and things like that, then I'd go be with my white friends and they'd feel like, "Oh," you know, "that's the way she's going to be." Eventually they realized that [thinking that way] was accepting me for who I was. They accepted the fact that I was one person altogether.

It probably took the black kids longer. They thought I was being an Uncle Tom, you know: falling down to the white man's word. They were holding that white aspect against them. I tried to get the two groups to meet, and now it's basically one big group. They had to get to know each other; they had to look past the color aspect, both blacks and whites.

Karen's mother's emphasis on developing a personal value system ("No matter what they say, you have to do what you think is right") allowed her to overcome pressure from her black peers and continue playing the sport she enjoyed and excelled at. Extraordinarily, it also helped her to bring about change for the larger good: at the end of her story, she felt confident that she could have both black and white friends and still maintain her black identity. She had also been able to persuade both groups of friends—perhaps by her conduct as well as her words—"to get to know each other . . . to look past the color aspect." She demonstrated her connection to, and reliance on, black folks' knowledge: "Blacks can understand a level that whites don't about themselves."

I met with 15-year-old Janice after classes on a chilly February afternoon. We were near the school bus stop, and as the students boarded their busses for home, Janice would point out and comment on her classmates. A small group of white kids rushed on board and Janice turned to me. These were the kids, she told me, that she and other blacks at the high school found most confusing: the white kids who associate exclusively with blacks. She reflected on why this might be so:

Maybe they're not getting something out of their own people. They like being around us. Some of them do like to learn more about where we come from, and what we have done in the world today, but some of them just want to be like us, and they don't want to learn more about us. It all depends on the person and how their parents raised them up.

Many black teenagers today are annoyed with the Afro-Americanization of white American youth, at whites playing at being black by adopting black ways of walking and talking and donning the clothes that symbolize black urban youth culture. Such playacting poses a threat that is experienced at a deeply psychological level: what blacks have created is being appropriated by those who don't merit it, and this loss of identity provides all the more reason some of our teens cling tightly to it, even if it is narrow, confining, and oppressive to other blacks who choose to be black in their own way.

Even Janice has felt and had to circumvent some of that anger. She told me about a time when her black friends tried to reject her for associating with whites, but their efforts ended up being counterproductive. At the outset, she said, she saw the conflict as whether her black friends "would talk about me if I went to play with these people." She described the pressure she felt.

Would the black group be saying, "She acts like she's white now, look at her. Look where she lives at, she acts like she's white." When people do that, that kind of pushes you toward the other group, because you feel like you're just not going to be any place with the other people. It pushes you toward the whites when the blacks reject you. There's only so much a person can take, so much of being rejected, that they just give up.

For 17-year-old Cara, the issue of exclusion became a question of choosing between ridicule or isolation.

I didn't used to hang around with black kids as much because they used to tease me or give me a hard time. So I usually kept to myself until now, this year, I found a friend . . . that I can really communicate with, that understands me. But she is white. We became best friends this year and that's kind of affecting my black friends because they've been saying, "Oh, Cara. She's racial now. She's hanging with a white girl. And [they said] we should stay away from her because she might turn against us." So I . . . had a choice [of] not speaking to her [so I could] hang with my black friends. But I didn't want to hang with my black friends because they treated me as bad as a real racial white person would. I didn't want to be that type of person.

The conflict was whether I should stay with this girl who's my best friend and ignore the rumors, or what they think, or be by myself and not have any friends at all. What happened? I kind of ignored what the black girls said. They talk behind our backs and stuff, but I don't care, because I think her friendship means more to me than any comment anyone else is saying. I finally have someone that understands me, likes me because of what I really am. Not enough black kids ever attempted to do that with me. There are a couple of black girls that talk to me, but I still can't relate to them as much as I relate to her. What gets in the way? I can trust my friend. I've never been able to trust anyone. And the black kids, I still have doubts. They might go back and tell someone else. They can't keep things confidential.

When I asked her whether she felt her decision had been the right one, she said, "Yes. We have a good relationship together and that's good. It's better than staying by myself, because who wants to be lonely all their life? You've gotta have a friend sometime."

Cara's experience, like Janice's, demonstrates the fallacy of defining blackness in strict and narrow terms. Like Janice, Cara felt that her black peers had pushed her away from their group rather than pulling her in. She was in the process of developing her system of values, of learning to understand what was important enough for her to defend. In this instance, it was honest, authentic friendship, and rejecting the notion that it was more important to be accepted than to be honest.

I was surprised by the depth of this teenage perception that whites will erase them so readily that exposure must be avoided at all costs. The idea seems to resonate with them at a gut level, like stories of zombie soul-stealers in low-budget horror movies. The teens who feel this way are often in a state of hypervigilance about what they consider an "authentic" black identity—the badges of membership: the walk, the talk, the clothes, and the identification with high-profile blacks in music and sports. Increasingly for many black youth, and for a variety of reasons, the identity they guard so closely and embrace so tenaciously is an identity that celebrates brashness, defiance, and, increasingly, anti-intellectualism.

Although the identity is immature, that is, unexamined and unreflected upon, it is real to many of our teens. And, having taken it on, they defend it at all costs, with the astonishing zeal that teenagers bring to their activities, like sports or arguing with their parents. They scour the social climate for evidence of white peer pressure to abdicate the identity, and they hold strays accountable, using social control mechanisms like gossip, rumors, and threats of alienation. They've taken on the message of their baby-boomer parents: be black, be proud, but know that you're in an environment where you'll have to fight to achieve this. So the energy of the "fight" is there, but expressed in the only way the teenagers know how to express it: as an immature, superficial black identity they feel justified in imposing on other blacks.

Charlotte Jefferson told me about the problems a friend of her young teenage daughter faced:

My youngest daughter, Lecia, just turned 13. There's this black West Indian girl in her class that's new to the school. I encourage Lecia to be friends with this girl because she's a nice girl, and to be honest, she really needs help.

The trouble is her parents act like they don't want to be black. They don't talk to the other black families, they don't accept our invitations. The long and short of it is that they act like we're *too* black. Hey, to each his own I say. But, like I said, there's a problem with their daughter that Lecia keeps telling me about. She says, "Ma, Kathleen is up at the school crying in the bathroom between classes. She's really sad. We've got to do something"—and all that. So they had this event up at the school and I decided to take the girls out afterwards for pizza. So Lecia and Kathleen start talking about some of the tough black kids in their class. Kathleen says, "They hate me. They hate my clothes, they hate how I talk. They call me a white girl. And I don't know what to do. My mom says stay away from those American black kids. They are bad kids and they'll only pull you down."

Now I know the kids she's talking about, and they're not *that* bad. It's just that they're working their own stuff out. I don't want the girl to avoid all blacks just because of her bad experience with this small group. She's gonna need them black kids one day—you know what I'm saying? And besides, what kind of message is that to give to a child? Her parents are telling her to stay away from the black kids because they are *too* black, and the black kids are making her life miserable because they say she's not black enough. No wonder the girl's confused. So I talked with her about it. I told her that she has to be happy with who she is herself and with the kind of choices she makes. And I told her there's no one way to be black. You don't have the right to tell other people how to be black and they sure as hell don't have to right to tell you how to be black. I don't mean to contradict her mama, but I did want to give her a perspective on black folks that she sure didn't seem to be getting at home.

Black teenagers who are controlling others by defending this "inauthentic" identity need to know the power of a truly honest black identity. Rather than adopting and imposing on others a racial identity that silences dissent and debate, parents, like Mrs. Jefferson, can teach them to understand what a sustainable black identity, worthy of defense, really is: an identity that is self-defined, provides a sense of being connected with others, and accepts that there are many ways to be black. We need to let them know that there are productive, effective means of communing as blacks—in Beverly Daniel Tatum's words, "all the black kids sitting together in the cafeteria"—that don't involve inhibiting diverse expressions of blackness or interfering with one another's efforts at self-creation.

Cara's, Janice's, and Lecia's parents were able to help their children understand that there is no single black identity, no one particular way to be black. They understand and strive to support the integrity of a teenager like Cara, who struggles to be herself at the cost of further alienation from her black peers, and who is building a value system that lets her enter into a friendship with a white girl founded on mutual respect. These and stories like them illustrate what I see as an essential parental responsibility: to make certain our children know that by assigning an inflexible, immature standard of identity to their black peers, they are behaving as oppressors in the same way that whites who attempt to enforce social control by assigning negative identities to blacks are oppressors.

We must also offer new models of identity to our teenagers, not just from the arenas of sports and entertainment, where strong black identities are appreciated. Models like these also promote the specious notion of color blindness—that blackness is irrelevant. We should instead ask our teenagers to admire and emulate those people who acknowledge and celebrate blackness, achievement, moral character, justice, and independence. For some, General Colin Powell may fit such a model. General Powell has, much to the chagrin of his political party, stood up and voiced his support of affirmative action, sometimes in very unfriendly social and political venues. He conveys an image of pride in his blackness and his accomplishments, without relying on this as his sole identity. There are many blacks—in and away from the public eye—who are leading lives of integrity and dignity, and who are willing to stand up for what they believe in and against people and forces that would deny them the right to be who they are and follow their dreams. They are in our government, our workplaces, our communities, and our families. As parents we must aggressively and constantly seek them out and offer them as models to our children while they work to integrate their personal and racial identities.

Media Images

Our children are saturated by the media: by magazines, movies, radio, and especially TV. In many households television serves as an additional—or substitute—parent, dramatically influencing our children's perceptions of themselves and the world. Black families seem especially vulnerable to TV. According to Nielsen Media Research, black households watch an average of 73 hours and 30 minutes of television each week. That's well above the national average of 48 hours and 25 minutes for all households. And blacks are especially vulnerable to stereotyping and distortion by the media. In 1997 *Time* magazine reported that "62% of stories on poor people in *Time, Newsweek* and *U.S. News and World Report* were illustrated with photos of African Americans, yet only 29% of poor Americans are black."

The media's most frequent representation of a young black woman is a teenage mother, who is usually presented as a low-income future welfare recipient with minimal education and few skills to bring with her to the workplace. She is sexually irresponsible and easily manipulated by the men in her life. Solely responsible for her plight, it is her fault and her fault alone that her future options are so limited. Black teenage boys fare just as poorly. On television they are violent and emotionally bankrupt, so far beyond hope or redemption that they are outside the social order altogether.

Most commonly, since TV rarely acknowledges cultural differences, blacks are presented as disconnected individuals with no racial affiliations. Racelessness is rewarded and reinforced in the medium. Black teens absorbing these images learn that white people prefer black people in isolation, disconnected from their communities of origin. They also learn that acceptable blacks align themselves with the norms of mainstream society and don't question or even notice social inequities.

Criminals, irresponsible welfare cheats, raceless "only ones"—the relentless perpetuation of these negative images and the exclusionary practices of the media significantly shape white America's attitudes about blacks, as well as attitudes blacks hold about themselves.

Media stereotyping, and some blacks' willingness to take on characteristics of the stereotypes, clearly pains and disheartens our teenagers. In response to my question, "What about black people makes you ashamed?" Kayla, a 17-year-old girl in Albuquerque, answered, "Blacks who act out the stereotypes whites hold about blacks. Especially if they weren't that way to begin with. We are better than that. Why sink to their standards?" In making the connection between the images people see on television and the situation they see in real life, a 17-year-old in Boston told me, "When people see black teenagers on the streets they say, 'Look at that black bum.' Then they look at us all as poor and lazy."

Negating Negative Images

In one of my interviews, a father and son told me a disturbing story about the night a white policeman tailed them as they walked from a high-school event to their home in an interracial neighborhood outside of Raleigh. When the cop stopped his cruiser, the father educated his son: "Don't stop. Don't ever do that. If he doesn't turn his light on, and he stops . . . don't you stop." After they were in the house the policeman knocked at the door to make sure that they lived there. When the father told the officer he was angry, the officer replied, "I'm sorry, sir. We've had a lot of break-ins." "That's true," the father said to me. "But he assumed because we're black . . . Here it is in the nineties and you still can't live in an integrated neighborhood without being identified as a burglar or a mugger or a robber because of the color of your skin. And that was pure racism."

This father had taken the opportunity not just to teach his son a practical short-term survival skill ("Don't stop" in a situation like that) but to bring up a longer-term resistance skill as well: he talked with him about the stereotyping the cop had used, the inaccuracy of his assumptions, and the fact that to the dad they indicated racism. He opened a door for his son to understand his racial reality and how perceptions of black men are distorted by the negative images we all consume.

It is critical that all of us, like this father, help our children from an early age to resist the denigrating images of blacks that assault them from the moment they can focus their eyes on a television screen, images that, as we saw in the case of Emma, can be toxic if swallowed, or, as in the story of the tailing police officer, can lead to humiliation and abuse.

Today's parents suggest several strategies for resisting the negative influences of the media on our children. One strategy, helping children and teenagers understand media politics and the interests that are served by negative stereotyping, requires talking with children about the stereotypes they see—the teenage mothers, the criminal boys—and helping them understand not only their falseness, but why they persist. A mother of a preteenager told me how she'd helped her son think about stereotyping by the news media:

> We went through a period at home a few years ago when my youngest was about 11 or 12 years old. I like to watch the 6 o'clock news at night while I'm fixing dinner, and Bobby would be in the kitchen with me helping out—setting the table, or he'd be working on his homework or whatever. But after a while it got so I couldn't watch the TV anymore. It was like every night there'd be a report about some gang shooting, or some drug bust, and every time I'd look up there'd be a picture of some young black guy being led into a police car with his hands cuffed behind his back.
>
> Now, we live in Philadelphia, and I know a lot of the crime here is in black neighborhoods. But, I'm sorry. Something is wrong here. And it got to a point where my son, he was noticing it, too. He'd ask, "Mommy, how come all the criminals are black?" And I had to tell him, "Son, not all criminals are black. The people who put on the TV news may make it look like they're all black, but that is not reality." And he's a smart kid. He's putting the pieces together, and I help him with that.

Mrs. Hooks helped her son develop the ability to think about possibilities, to think beyond what is presented by the media. Children who are helped this way become increasingly able to examine complex issues like racism and politics. As parents, we need to watch television with our children and discuss with them what they are seeing. We need to talk about why it is that black people are so often overrepresented in stories and images of poverty and crime, or why there seems to be an underrepresentation of positive black role models on the news. As you and your child "read" the television shows and films together, you might ask yourselves: Whose interests are served by perpetuating these stereotypes? Does the presentation of demonized versions of poor black folks pave the way for nonblack people, or middle-class people, to distance themselves from the concerns of the poor and ignore the sociopolitical causes of problems like poverty? Do the misrepresentations we see and read make it easier to exclude blacks and others from the economic power base while taking comfort in the notion that those who are excluded are responsible for their often-limited options? It is essential that our children know that these stereotypes are not the whole truth and that these media depictions do not represent reality in its entirety. Developing media literacy skills—the ability to recognize and critique negative images—is the first step toward overcoming them. And it equips our children and teenagers with what they will need to be critical viewers in your absence.

The second strategy—exhorting children to "talk back" to the media, to confront and repudiate negative images, media stereotypes, and distortions—makes use again of black folks' truth. A mother of a 16-year-old girl told me how this works for her:

> My daughter loves that show *Friends*. All her little girlfriends watch the show each week and then sit on the phone talking about it with each other. So one night I sat there and watched it with her and I had to speak up. I said, "Celeste, what major U.S. city do these people live in where there's no black people? I mean you hardly ever see a black face on that show! They don't have any black friends, they don't work with any black people, nothing!" So she says, "Oh, Ma. It's just a show." I said, "I know it's just a show, but still, what are they saying here?" I said, "Where is this true? Whose reality is this? Is this what we want? For white people to only have white friends?" She goes, "No. But there are a lot of white people who don't know any black people." So I said, "And is that a good thing?" She said, "No. Because then the whites never get a chance to have black friends." I said, "Bingo."

See, you've gotta challenge the reality of these sitcoms. I know it's just a show, but you have to think about who is watching these shows and what they are learning about the world from what they are seeing. My daughter likes to write stories and stuff, and so I told her, "Maybe someday you'll grow up to write more realistic scripts for that television station, because this has got to go."

Rather than allowing her daughter to be a passive media consumer, Celeste's mother challenged her to oppose the industry's limited representation of who blacks are and replace it with images and story lines that are diverse, honest, and reality based. She helped her do a reality check on what she saw: to consider from whose point of view shows like these are written and whose point of view gets silenced in the process, and to make connections and imagine alternatives.

Consciously "sharing parenting" with the media as a resistance strategy means making efforts to counter negative, limited, and limiting media images with stories of African American history and courage, leadership, and change. One mother, Mrs. Harding, described the education she ensured for her children when they were young—an education full of antidotes to media presentations of blacks.

When my kids were young, they went to an all-black school . . . a little private, parochial school that was a community school. It was during the seventies when we were coming off the high ride of the black national movement, so the kids were learning African languages, African customs. I was an activist. I was always getting people fired up at me because I was very political. We participated in a lot of black things. We took the kids to black plays, did black poetry, got involved in lots of black community events. We were constantly reaffirming the struggle of black folks always trying to improve themselves.

In one of our discussions about the media, a Philadelphia father of three jumped up from his seat and walked over to the framed photographs that were spread out across the top of the family's upright piano. "Let me show you something," Mr. March said, and with that he handed me a tattered and faded picture of an old black man. He explained that this was his wife's father's great-grandfather, and that he had fought with the Massachusetts 54th. "The family," he told me, "knew of this honor all along."

We kind of took it for granted. The kids were like, "Yeah, okay, I've heard it." Then a few years ago Hollywood decided to make a movie, *Glory*, with Denzel Washington, and suddenly it became a big deal. Once Hollywood said this story had value, then the kids said it must be true and important. And that's what we are up against. I think it's really important that we tell our stories to our children, and teach them to take pride in those stories with or without Hollywood's help.

A Boston mother, Mrs. Saunders, reinforced Mr. March's messages that we must realize our own role as historians, telling our children our own stories of accomplishment, sharing with the next generation the narratives that shape our future by telling us where we've been. She described a ritual important in her family: each year at Kwanza the adults in the family take the opportunity to tell the family's history, to remind the children where they come from and who they really are.

These parenting strategies, of teaching black youth to recognize and understand negative media imagery; of confronting those images by "talking back" and drawing on black folks' truth; and of providing a constant counter to media distortions with real black stories and history, are critical to raising resisters: children who are socially smart, psychologically strong, and able to create a self in their own image, not one inflicted on them by the media. We must equip our children to understand the limitations the media imposes on blacks through television programming that shows blacks as the only one in a situation, utterly disconnected from his own community, family, or other black friends; or as frightening, violent, and irresponsible. And we must offer alternatives to these assigned identities and teach our children to assume and take pride in a black identity that negates the neutralized or negative ones promoted by American society today.

RESISTANCE STRATEGIES

Unhealthy (Short-Term, Survival-Oriented) Strategies

- Passively consuming media images

- Internalizing negative, denigrating media depictions of blacks as lazy, criminal, and marginal, and becoming dissociated or contemptuous of oneself in response

- Taking on a color-blind perspective (often encouraged by schools) that erases one's racial self, as a response to the confusing, negative images offered by the media

Healthy (Long-Term, Liberating) Strategies

- Helping teenagers to understand media politics and the interests negative stereotyping serves

- Encouraging children to "talk back" to the media, to confront and repudiate negative images

- Instead of allowing the media to parent children, parenting them at home with stories and history that help them know who they really are

- Providing positive models of blacks of achievement, inside and outside the family

Psychologically Strong, Socially Smart

A psychologically strong, socially smart teenager has an understanding of the sociopolitical issues negative media images engender. Such a youngster is able to view media images critically rather than simply accept them, recognizing the point of view from which they are presented, and imagining alternatives.

7

DATING, FAMILY FORMATION, AND CROSSING OVER

Washing the dishes while we talked, the mother of a 16-year-old girl told me,

> I'm always teaching my daughter, Tonya, to assess things correctly, to be on her guard. She has this girlfriend, Alison. Alison, who is white, says she likes hanging with my daughter and going to parties with her because Tonya goes to black parties and Alison says she can meet lots of black guys there. Tonya told me this girl says she only dates black guys. She said she thinks they are cuter and sexier, and good in bed and all that stuff. I said, "WHAT?" Now that girl may have thought she was paying black boys a compliment, but the truth is that she is reacting to black boys based on these old tired stereotypes. I want my daughter to see through this. Honestly, I don't know if the white girl is aware of the racism in her way of thinking. But I definitely want my daughter to know the real deal.

Most black parents want their children to know the "real deal" about sex, love, and relationships. Most want their children to become mature adults, able to create and sustain lasting relationships that can endure the rough-and-tumble ups and downs of marriage or a long-term loving and committed relationship. Most hope—usually out of a sense of fear and a desire to protect their children from homophobia—that these relationships will be heterosexual ones. We also realize that today this ideal is realized less and less often. Some say this is because today's young people are too individualistic and too self-centered, that they don't understand what commitment truly means, and that they're unwilling to make the personal sacrifices that sustained, loving relationships require. Our young adults have neither the stamina nor the endurance for the long term. Hence, today's rising divorce rate. And if large numbers of us are failing in our marriages, even more of us are not getting married at all. Many of the teenage girls I talk to (and often their moms) say that although they would like to marry, they can't find the right mate.

Most of us hope that our grandchildren will be born to two parents, preferably living together, who will love them more than anything else. Yet at the same time we also acknowledge that relationships like this won't be the case for all of today's young black men and women, just as they weren't the case for many of us. The parents I talk to worry about their children and their future relationships, and they are quick to point out potential pitfalls. They fear that their children will launch relationships before they are ready, emotionally or financially, and they worry that they will make bad decisions about whom to love and why. They acknowledge that too many black children are raised in poverty, and in families that are under stress, or where parents are separated, or where a child is estranged from a parent. Some parents speak from personal experience, and they harbor hopes that their children won't repeat mistakes that they themselves once made.

Black parents are also extremely worried about today's highly sexualized youth culture, and about whether our children are responsible and mature enough to make decisions that protect them not only from unwanted pregnancy, but from potentially life-threatening disease. We know that sex is used to sell everything today, from jewelry and jeans to self-esteem. We recognize the intensity of the sex drive in adolescence and young adulthood, as well as the terrifying threat of AIDS. The stakes are dizzyingly high here: we must teach our children to resist the sexual irresponsibility that clouds judgment, and to resist making babies they can't afford to raise. We know we must make our teenagers understand the reality of the costs of raising a child: that the cost of raising children escalates, and that parents without escalating paychecks are doomed to fall behind.

We also know that we must raise our sons to resist the temptation to abandon their families. They should be made to understand that too many black children are raised without fathers, that the lack of a father's paycheck leads to poverty for most black mothers, and that poor children are at risk for myriad social problems, from poor health to abuse to academic failure to involvement in illegal activities. And we know, too, that we must teach our daughters to resist equating motherhood with womanhood, to resist making a child in order to have someone to love who will love you back, to resist sleeping with a guy just to hold on to a relationship—because he says he loves you, or because being in a relationship makes you feel more grown up, or because you don't know how to say no or don't respect yourself enough to do so. All the black parents I've met want their daughters to resist making babies simply because they want to fit in with the other girls or women they run with, and they want their daughters to resist choosing their baby's father based on how he looks and whether he will make pretty babies, which may elevate the mother's status and provide an ego boost (however short-lived) for the young parents.

The parents I talked with want their children to be able to stand up for mature, committed relationships based on knowledge of themselves and each other, who come together with a solid sense of identity, knowing what they want and what they are willing to give up or compromise on, because they know they will have to eventually. Ideally, parents say, they want their children to enter a relationship after they've completed their education and have stable, promising jobs that put them in a financial situation that makes raising children realistic.

The same parents acknowledge that for their daughters who don't marry but have children, the task will be even harder, and they want their daughters to be aware of this reality. They want their unmarried daughters to know that if they have children it is their responsibility to be forewarned and prepared before they are born. That is, they must be financially able to handle the costs of parenting, and have strong social support. They also need to know that they should stay connected to their child's biological parent, or have a surrogate parent available and willing to step in when needed.

The next generation deserves the best we can offer them. This doesn't mean lots of things or lots of money. It does mean love, commitment, security, and parents who don't just make a way for their children, but make the best way possible. Doing this requires thoughtful planning and a certain kind of readiness—including self- and group knowledge, education, stable employment with a future, and social support. All in all, parents and teenagers alike say we must take an unwavering stand for strong, secure, and stable black families.

PROMOTING RESPONSIBLE, REALITY-BASED PARENTING

The teenagers with whom I spoke, including the teenage moms, told me that their parents emphasized responsibility in the messages they communicated about sex. Dwania recounted the list of messages she remembers hearing as a young woman. Her parents told her "to be responsible to your community, the black community." They also told her "the message of respecting people's differences. You know, messages of being humanitarian. They talk a lot about sexual responsibility—about who you choose to have sex with, whether you choose to have a baby or whether you choose not to. They say, just be responsible." The thrust was clear: she was to embrace responsibility and respect.

One mother, Mrs. Banks, has an 18-year-old daughter. In her conversations with her daughter, which she makes sure take place often, she constantly emphasizes the importance of resisting sexual irresponsibility and premature motherhood:

> I like to know what's on my kid's mind all the time, or as much as I possibly can. We talk about sex, and I told her, "I don't want you to have sex, but if you feel as though you can't resist, make sure he has a condom. Or you go get birth control pills. But don't bring me no grandkids until you're out of college."

Mr. Ellis described the clear, no-nonsense messages he gave to his son about responsibility in relationships, about resisting premature fatherhood, and about dealing with the consequences of fatherhood:

> My son learned to do the dishes and to iron his clothes and clean the house just like my three daughters. It's like, "Look, we're all people in this house and we'd better do this thing together." I gave my son the message my father gave me: You shouldn't go out with any woman you didn't feel was good enough to marry. And I told my son early on I didn't want any kids out of wedlock. If he slipped up—I didn't care how old he was—he was going to support it. He wasn't going to quit school, and his grades better not slip either. "So the best thing for you to do," [I told him] "is not to do anything."

He described, too, his frank discussions with both his sons and daughters about sex: "I told all of my kids about sex. I said, 'It's not that difficult. You don't need to practice it. It comes naturally and you'll get the hang of it once you get married.'"

Unfortunately, double standards are clearly still alive and well in too many of our homes. Seventeen-year-old Flo says she hears double standards articulated by girls and boys all around her at the alternative school that she attends for pregnant and parenting teens. As she said,

> A lot of girls I know they say, "Well, I'm lucky I have a boy because he won't be bringing any babies home." I say, "Don't tell your son that! That's like giving him a license to say, 'Here, you go get as many girls pregnant as you want, but don't acknowledge any of the pregnancies or anything.'" So we'll have another generation of unwanted babies. And then there goes another generation of black people in jail, black people on drugs, black people undereducated, illiterate, black people in drugs and prostitution. You know what I'm saying?

Flo was a very smart, thoughtful young mother, who understood how the irresponsible messages embedded in double standards about sexual responsibility give boys freedom to hit and run. She told me that she grew up in a family where adults and children talked about their racial reality frequently. Her mom, an artist, encouraged her to think hard about where we are headed as a people, and what we can do to turn things around. "We used to talk about it before," she said, "but now that I'm pregnant, we talk about these things even more." It was Flo's mother who helped Flo clearly see the connection between early, unplanned pregnancy and the decline of black individuals, families, and the community. And Flo says its because of these conversations that she's more determined than ever to attend college and offer her baby the best life she can.

Although we often act as if adolescent motherhood is something new, it's hardly that. And, as more than a few young women have reminded me, large numbers of adolescent women (including their own mothers) have raised children and turned out fine, thank you. It can be really tough to deliver a message of restraint in the face of a reality of children who have limited real-life experience and may not know what their options are or could be in the future.

When I talk to middle-aged black women about teen pregnancy, they inevitably share their own experiences as teenage mothers. These women often welcome the chance to share with teenagers the hard-learned lessons about becoming adults, which they feel are important to pass on to the next generation.

Mrs. Trotter, 41 years old and with two sons in their early twenties at the time we spoke, described the period she became pregnant with her sons as a time when she was "side-tracked" and "lost herself." Attracted to boys at an early and vulnerable age, she spent much of her adolescence in pursuit and being pursued, and the following two decades raising kids and keeping house. The responsibility of child rearing and housekeeping demanded that she put aside her own needs for self-exploration and development. Pretty soon she didn't know who she was or what she desired. Now, in midlife review, she thinks often of the years of self-discovery that were lost, and she sees the need to resist a loss of self as the key lesson she can pass on. This kind of "recovery" speaks to a recognition of loss that for some compels us to honor what's been absent and to reestablish it, sometimes physically, sometimes psychologically or socially. And sometimes recovery means a reaching back in order to move forward.

Knowing that others can learn from their struggles is an important part of the process. One key message these mothers conveyed was this: all see the need to reestablish the kinds of kinship and social supports for young mothers that we had in our families and communities in the past in order to ensure the health and well-being of future generations.

Mrs. Young also became a parent while she was still a teenager. She acknowledged how difficult the task of raising a child can be for such a young woman, but she also pointed out the support and models she had in her own mother and other members of her family:

> I was 18 when I had my first child. But one of the things I had was the sense of how to be a parent. I had the sense of what it would constitute to be a full, complete woman, you know, in terms of accepting that responsibility—to care for your own children, to care for your husband, to nurture them, to be able to balance a child and work, if that was your option. I mean, we've never had too many choices in terms of that. [It] was a given. So I had seen my mother do it, and her mother no doubt had done it. I had not seen her [my grandmother] do it, but I know when I hear the stories about what she went through to keep her family together, I know that she did it.

The support that Mrs. Young had from her family is considerably harder to come by today, when fewer and fewer teenagers have the good fortune to be part of a caring extended family in the immediate area. With the loss of the extended family and of community supports has come the loss of models and stories for parents, no matter what their age, to learn from, and little that's been helpful has sprung up in its place. Both Mrs. Trotter and Mrs. Young appeared aware of this, and both emphasized the critical importance of forming a strong personal identity at a young age, of knowing who you are, and of supporting each other.

Another mother, Ruthie Walston, told me a similar story about what she had learned from reflection on the loss of her marriage and the recovery of her sense of self.

> Today, I just believe in doing the things you want to. That's my whole thing. This is what I would tell black girls: "I lost myself. The last time I was married, I was so in love with him that nothing else mattered. I put this person before myself, and I felt like my happiness was just in this man. And now, since I've been divorced this last time, I realize that you've got to be happy within yourself. And that's something I was not. I just thought that oh, as long as I had a man, the man I wanted, that would make me happy. But when you change your identity to have someone, you don't need them. You've got to be yourself." I always say, in order to be free, I've got to be me.

DATING AND FINDING A MATE

Often my talks with parents and teenagers evolve into discussions about dating and, for some, future marriage. Families with older teenagers are well aware that their children are at a stage when they are developing their capacity to achieve mature intimacy and commit themselves to someone. As one adolescent developmental psychologist describes it, "Dating is a means of personal and social growth. It is a way of learning to know, understand and get along with many different types of people. Through dating, youths learn cooperation, consideration, responsibility, numerous social skills and matters of etiquette, and techniques for interacting with other people."

All of us hope that our children will find partners who will treat them well and who understand the importance of respect and mutuality in a committed relationship. One father, Mr. Harris, talked about his aspirations for his children, both girls and boys, and what he emphasizes to them when he talks about relationships:

> I talk to both [my daughters and my sons] about roles—how they both can contribute and not take advantage of the other. I tell my daughter to find a man that respects himself and loves himself first. Because without that, they can't love you. And if you find a person that's got to dominate you, where you've got to spend all your time in the kitchen and not be treated as equal, that's the wrong relationship for you to be in. [To my] sons I say, "Don't dominate the ladies. Don't push the ladies. You treat them with respect, the same way you would treat your mother or even your sister." I know I won't be with them all the time . . . but I try to monitor their behavior. What I instill in them is, "Don't bring no junk home, because you're not going to get my approval."

When parents are talking to boys, Daneesha, an 18-year-old mother, says they should emphasize family and education. As she said,

> The absence of black men is a really bad problem. Every black girl I know knows a guy that she has dated who has been in jail. Personally I know three guys that I used to date that are in jail now. Teach boys the responsibility of family. It's okay to cook, clean, take kids to the park. It's okay to love. Then they wouldn't do drugs, jail, cuz they'd have something to fall back on. I mean if a man loves his family, he wouldn't do that [stuff].

A social worker I know tells me that in her clinical practice, she is seeing more and more black families who appear to be discouraging their young adult sons from leaving home. Sometimes it's about protection, she said, and safety issues, and sometimes it betrays the parents' fear that because of the poor, low-paying jobs that are available to him, a son can't make it in the outside world on his own. Some of the young men, she told me, become too comfortable to leave. What they lose is independence, that critical learning of how to sink or swim on one's own. Over time the situation also contributes to a decline in financially stable, potentially marriable black men.

Mr. Franklin is struggling to raise three sons. He sees the difficulty teenagers face in getting past the superficial, in knowing how to understand what is important in a relationship—like love, sharing, mutual trust, respect and, loyalty—and what isn't—like skin color or social-class status.

> The bottom line is who the person is. It's so difficult to overcome the superficiality that young adolescents are introduced to around male/female relationships, because of early sexual activeness, and I think it creates a lot of confusion. It lets the sex drive and other things take center stage, rather than the drive of understanding [someone's] personality and the like. And it allows them too often to drift into an immature sexuality and the beginnings of an immature set of early relationships that take a long, long time to recover and regenerate. I hope my kids get past the superficiality—that you select somebody because of their class, their color, because they're going to give you some cute children. . . . I hope . . . [they avoid] the differences and alienation and put-downs that I have seen in my lifetime. I hope they get around some of that. And I hope also in my guts that they do not choose a white mate.

DATING ACROSS THE LINES

The subject of interracial dating and marriage still haunts us. I continue to hear, from both parents and teenagers, strong prohibitions about crossing that line. In particular, many of us still believe that black men should marry only black women. Arlene, a 16-year-old, summed up the sentiment of all the girls I spoke to when she said, "Black boys need to stay with their black women."

Until very recently, we as a group have tended to leave black girls and women out of our discussions about interracial dating. Talk about dating and marriage between black girls or black women and white men tends to arise when we express our worries about the dwindling number of available black men; this predicament, we say, might require black girls who wish to marry to look outside the race. Those discussions are supported by current statistical research that shows that most black women will marry either later in life or not at all. (According to the March 1998 U.S. Census Bureau Report, 53 percent of African Americans ages 25 to 34 have never married.)

Mr. Franklin, who had said that he "hoped in [his] guts" that his children didn't choose white mates, also shared with me his own experiences dating white women when he was in college. He said that although he did date white women for a while, he eventually knew he had to "confront reality"—that is, the future. He stopped dating one white woman in particular because he knew he would never be accepted by her family. And his own parents told him many times not to look at white women in terms of long-term commitments, that to do so would be an offense to black women. He was also influenced, he said, by the climate of the times: this was the 1960s, when the black nationalist movement characterized interracial dating as a rejection of black women. While he accepts his own and the attraction of other black men to white women as honest and genuine, he continues to feel that his decision (not to marry outside the race) was the right one, and he hopes his children do, too. He wants to teach his sons the reasons to marry within their culture: to support and build strong families that will sustain and support resistance to all the barriers blacks have and must still conquer as a people.

Mr. Ellis, on the other hand, saw marrying a white man as a possibility for his daughters. He talked about listening to a discussion among six 13- and 14-year-old black girls at his daughter's school cafeteria. He described the conversation:

[One turned to me and said,] "If you're smart, you end up in jail for black males. If you're cute, they kill you. If you're dumb, you ain't worth it. And if . . ." After they ran it down, eliminating all these black males, they said, "Who are we going to marry?" I said, "Well, I guess it's about time for you to look for some white males, then. Don't rule that out because you look out here and you see how these white girls chase these black boys." I said, "Don't rule out your marrying a white male." But they had ruled them out. They said that by the time they finished with the black men who were gay, black men who were in jail, black men who get killed, and those that are just plain not worth the effort, there's no one left. And these were 13- and 14-year-old black girls talking!

It's one thing to be in your thirties and have the fear—that there are absolutely no marriage possibilities on the horizon—hit you upside the head, but it's quite another to face that reality at age 13 or 14, when these issues seem new, extremely important, and maybe even insurmountable. Mr. Ellis thinks black girls should of necessity think about "broadening their options" and reconsider marrying outside the race.

Men are absent from many black women's lives, and as a result, many black girls grow up fatherless in female-headed households. Those who do have fathers in the picture often say that their fathers become increasingly uncomfortable interacting with their daughters, particularly after puberty. And now as the girls approach young adulthood, many find themselves unable to date because of the paucity of available young black men.

Anxiety about lacking partners appears to be setting in at an earlier age. Some girls tell me they fear being alone in a culture that emphasizes couples. They are apprehensive about social disapproval for single parenthood, yet they are aware of the important cultural value placed in the black community on fertility and having babies. Increasingly, our daughters feel they simply can't couple even if they wish to do so. Some, feeling desperate, make poor dating and marriage choices. Their alternatives? They can wait for black men to appear (and risk being alone forever) or they can cross over.

As Shawnee told me,

> A lot of black girls feel as though they should have black boyfriends. I rarely see girls that have a different race for a boyfriend. Because they feel that people will talk about them. [They think] people would talk about you. You know, like the movie, *Jungle Fever.* That's why everybody don't want to be around this stuff. But that don't make me no difference. I mean, because you're white, I mean I'm not going to treat you no different from a black guy. If a white guy was to approach me, and he told me he liked me and wanted to take me out, I would go out with him. Because he's white, that don't make no difference.

One young woman I interviewed asked me what I thought about dating outside of the race. Not at all sure of where she was headed with this line of questioning, I stammered out a lame, poorly thought-out response to her question. I don't even think she heard what I said, for before I could finish, she launched into a story about a young Latino man she had recently been dating. Then she described what had happened at her house when she brought him home. Her dad, she explained, was polite while her guest was there. But after the man left, he pulled her aside and told her in no uncertain terms how disappointed he was in her choice of dating partners. "I expected this from your brothers," he said, "but I never expected it from you."

Traditionally, we African Americans as a group have been highly reluctant to endorse interracial marriages in which black women are marrying outside of the race. The situation brings back to our collective consciousness terrible memories of black women being raped and coerced into sex by white slave masters. It invokes images of powerlessness—of black women used and abused. In addition, we think of black women as the carriers of the culture, the parent most responsible for passing on the traditions, values, and consciousness of a people. How can she do this when she is coupled with a white or nonblack man? And to many black women, white men are seen as the ultimate oppressor, members of the group that receives all the power and privileges this society has to offer and holds that power close to the chest, preventing everyone else—especially black folks—from getting close. Who can imagine sleeping with the enemy?

There is a problem here. Too many black girls and women have grown up thinking of white men as the enemy. When it comes to mate selection, we exclude them from our consideration *just because they are white.* Upon closer scrutiny, this is, of course, a troubling, prejudiced notion. We are making assumptions about individuals within the group based on ideas we hold about the entire group, conduct that exasperates and angers blacks when we are the objects of it. But when it comes to dating outside the race, we often hold a double standard, especially when it comes to black women and nonblack men.

Black girls and women are thoroughly conditioned to avoid thinking about dating nonblacks. In many of our families we don't even talk about it: the prohibition is assumed to be true, right, and just. End of story. But based on contemporary conditions, including the dearth of black men to date and marry, the declining rates of marriage and remarriage in the black community, the increasing number of black children born out of wedlock and/or raised without fathers, many black women may now be thinking that it's time to begin the conversation. It's clearly a subject that would benefit from more discussion in the black community and in our families.

MAKING SMART CHOICES

At the very least, we must reiterate the fact that our girls should resist excluding white men for the wrong reason—simply because they are white.

Then we need to talk about dating outside of the community: the implications, the consequences, the pros and cons. We need to talk to our daughters about being open, flexible, and careful. We need to tell them that even if they date or marry outside of the race, it is important to stay connected to family if they can, and to the larger black community as well. Finally, we need to help our daughters to support one another in whatever decisions they make.

But what about our boys? The issue for them is, I believe, very different. In talking about this subject with parents and teenagers, I often feel as though I've stepped into an argument with a history, one in which people have long since chosen the side they're on. In fact, nearly everyone who brings up the topic feels that when black men choose to date and marry white women, it is tantamount to a rejection of black women and the black community. They think that dating white suggests all manner of negative things about the men who do cross, that it denotes a lack of racial identity and self-love. Some put the issue in more urgent terms: If the race is already under siege, how can we afford to lose even one?

A father in Raleigh told me he tells his young son, "If you can manage to—when you do start dating—look around, look at all these beautiful sisters before you go out with a white girl." He added, "I wouldn't say no if he wanted to marry a white woman. I wouldn't tell him not to, but I'd rather see him marry a sister."

A New Mexico woman described how the past and present collided in her mind when her high-school son began to date a series of white girls. Like many of us, she had, in her twenties, rejected the "marry within your race" imperative passed down by an older generation. Love, she taught her own offspring, was about respect and mutual compatibility, not skin color. Today, however, in her forties and resentful of her son's dating choices, she finds herself questioning her beliefs. Had she failed to teach her son to embrace positive images of black women, to resist common cultural biases? Had she failed to give him the tools to resist?

Her story and a North Carolina woman's combined to sum up the issue as a dilemma of the post-civil-rights era. The North Carolina woman, who was raising her family in a predominantly white, middle-class suburb, told me a story about her son's dating partners, and the discussions about interracial dating that she and her husband have with him and his brothers. The son, who was in the room as she spoke, was extremely embarrassed by the conversation and cut in on several occasions. Their conversation was a fascinating example of parent-child verbal volleyball. The mother talked first:

First of all, we talk to make them aware that they are black males and that black females resent the fact that these white females are [approaching them]. Our sons are athletic, they play on the varsity and junior varsity teams, and they are spotlighted. That makes them appealing in another sense. And we try to make them aware—make sure they understand why she's approaching you. I didn't want them to be confused when the girls ran up and said, "Oh, you're so cute! I wanna know him because he plays varsity at Central." Don't be stupid about that!

Once I asked him, "What is it about these white girls that is so appealing to you?" [Son groans and mumbles, "Why are you doing this to me?"] This one says, "Mama, they're good for your ego. They just pursue you and they just get so excited."

Then one of the sons said to his mother, "Mom you have to understand that being an individual, sometimes you need that ego boost. You need somebody to say, 'You're somebody.'" The mother continued, "But the black girls say that, too. You just don't hear it."

As the conversation progressed, the mother described the dilemma she and many black parents face when it comes to socializing children about race as it relates to dating issues:

See, I'm going to tell you where the contradiction comes. It's difficult to try and raise your children as Christians with a philosophy of love, and then with the philosophy of being black men. We don't have enough of those black men for the black females. And it's hard to tell a child we would really rather you just date black girls, because we want you to have a black wife when you get married, while at the same time you also try to teach them to look at the person's heart.

If I'm totally honest, I want the boys to find somebody with a good heart who's black. That's just the bottom line and maybe that's not right. But see, when we were growing up there was no choice—we didn't even think about that. But because of the environment they are in, I mean it's hot pursuit. And sometimes its hard when those hormones start kicking in and all those emotions . . .

At this point her son broke in to say he likes to date black girls *and* white girls, to which she replied,

> When you go back and forth, if your emotions get caught on the forth side before you come back, then it may be real hard to come back. And that's all we're trying to get you to see when we have these conversations with you boys.

These interracial relationships do, as this mom attests, try us in any number of ways. Although statistically the numbers remain relatively small, the vast majority of interracial marriages are between black men and non-black (usually white) women, a phenomenon we've been observing and talking about for quite some time. Some of us are adamantly against inter-racial marriages, some of us are on the fence. We don't like it in principle, but when it comes down to our child—our son and daughter-in-law—we give it a conditional okay.

As the North Carolina mother pointed out, parents often stress to their sons that they must resist loving white women for the wrong reasons. These wrong reasons include valuing a white standard of beauty over all others: buying into the notion that white women are more beautiful than black women, or any other group of women, just because they are closest to the image that advertisers say is ideal. The wrong reasons also include believing that white women are smarter, more refined, or more "feminine" than any other women, or being attracted to white woman for the "ego boost" some black men can get from being chosen by a white woman. That is, because black men know that white women are subtly conditioned to steer clear of black men, the fact that a white woman has chosen a black man must mean he is really remarkable. Another wrong reason is the ego boost associated with the assumption of black male virility that is embed-ded in the black male stereotypes about sexuality. Still another wrong rea-son is thinking that having a white woman on one's arm at the company picnic will enhance one's position in the company, raise one's status, or show people that you have arrived.

Finally, it's critical to resist dating or marrying a white woman because you think the relationship will help you to escape the stress and strain of be-ing black, or of being a financial provider. Some people think that in an in-terracial relationship these problems will disappear, or will diminish in importance because you have different challenges—challenges that are more acceptable, like the romantic stress of loving a white woman—instead of the boring, everyday stress of being a black man, or a black father/provider. All in all, these notions need to be resisted because they are not about love, mutual compatibility, and respect, the elements that are essential to building a strong, committed relationship.

RESISTANCE STRATEGIES

Unhealthy (Short-Term, Survival-Oriented) Strategies

- Engaging in unplanned, unprotected sex

- Succumbing to peer pressure or pressuring others

- Forming relationships before you are emotionally and financially equipped to do so

- Having babies as a way to fit in with other girls or to have someone to love and love you back

- Sleeping with boys or men just to hold on to a relationship, because it makes you feel more grown-up or because you don't know how to say no or don't have enough self-respect to say no

- Abdicating responsibility for the children you have fathered

- Dating or marrying a white woman because she meets a white standard of beauty or femininity, for your own ego boost, because you think it's a status symbol, or because you think it will help you avoid the pressures of being a black man

Healthy (Long-Term, Liberating) Strategies

- Teaching teenagers to embrace sexual responsibility and respect, both for themselves and others, through open, honest, and constant communication

- Teaching youngsters the reality of entering into relationships and having children: the financial costs, the necessary commitment, the requirements of sacrifice and compromise

- Teaching daughters that if they expect to have babies without marriage, they must plan ahead: they must know who they are, and they must be educated, have stable employment with future prospects, and have sturdy social supports

• Teaching teenagers to embrace high expectations in mate selection

• Helping teens understand the importance of embracing the black family

• Helping daughters to understand that they shouldn't exclude the idea of marrying a white man simply because he is white. This should apply to men from other racial and cultural groups as well.

Psychologically Strong, Socially Smart

A psychologically strong, socially smart teenager enters into a relationship fully aware of the commitment and long-term responsibilities it will entail. He or she resists immature relationships that bring short-term satisfaction at the expense of long-term love and support, and makes decisions about dating and forming a family with long-term goals in mind, including the responsibility of raising the next generation of black children.

PART THREE

SPENDING AND FINANCIAL GOOD SENSE

Therese, a hard-working mother of a teenage boy and a younger daughter, was venting to me about the story a coworker had told her about her 13-year-old son:

> This boy had been badgering his mother for I don't know how long about buying him brand-new $130 Michael Jordan sneakers. Now she's a single parent with three kids, right? She works full time at my company and I know she could not afford these shoes. So what does she do? She takes another part-time job somewhere else just so she can buy her boy these things. Okay. So the boy finally gets his sneakers and he's at the gym, on the basketball court, you know, showing them off. But then—and I couldn't believe this—she says, "The next thing you know he starts teasing the other boys, calling their clothes 'cheap' and 'ghetto' because they didn't have the fancy shoes he had." Can you believe it? Yesterday he didn't have them himself. Then he gets the damn shoes and suddenly he thinks he's better than everyone else. And what's really bad is that this boy didn't have a clue about what his mother had to go through to get those sneakers.

She threw up her hands in exasperation.

That's why I talk with my boys about money and the cost of things these days. We don't buy things just because they're in, or they see them on the commercials. If they outgrow what they have, or if it's a special occasion or something like that, fine. But to buy just to buy— no way. And then to rub someone else's face in it. Uh-uh. No way.

Like Therese, many black parents talk about the importance of making sure children know where money comes from—hard work and sacrifice— and of the importance of knowing not to waste it by buying frivolous, unnecessary items, or to use it as a wedge between people, especially other black people who may have less than you. Their comments reminded me of the story I heard from a black social worker in Boston. She had saved for years to buy a Mercedes, and when she finally brought it home, she found that several of her black neighbors assumed she'd paid for it with gambling winnings, or by dealing drugs. That she had actually scrimped and sacrificed for it simply didn't occur to them. She attributed their bad feelings to envy and resentment, which surprised and disheartened her. "We can be our own worst enemy," she complained.

Spending the Future: Teens and Money

A Philadelphia girl was murdered over the gold chain she wore around her neck. It was a bleak, sad story. A boy demanded her necklace, she resisted, and so he shot her. For me it became an allegory for the kind of unfettered materialism that defines black youth today and threatens their futures. Many of us now raising kids agree that our teenagers are too often chained by gold necklaces to lives of meaningless materialism and waste.

The Philadelphia girl's story wasn't new. Black children and teenagers are killed, maimed, and assaulted daily across the nation, not just in the inner cities of Philadelphia and Boston, but in racially mixed and predominately white suburban schools in and around Raleigh and Albuquerque as well. And the violence is all too often tied to the possession of objects: sneakers, leather jackets, gold chains. Parents all over the country lament the culture of materialism among blacks, especially among young blacks.

Mrs. Patterson, a 58-year-old Boston mother, is "proud about our strength, our ability to overcome odds, [and] that inner strength and courage." But like many others, she worries that our children are losing sight of those attributes: "Kids today," she said, "don't realize that's what it took. That thread has been broken. We've relinquished our traditional heritage . . . in a rush to become urbanized we left a lot of the values and the morals.

These kids were not rooted and grounded in anything." She, like many of us, blames her own generation, at least in part, for the problem: "After Martin Luther King's assassination," she says, "we fell apart. We passed on the black-power salute, the Afros, outward symbols of being black. But nothing substantive."

Many African American parents believe that financial responsibility is actually about self-determination, at both the personal and collective levels. We want to help our teenagers with their developmental task of achieving economic independence, and in order to do so, we know we must help them clarify their thinking about material acquisition. We also know, and want our children to know, that financial responsibility is related to both family stability and the black community's economic health. These are the things both parents and teenagers tell me we need to take a stand on.

Many talked about the necessity of good, thoughtful, future-oriented money management. Some told stories of how family members had been swindled (almost always by unscrupulous white people) out of land or valuable possessions due to their ignorance of money matters. That history, which is still fresh in our minds, demands that we pay much closer attention to our money.

A mother in Boston shared a widespread complaint when she stated that our children aren't taught the folly of materialistic values. Like other parents, she worries that this generation of teenagers, who are growing up in a materialistic, consumer-oriented culture, and who so often have never been required to spend their own money on anything but discretionary items like clothes and stereos, have a severely distorted financial perspective. Although they know how to buy, they don't know how to budget, prioritize, sacrifice, or save. She worries too about the fact that so many teenagers appear to learn their bad financial habits from their parents and other family members—the very people from whom they should be learning financial responsibility.

Consumerism is endemic among Americans of all races. But for blacks the statistics are particularly disturbing. According to the economist Julianne Malveaux, writing in *Essence* magazine, "right now Black people are 12.7% of the population of the United States. We earn 8% of the income, but own just 3% of the wealth of roughly $2 trillion in assets held by American households," and "on average black households spend 25% more than white households on color TV's, but are 30% less likely to have savings."

We, and especially our teenagers, are locked in a relentless cycle: we want as much as the next person, and when we get it, there's always someone standing by with even more for us to compete for. We want the right selections and the latest cars, and we want to wear fashionable clothes with someone else's name emblazoned across our chests and backsides.

Marketing demographics show that blacks are into looking good. Our spending last year topped $400 billion annually. We define ourselves all too often by our cash supply and our things, confuse identity with ownership, and status with fashion. And to maintain our self-created image, we buy more. And more. And more.

One Philadelphia mother used her own family as a point of reference when she discussed money, spending, and values. As examples of misplaced values, she told me stories of her relatives, whom she described as people who held good jobs with good salaries, and who overemphasized expensive clothes while they deemphasized and even ignored school achievement. "It's so easy to run into blacks who are shuckin' and jivin'," she said, "and think life is one big party. And sometimes I see some of these black mothers [who live in her neighborhood] who tend to be so materialistic. They wear Gucci, Pucci, and all that stuff. They don't even worry about the kids.".

We can all share stories about mothers who could stretch a dime halfway to China, and about fathers who sacrificed, pinched, and saved to send a child or two to school. Those stories of sacrifice and honor often stay with us. The truth is, poor people can't afford to make poor choices. Although we have more disposable income than ever before, many feel there's been a loss of these values and behaviors today.

A lot of us grew up in poverty and know firsthand about the stresses that poverty places on black families. We were raised with a mentality of survival, of never having had enough. Our own parents grew up seldom having money; when they did have it, they spent it only on items that were absolutely necessary. Some of us can recall our parents participating in bizarre spending rituals that grew out of having so little, like buying and hoarding because they were afraid they'd lose what they had worked so hard to attain, or buying "nice" items—like fancy china, or draperies—never to display them until the right time, which never seemed to come. Others of us grew up in frugal, even stingy families. On the other hand, some of us grew up with relatives who couldn't hold onto a buck even if their life depended on it.

Those of us who grew up with these kinds of concerns about money don't ever want to return to never having enough, never knowing when or if we'll ever get what we want or need. And we want so much more for our own children. Many of us hope and believe that through our children we can have experiences we were denied when we were young. We buy into the guilt trip society inflicts on working mothers, and we try to make up for this perceived (and sometimes real) lack of time with our children by buying them things: toys they seldom use, clothes they seldom wear, videos they seldom watch. And many of us hold down multiple jobs in order to buy even more.

This chronic need to buy more and generally higher-and higher-ticket items is a shortsighted form of resistance—to invisibility, marginality, and low self-worth. It's a quick-fix response to not being allowed to play the game, or to fully participate socially, economically, or politically. It's an attempt to buy recognition, status, and self-esteem to impress each other and to feel good about ourselves. And purchases often do make us feel good, at least until those monthly charge card payments come due. Then we pay the real price: the emotional, psychological, and family turmoil caused by debt. We pass these self-handicapping strategies along to our children, in the form of crippling attitudes and values about money, like "easy come, easy go," "buy now, pay later," maxing out our credit cards, buying because there's a sale, buying to be hip, buying just to buy.

Mr. Lawrence remarked that what used to be a code of manners is today a code of cash. His daughter had begun to date, and he had many complaints about the boys who came to the house—about how they dressed and especially about their lack of respect and their bad manners. When he was growing up, he said, a young man was expected to walk up to the door, ring the bell, meet, and (despite every disinclination he might have) carry on a conversation with the girl's parent. The boys who date his daughter, he said, sit in the car and honk the horn for her to come out. Or they come, as he put it, "with their posses"—a whole new spin on group dating. He was clearly and thoroughly disgusted with what he perceived as the boys' materialism and rudeness.

There's no code being put out there. And not just put out there, but being enforced. If you don't follow a code, there are also some repercussions thereof, and they don't see that now. What they see is "if I don't have a dollar," the repercussions thereof. So whatever the code is that says, "this is how you get a dollar," that's the code everybody is adhering to.

According to Mr. Lawrence, and to other parents as well, the code of conduct has changed. When he was a young man, boys were expected to show respect and worthiness when they dated. Interpersonal respect has been lost to a rage for money and the activities that produce it. That's why he insists that he meet the guys his daughter goes out with at least once face to face.

I don't care how much money he has, and I hope my daughter doesn't care either. He's only 18—how much money can he have? I mean legitimately. It's not about the money, it's about respect, and I want these boys to know they got to have respect for my daughter and her family.

The media (television, movies, advertising, billboards) fan the flames of this consumer fire. Fashion has become a major part of the entertainment world. The expensive sneakers, hip-hop sweats and sports clothes that black teenagers wear quickly become standards for black teenagers across the country, and more recently, to white teenagers as well. A Boston father, Mr. Francis, told me that his own sons were teased at school by other blacks because they weren't as he put it, "slaves to fashion." Black fashion parades as black "authenticity," and our children want it—at younger and younger ages. But can you really buy a sense of self at the store?

WHAT MONEY SHOULDN'T MEAN

The effects of this jacked-up consumerism are insidious and profound, our values become confused. We and our children start to equate looking good with maturity, having things with being good, self-esteem with appearance. Kate Jordan, who was particularly incensed with "the hot pursuit of the Benjamins," tells her children about a boyfriend she once dated who "failed in life" because of his need to keep up with the Joneses, to look good, to "be the man" at any price. This young man spent too much of his youth making sure that he always looked good or better than everyone else. He always had to have the fancy clothes, the latest car; he had to be "the man" at any price. But eventually the price got too high. He had overspent. When the company he worked for was sold, he lost his job and eventually everything else. He never bounced back from that blow to his self-esteem. Today, still unhappy with his situation, he remains essentially unemployed, bouncing from dead-end job to dead-end job, unable to commit to anything because he doesn't feel he's a man.

This is particularly problematic when it comes to forming individual relationships. If a teenage boy chooses his friends based on what they have and wear, will he experience any of the real rewards of friendship, like loyalty and support? If a teenage girl selects her boyfriend based on his possessions, how likely is it that the relationship will be a loving one? Teenagers, intent on "fitting in" with a group, find it easy to identify desirable groups based on what they own. The price of admission to a group may simply be the right clothes, CDs, or concert tickets. Selecting friends and choosing whom to date based on material possessions may provide short-term companionship, but in the long run it may mean a lifetime of perverse and distorted values.

One mother told me that even her young teenage daughter feels the influence of money in social situations:

> Ellen, my 14-year-old, has recently become interested in boys, so we talk often about how to choose the right kind of boy to spend time with. She isn't really dating yet—I wouldn't allow it at this age—but she'll go with maybe a small group of kids to the movies or something. There's a lot of emphasis with these kids on money. Too much for my taste. At her age, I tell her that she should be concentrating on what the boy is like, what his personality is like, do they get along, do they have similar interests. Money, I tell her, should be way down on the list.

According to Joy Patton, the task grows even harder and more complicated as teenagers get older. The mother of a 16-year-old, she knows that it's especially hard to pit her own messages of restraint against the messages about how to behave in relationships that her daughter receives from soap operas and CDs. Joy spends a significant amount of time, she says, countering the messages of rap lyrics, which she thinks provide a warped, unhealthy view of relationships between males and females. All too often, she told me, they suggest that a girl's primary goal is to find a guy who will buy her things—not just any things, but expensive things. Any guy who can't rise to the task is, as the song by the group TLC terms it, a "scrub." She went on,

> Half the time I don't know what these rappers are saying. The music's too loud. They're mumbling. Then every now and then you catch a

phrase and . . . Say what!?! Come again??! So what I've learned to do is this: I read the lyrics. Even if I don't wanna hear it I make sure that I know what she is listening to. Then if there's something in the song that I think she needs to think twice about, we talk about it. I say, "What do you think about that? Do you think that's right?" And stuff like that.

Another mother, Ms. Graham, told me about her 15-year-old niece, who is attracted to bad boys with $100 sneakers. She described the problem as a destructive cycle. According to her, if girls are attracted to boys with money, then boys who want to attract girls will do whatever it takes to get that money. For teens who are shut out of the legal economy, this often means resorting to the illegal economy: the drug trade, hustling, and selling "hot" goods.

Helping our children resist the siren call of the shopping mall means mounting a campaign on many fronts. Many parents stressed the importance of developing family traditions that reinforce core values like saving and sacrifice and provide a counterbalance to values driven by the marketplace. Ralph Jackson, a 41-year-old mail carrier outside of Albuquerque, described what he thinks is missing from many teenages' financial education today, and what should be done about it. When he was growing up, he said,

in my neighborhood, we had a big family, and to most standards, I guess you would say we were poor. But my mom could do more with a dime than any woman I ever seen in my life, you know. She could take a dime and make a dollar out of it, and save money and don't take nothing from nobody. [Black teenagers today]—they see the nice things, they have to know it's not a gift. They have to learn how to get those nice things. Teach them how you got them. And teach them to appreciate what they have.

Many parents advocated making money real to children and teenagers: making sure they know where it comes from and know how to earn it. For instance, Mr. Jackson described how his own father taught him to learn how to make money and then how to appreciate what he had. He told me that when he was growing up, he wanted a bicycle more than anything, so his father helped him make one from old junked parts. "I'd get a bicycle frame here, a rim there, a tire here, an inner tube there, and I fixed one up." One day his father called him over, pointed to a shiny new three-speed bike left on the curb, and said, "Now anybody around here could come by and take that bike, couldn't they?" Then he asked Ralph, "Where's yours?" To which he replied, "Chained to the fence." Right then, Mr. Jackson told me, it struck him that the black boy who owned the bike, whose family had more money than his did and who probably bought the bike for him just because he'd asked for it, appreciated it so little that he was careless with it.

Ralph Jackson's father also used the boxer Joe Louis's story as an example. He told him, "Know how to make money, and don't be foolish enough to lose it. Look at Joe Louis. He made so much money as a black man. But he died poor and broke. Know how to manage it so you can keep it." Other parents, like Lee Elmore in Philadelphia, told me that they take their children around the community, pointing out the black people they grew up with who had made poor choices, entered the illegal economy, and spiraled downward. This personalized approach is a powerful one; it shows that financial disaster can happen to anyone—no matter how smart or attractive they are, or what kind of family they come from—who doesn't have the determination to be financially responsible.

Kay Smith, a mother from a suburb outside of Philadelphia, stressed the importance of refusing to buy the best, the most expensive, the most fashionable for her son, even if she can afford it. She doesn't want to deprive him of the pride he'll feel later on if he can buy high-quality things for himself. As she put it,

> If I can afford the best for him, I'm not going to give him the best. Because if I always give him the best, he's not going to know what it's like to buy anything when he goes out on his own. My goal is that first you get the basics, and then, when you get in a position, as you grow older and you get your education, you can get what you can afford to get. I think that's a lot of our problem—trying to keep up with the Joneses, and I know I can't.

A mother of two teenage daughters, Esther Pierce, finds it crucial to teach children that who they are doesn't depend on how they dress. She laughed, "My children wore designer clothes all right: I designed them." And Mr. Lowery emphasizes to his teenagers that money is not what makes a person special. As he says, "The rich guy may not necessarily be content at night. Kids have to know what really counts."

Although we often complain about the consumer-driven culture we see as undermining our children's values and financial futures, we can also envision clear strategies for resisting. Most of all we must continue to engage in those critical discussions with our teenagers about what is really important in life (sound relationships, education, hard work) and what is not (appearances and possessions). It is only through thoughtful, thorough, constant emphasis of core values that the material culture can be resisted.

RESISTANCE STRATEGIES

Unhealthy (Short-Term, Survival-Oriented) Strategies

- Using material goods to provide a sense of self in a society that devalues the black self and views it as essentially worthless

- Keeping up with the Joneses

- Envying and resenting those who have more than you

- Finding possessions more important than staying out of debt

Healthy (Long-Term, Liberating) Strategies

- Developing family traditions that reinforce core values and offer an alternative to the values of the marketplace

- Discussing money-related issues with your children, including budgeting, saving, resisting impulse purchases, buying black

- Having ongoing talks about the importance of defining themselves and others not by appearance and possessions but by character and values

- Teaching children to be aware of how the media promotes unfettered consumerism and distorts values

- Teaching teenagers to value what they already have

- Serving as models for our children by aspiring to spend our earnings in more profitable ways, including investing in the future (in higher education, in homes and stocks, in black businesses and communities) instead of in high-ticket items that quickly lose value, and understanding for ourselves and teaching our children the difference between want and need—that if you can't afford it, you don't buy it

- Helping our children understand the power of buying black to strengthen the black community by putting money into black-owned businesses. (The black-owned clothing company FUBU [For Us By Us] has been so successful because it has heightened black youths' awareness of buying black by tapping into their sense of racial pride and solidarity.)

Psychologically Strong, Socially Smart

A psychologically strong, socially smart black teenager knows how to resist peer pressure and to control his own spending impulses. This child understands racial reality, which means the facts about black youth unemployment, and knows the importance of acquiring marketable skills. He or she also understands when after-school employment is necessary, and when it isn't; that is, that money earned for image-maintenance at the cost of schooling is money lost.

DISSING, BOYS, AND DESTROYING
THE TIES THAT BIND

On a recent trolley ride a group of black students boarded the car I was in, swearing and carrying on, using the "N" word loosely, loudly, and far too much. The adults in the car seemed annoyed and embarrassed; some made efforts to move farther away from the teenagers. No one spoke up; we all just waited until the moment would pass and the offending teens would leave.

This is one example of the kind of behavior that many parents and teenagers described as troubling, embarrassing, and on the increase—part of what many of us perceive as a generalized lack of civility in the black community. From rudeness and vulgarity, which many attribute to the undue influence of the media and peer culture, to incendiary language and posturing, such behavior is frequently seen as destructive to the black community, contributing to black-on-black crime and rupturing the ties that are critical to black community cohesiveness.

Although we as adults can fall victim to a tendency to romanticize the past, selectively remembering only what makes us happiest to recall, parents in their forties and fifties do believe that a generation ago we were readier to respect one another's differences, less likely to hurl insults, more deferential to respected figures of authority. We weren't so quick to insult, or to grab a weapon. We swore all right, but not at the top of our lungs, all day, and indiscriminately, and certainly not when we were so very young.

This issue of incivility is highly charged and close to the surface for black parents, and it unleashes a torrent of responses on the subject. While girls are not immune, most of the criticism we hear is aimed at the behavior of our boys. And bad behavior is universally acknowledged as an impediment to healthy psychological growth.

Kathy Trainer is a divorced high-school teacher with two sons. At the large urban high school where she works, she sees a lot of loud, rude, and disrespectful behavior, sometimes directed at authority figures, but usually hurled from one teen to another. As one of the on-site mediators at the high school, Ms. Trainer is often called upon to help resolve interpersonal conflicts between students. "I don't mean to suggest that it's always our kids, because that's certainly not the case. But it really hurts me when it is, when we're talking about each other, putting each other down. Because to me, they're putting us in the role that other races put us in. They're joining right along with them in putting us down, you know."

"Black crime on blacks," another woman, Mrs. Davis, complained. "We are victimized more by our own. The crime, I guess, and the drug problem."

Vivian, a 16-year-old in North Carolina, articulated the concerns of many blacks, with an understanding that belied her years.

> I don't see how anyone else can accept you if, you know, you can't accept yourself. You have to accept your own culture before anyone else can accept you. And as long as we're sitting around here fussing and fighting and acting crazy toward [each other], no one is ever going to give us any kind of respect that we certainly need. Because instead of trying to help each other, we're too busy fighting each other. When we need to be going together. I cannot understand what the problem is. A lot of times it's over little stupid stuff that they get into things over. It's materialistic things they fight each other over, seeing one person with more than what you have. And they fight over stuff like that . . . thinking it's going to prove something. That they are strong or something like that. When actually I think it just proves ignorance.

This notion of respect came up again and again. People talked about it in many ways—self-respect, respect for others, demanding and deserving respect—along with its antithesis—a generalized disrespect toward others, or, as the teenagers today term it, "dissing." It means ignoring, insulting, or demeaning another person, usually to make yourself feel or look better. It is often used as a form of psychological warfare, to unsettle someone else, or to put him down or in his place.

We've had a long, culturally rich history of "playing the dozens" (a kind of verbal sparring to determine who was the wittiest, quickest, cleverest, funniest. It used to be about nothing more than a playful release of hostility. Now it often turns abusive, humiliating, and emotionally devastating; it's a form of violence, with the object of destroying the opponent. Many young people participate in dissing others, but when they are dissed themselves, many feel wounded to the core. Nowadays, it's reason enough to fight—even kill. It creates an atmosphere of fear. Teenagers fear that the "dis" from a particularly vicious opponent might not only leave you psychologically wounded, but maybe also dead.

As the psychologist Ann Ashmore Hudson says, in this climate, conversations and relationships become stilted and constrained. Honesty and openness are closed down; secrecy is promoted instead. Dissing isn't just about fitting in, being seen, showing off, or gaining status. It is often the result of, and a reaction to, rejection and fear. Black teenagers, feeling invisible, marginalized, and unworthy, look for recognition—even negative recognition like fear and loathing—where they can get it.

Boys' Development

In an address at Princeton University a few years ago, the noted playwright and author August Wilson, in reflecting upon the impact of the black power movement and the 1960s on his own development, wrote that this period

> was the kiln in which I was fired, and has much to do with the person I am today and the ideas and attitudes that I carry as part of my consciousness. The ideas I discovered and embraced in my youth when my idealism was full blown, I have not abandoned in my middle age when idealism is something less than blooming, but wisdom is starting to bud. The ideas of self-determination, self-respect and self-defense that governed my life in the '60s, I find just as valid and self-urging in 1996. The need to alter our relationship to the society and to alter the shared expectations of ourselves as a racial group I find of greater urgency now than it was then.

A great many black men and fathers share August Wilson's desire to pass on to their sons the wisdom they have gained in their attempts to live rich and meaningful lives as black men in the post-civil-rights era. Parents, but particularly black dads, feel they have learned new lessons based on contemporary realities. They must use these lessons, they believe, to protect their sons from a pernicious racism that at times threatens their very survival. They must also use them to shape their sons into the men we as a community need, want, and deserve.

One father, Mr. McKinley, told me how hard it was to see his youngest son, at nine, beginning to take on the physical characteristics of a teenage African American man. The boy's developing body, Mr. McKinley felt, heightens social anxieties. From his experiences as a youth worker and the father of two older sons, Mr. McKinley knows that as boys mature physically and socially, society perceives them differently, usually as a threat, based on assumptions and presumptions tied to their bodies, and what they can and are thought to be doing with it. Mr. McKinley, like other parents of black boys, is filled with rage at this idea. How dare they make these assumptions about his child? He worries for his son and feels he must socialize him, quickly and well, about the effect his mere presence has on others.

Black teenage males face a disproportionate number of obstacles to achieving social and economic success. The transgressive teen defines how we think of all black adolescents, but particularly black boys. Black teenage boys, and even preteens like Mr. McKinley's son, are in dire need of respect, education, and support in understanding what is expected of them. They need to understand their racial reality, including the negative role society has read for them, and the necessity of being able to repudiate that role. They also need to know what we as responsible blacks expect them to grow into and stand for.

We are so painfully frightened, so focused on just making sure that our boys simply survive—quite literally—until manhood, that many of us just can't find the energy and confidence to come together and find agreement over the characteristics we want our black boys to grow into. But come together we must, to provide new models of black manhood, to articulate positive, purposeful expectations, and to help our boys know they are loved and that something beyond survival is expected of them. Mr. Haley, a 43-year-old father, didn't finish high school himself. He spent many years unemployed, wasting much of his young adulthood on the streets. Eventually he found a stable job with the sanitation department and is now consistently contributing to the financial support of his children. As he put it,

A lot of us grew up in a matriarchal sort of family. It's important that males understand that they, too, are of value, and that they, too, can contribute, and that they don't have to dictate. I think it's important for them to have an education and value it. And without an understanding of that, then you generally get what you get in the streets. I had both of those experiences. There's no guarantees, but you must be educated.

His daughter, 16-year-old Kaydeen, who was listening from her upstairs bedroom, joined us in the kitchen. For her, as for most teenage girls, discussions that focus on boys are like a magnet. This one drew her in. She told me about the boys at her large public high school. She also told me that she had recently attended the funeral of a boy in her math class who some say had been running drugs at a nearby university. I asked her what she thought we should be saying to our boys about growing up black. She repeated what her father had said, and she emphasized education as a way to counter peer pressure:

> I don't have any brothers, but I have some guy friends who are around my age, you know. And it seems that guys like the easier way out than girls, like not finishing school and just selling drugs and not getting a legal job. We should tell our boys not to be influenced by other blacks, like drug dealers, because that's easy money. Black guys are more influenced by other black guys that are dealing drugs because you see all the guys riding around in nice cars and stuff and they are influenced by that. They should be taught to get the things they want by working for it.

Another father, who had recently turned his life around, talked about the importance of a social, political, and gendered education for black boys, which will help them become socially smart. He, like many others I talked to, felt that black boys must resist negative influences that derail them—the lure of quick cash, the stress of negative peer pressure, the easy out of quitting school—and they need help in understanding how to do this. "Making it" (the coping strategy that has worked for so many immigrant groups) is hard to adopt when you believe the system is stacked against you, or is rotten to the core: corrupt, illegitimate, and unjust.

Black teenage boys also need to face facts. According to Sonny, a 17-year-old, it's important to be realistic, particularly when the reality is inescapable and brutally unfair:

I think your sons, you have to let them know that it's going to be hard on them because of being a male and black. You need to know that . . . as you go on up to the neighborhood, there's going to be some obstacles. I mean, people want you to see drugs, people want you to use drugs, the police want you to mess up so they can lock you up. I mean the police are going to harass you. There are going to be certain obstacles in the neighborhood, no matter where you go. You can be in a white neighborhood, and it still happens. And you have to let them know who they are. I mean, I think that's the whole survival point.

Besides being marginalized by the culture at large, many young black males are expected to mature and take on a productive, responsible role in society, despite being uncertain about what constitutes a proper and successful role for black men in the lives of their own families and communities. Many grow up without the benefit of a father or other male role models to help them define what it means to be a man in a culture that blocks access to mainstream avenues of success. As Eric, a 19-year-old sophomore at a junior college outside of Philadelphia, told me,

Like on my block right now, when I say to other people, "I was doing something with my dad," other kids say, "Your dad is the only one left on the block, you know that?" Everyone says that. It's not that they don't notice. They do know. My father lives with us. He's the only father on the block and I'm the only black boy in college from that block. You can say it's a coincidence, but I don't think so.

Eric's dad has taken it upon himself to become a community dad. As the only black adult father available for the young men in the neighborhood to observe and interact with, he is trying to be a father to as many teenagers as he can. Eric told me that throughout his childhood, when he and his dad went to a ball game or took in a movie, his dad encouraged him to bring along a friend. Our community has long referred to this as communal parenting. And countless African American mothers in similar situations have successfully enlisted the help of the adult males in their lives, neighborhoods, and church communities to serve as substitute uncles and surrogate dads.

Researchers believe that much of the negative behavior of black male teenagers is the result of their powerlessness and economic isolation and that much of their confusion about the proper role of black men and fathers in family life arises out of the peripheral, inadequate, and inconsistent performance of their own fathers. As one mother said to me,

> Our men have got to get their acts together. They can't lean on and dump on black women so much. We've gotta get out of this "papa was a rolling stone" mentality and teach these black men to be supportive with their black women. In many cases the male doesn't play a dominant role. Dad shows up whenever, daughters grow up watching their mothers deal with this, and then they repeat the pattern in their own lives. Black men should teach their black sons to be a man. To stand up—be a father.

Black boys, like everybody else, need to feel strong, in control, powerful, and courageous. But for too many black boys these attributes translate to self-destructive, risk-taking behaviors like physical aggression, domination, and sexual conquest, which they mistakenly equate with masculinity, the one and only way to be a man. Many blacks with whom I spoke attribute this distortion to the fact that society blocks access to positive gender-role achievement for black males. Unfortunately, it is only a cover-up, and the insecurity and vulnerability that it masks can, over time, leave black men feeling alienated from their true feelings and detached from others.

Mr. Nickerson, a 54-year-old father of one son, talked about the difficulties of growing from a black boy to a man today, and described his perspective on macho posturing:

> You have to be careful with kids today. You promote this black thing and most of the guys, they have to convince people that they are male. They get into this macho thing. I mean, I'm as macho as the next guy, but there's a time and a place for it. I mean, if you're going to throw your macho in to buck the tide, you're fighting a losing battle. Your best bet is to go with the flow. Once you get in, you might see a different thing completely when you get inside. A lot of guys go overboard with the macho bit. [You must] be flexible and fair.
>   Some of these guys, they have a vendetta against the world—a bitterness. Some of these young men are so bitter you can't even hold a conversation. Like my grandmother taught me years ago, you

know, "you can catch more flies with honey than you can with vine-gar." I'm not saying you've got to be the sweetest thing in town, but hey, there's a time when you've got to kind of back off, you know.

He offered the following words of advice:

I tell any black man coming up today to assert yourself, be assertive, but don't overdo it. Let people know who you are, what you stand for, what you will take and what you will not take. There's some things you will stand for, and you'll take a lot, and there's others that you must draw a line. Let them know where that line is. Plus, you have to give them respect. "I respect you, I will not cross your line. You re-spect me, you don't cross mine." But respect is not something you can demand. It's something you have to earn.

"We'd rather curse each other and call each other bad names rather than deal with why we don't understand each other," hissed Sam Archer. In his opinion, the "cool pose" he watches his son's friends take on is grounded in "dissing": a generalized disrespect for others, which can, depending on the teenager, mean treating others unkindly, cheating, lying, stealing, talk-ing trash, walking around with an "attitude," listening to or creating disre-spectful song lyrics, and excessive cursing, especially in public.

One mother, Margaret Simpson, says she experiences this problem with her 17-year-old son. She explains the uphill battle she faces trying to counter her son's inclination to dissing and macho posturing, particularly if this is the code of the streets, and the norm of the neighborhood. "I try to teach my son that he is strong, but he doesn't have to use his strength to overpower." She reminds him that "you don't have to butt the door down all the time. You don't have to be so brutal with that strength. You can have strength and be nice, too. You can share. Don't try to grab everything for yourself."

Allen, a teenage boy in Raleigh, told me that boys need to be encour-aged to work their hardest. "Don't fall on the line of being a quote-unquote gangster," he said. "At school I see a lot of blacks with dreadlocks in their hair, with the attitude of 'I don't want to do that' and 'ain't nobody can tell me what to do.' But they need an attitude that makes them want to succeed, you know—do the right things."

The sociologist William Oliver has argued that there are two dominant identities offered to and expected from black teenage boys in our culture: the tough guy and the player, both of which are earmarked by macho posturing and both of which our sons must learn to resist. The tough guy is physically aggressive, and looks to dominate others through physical or verbal threats and armed force. The player's game is sexual conquest: seducing women, stringing them along, and knocking them up with the goal of acquiring a trophy shelf of adoring women he can exhibit and boast about. Both identities are extremely limiting and potentially life-threatening. Violent living and seducing other people's girlfriends both invite retaliation.

But a steady diet of degradation and humiliation feeds violence. As Sisela Bok has written, killing happens when the killer feels he is somehow authorized to do so, which in some cases means when a person has been humiliated. Shame elicits anger and rage, not personal responsibility and self-examination. And race-related anger leads ineluctably to self-hatred and racial resentment. Arising from a sense of vulnerability and powerlessness, race-related anger can cause black children to experience heightened stress; to hide it is to increase its force a hundred times.

That our young men are hostage to violence is borne out by dismal statistics: Blacks represent 12 percent of the U.S. population yet make up 44 percent of the inmates in state prisons and local jails. The tough-guy identity decimates the black community: the vast majority of homicides in the black community are committed by young black men preying on other young black men. Far too many see the gun as an instrument of self-respect. And the violence isn't only against others: the suicide rate for black and other minority males—who once were at much lower risk for suicide than their white counterparts—has increased markedly since 1986.

Thus violence is the ultimate disconnect from community and a profound moral problem. When we view it from this perspective, violence is a crisis of community, an abandonment of our traditions of caring, compassion, and interdependence. Ultimately, this relational breakdown represents a corrosion of social bonds, the establishment of a new anti-order where life is cheap, blacks live continually in danger, and a boy who feels disrespected—because someone has messed with his possessions, including his girlfriend—all too often lets the world know it with a blast from a gun.

Resisting the lure of a violent lifestyle, rejecting the tough-guy image or player identity, and envisioning a black male identity that both acknowledges social barriers and is creative enough to think outside the box create new roles and responsibilities. You don't get there by dwelling on frustration and disappointment; you get there through pathways of love, respect, and commitment to a belief in self far greater than anyone's disbelief. It requires thought and work, by parents and the community at large. Mia in Raleigh and Carolyn in Boston say that there is an urgent need for black boys to know the African American history of survival and accomplishment—a positive cultural continuity that will go a long way in helping them to pave the path toward manhood.

Mia offers this: "They need to know about the discrimination, that blacks have to struggle in the world. Boys might get it worse than we get it. I think they need to know about the violence out there and how we need to come together. And all of them need to be educated about their roots."

Carolyn has an even more specific suggestion. According to her, all black adolescent males "need to know more about their history and more about what other black males have done over the years. And what he should hope to accomplish. Show him the right way. . . . he needs to know the racial stuff that is going on in the world. Girls need to know this too."

Part of the problem with the socialization of black teenage boys is that too many rely too much on themselves and their peers; they are isolated from the adult base of wisdom and guidance. Jay MacLeod's research contrasted two groups of black adolescent males living in the same low-income communities. One group looked around at the high rates of unemployment, poverty, urban blight, and racism, concluded that the cards were simply stacked against them, and said they gave up. They rejected the dominant ideology of achievement, and eventually dropped out of school and the labor force. The other group of boys looked at the same conditions and concluded that although things look bad, as a people we are doing better. These boys saw themselves on a social upswing, as part of a "collective upward social trajectory." They acknowledged that their own families, many of whom had moved from the South to the North and were now experiencing better working conditions and expanded housing and educational opportunities, had personally experienced notable social improvement. Messages in their families emphasized resistance and exhorted them to keep striving. The focus for these young men was not just on surviving, but on keeping their hopes high and envisioning the future they want—messages that helped them accept, adopt, and live the achievement ideology.

Knowing and honoring our personal, family, and cultural group histories is about much more than self-esteem. As parents our job is to help African American adolescent children to adopt a sense of black history as formative. They must know that this is who you are, and that yours is a history of achievement and perseverance against the odds. They must see themselves as part of the social upswing MacLeod speaks of, with the skill and will to build upon family and cultural resources.

Moreover, they must become empowered with the knowledge that "I have the power to make it happen." As a 19-year-old young man told me, "If you know who you are within yourself, then it don't matter what other people say you are. Then they wouldn't have to worry about the struggle. Parents should tell you that you have the strength within yourself. That you know who you are and no one can touch that."

One father, an executive in a multinational corporation, described the idea of "knowing who you are within yourself" and maintaining a positive black male image in a heartening, vivid way. At 43, Dan Childs was the father of several children and one of just a few African Americans in such a high-level management position in the country. His corporate climb had taken hard work and had been painful at times. He had left one position because of what he described as his employer's denigration of affirmative action. Later the same corporation recruited him back at a higher salary and with more responsibility. "My record speaks for itself," he readily proclaimed.

During our interview in his large, light-filled office, he told me that he is teaching his sons how to be assertive, which to him means how to speak your piece while keeping the peace, a skill he has learned along the way. He told me he wants his sons to always remember that they are black men, and that they must let others know that they are black men, and exactly what they will resist and what they will stand up for. While he was telling me this, he was getting ready for a meeting with his executive staff, opening desk drawers and moving piles of paper, obviously looking for something important that he'd misplaced. Finally, exasperated, he called his secretary. "Where's my kente sash?" he said. "Bottom left-hand drawer," she yelled back. He pulled it out, smoothed the wrinkles, and carefully placed it over the shoulders of his dark navy suit, tucking the edges of it neatly under his lapels. "Nice, huh?" he asked me. "I like to wear this so they won't forget who they're dealing with. These white people remind me every day I'm black. I ain't here to be liked. I got a family for that. I'm here to work, and you better respect me. I let them know I'm black and I love it." He looked handsome, almost regal in the bright African colors. We both laughed hard.

I left the interview wishing that all of our growing black males could see a man like Dan every day: a man who is powerful, productive, confident in his black male identity, honest and outspoken, speaking his piece and keeping the peace. Unless our children stop the dissing—stop focusing their energy and youth on misplaced anger, disrespect, and violence—few will have the spirit, sense, or skills to take on a black male identity like Dan's: proud, secure, and connected to others in positive ways. We must teach our sons that although avenues to success are often shut off to them, they are not all completely blocked, and some, in fact, are quite open.

Our sons can take the right path; the power lies within each of them and those of us who raise them.

RESISTANCE STRATEGIES

Unhealthy (Short-Term, Survival-Oriented) Strategies

- Macho posturing as resistance to cultural marginality and as a way to cope with stress and anxiety and mask feelings of insecurity

- Becoming angry and bitter as a reaction to cultural marginality

- Acting on strong race-related emotions in ways that get you into trouble (hurting others or keeping anger locked up inside, which causes stress and depression)

- Resorting to violence and sexual conquest to acquire respect in a society that doesn't respect black men

- Becoming excessively self-centered as a response to feeling that no one cares about you

- Responding to disrespect by seeking to humiliate or shame others or wanting vengeance

Healthy (Long-Term, Liberating) Strategies

- Helping teenagers understand their origins and develop strong positive attitudes about themselves infused with racial pride (a strong, positive racial identity

- Encouraging understanding of the self as connected to other blacks, and honoring the connections through an ethic of care—for neighbors, family, and the community

- Helping teenagers counter definitions of themselves that are imposed by others, and instead creating and affirming their own definitions of self that can be sustained and defended over time

- Helping teenage boys recognize incivility as a major contributor to relational breakdown, destructive to the self and to the community

- Discussing causes and effective responses to race and gender discrimination, especially as it relates to the police

- Helping teenage boys take pride in controlling their strength, using it for positive ends rather than to overpower, bully, or intimidate

- Helping teenagers counter excessive self-interest by emphasizing group advancement and its importance as a source of individual hope

Psychologically Strong, Socially Smart

A psychologically strong, socially smart black teenager must understand the importance of resolving conflicts peacefully, averting domestic violence in our homes and in our intimate relationships and street violence in our communities. This means that he must learn how to let go of bitterness, attitude, and anger before it is transformed into rage and self-destruction. This teenager has learned about the history of black achievement and successful resistance, the history of discrimination and its modern manifestations, and the critical importance of a good education.

DISCONNECTION: UP AND OUT OR LEFT BEHIND

There may be nothing more important than helping our children recognize the importance of balancing individual and collective responsibility in their future lives as African American women and men, and as parents of the next generation.

In their powerful study of racism in the lives of middle-class African Americans, Joe Feagin and Melvin Sikes argued that according to conventional thinking, the black middle class has achieved the American dream. The gulf between the social classes is described as "the pampered and prosperous middle class and the pathological black underclass."

Politicians, economists, and social scientists point to the sizable black middle class as proof that social and economic conditions have improved dramatically for black people. On the other hand, some look at the same economic indicators and express deep concern about the fact that a full 45 percent of black children are born into poverty, and that we now have the fastest-growing black underclass in history.

The definitions of social-class status in black communities are slippery at best. Although there is much talk in the social science literature about a growing gulf between the black haves and have-nots, in reality social class in black communities—even within individual black families—is in a fluid state. Blacks move in and out of social class in a way that whites usually do not, and many of our individual families contain several social classes. Family members interact across class lines and integrate into a multiple-class perspective.

Thus for many of us, specific and inalterable class identities are seen as problematic, creating divisions in the community that don't feel right, honest, or fair. For one thing, they are too often based primarily on the superficial and ephemeral—more specifically, money, which comes and goes. Blacks recognize, of course, that important differences among African Americans do exist: in educational background, possessions, personal taste, interests, access to resources, and future orientation. But beyond all this, what the black parents who wish to raise caring, smart, and responsible resisters say really matters are the strong values that support and sustain individual development, community development, racial connectedness, and interdependence.

Social scientists spend a great deal of time talking about the black poor, especially the underclass. They focus on cultural deprivation, blocked opportunities, and the culture of poverty. The black poor are "othered"—fitted neatly into the "us versus them" dichotomy. In the intimacy of our interviews, I discovered that black people generally reject this distinction. How can we do otherwise, when we know that the "them" in one conversation can so quickly refer to the "us" in the next? We know that negative pronouncements about lower-social-class behavior too frequently spill over to cover the undifferentiated black masses across social-class locations. Moreover, we know that our disadvantages are less often of our making, because they have been built into the social structure. Even when we enter the job world buttressed with educational achievement, our education doesn't always yield the high incomes of our white counterparts. Our income is rarely tied to real wealth, like real estate or income from stocks and bonds. Our history has been one in which we have always had to work harder for fewer rewards.

"I went to Tuskegee Institute in Alabama," Billy Jean Ryan told me. "There was something Dr. George Washington Carver was fond of saying:

'Never look up to the rich or down on the poor,' and I believe in the wisdom of those words." She went on to tell me a story of the challenges she faces trying to orient her daughters to social-class differences:

> Our church has a BYF [Baptist Youth Fellowship] and my two kids do a community service project through it. One afternoon I agreed to drive them to this other church across town, in a poorer section than where our church is at. I could hear the kids in the back of the car talking about "those people." Those people don't have this, they don't believe that . . . I had to interrupt and ask them, "Those people? You mean those *black* people? You're talking about them like they were from another planet. I don't like that. Those people are us. They may live differently than we do, but they're still part of us, part of who we are."

We welcome the higher incomes, access to resources, increased opportunities, and privileges, but, like Billy Jean Ryan, we worry as well. We fret with one another about the feelings and reactions of those blacks who are left behind to suffer continually deteriorating services and increased crime, but who, by acquiescing to an environment that is hostile and forbidding to others, deprive themselves and their community of the benefits outsiders might bring. We speak with a sense of connection to low-income black families and a heartfelt understanding of the pressures these families are under and the choices some feel forced to make.

Descriptions of low-income African American teenagers fill our newspapers and magazines and spill across the evening TV news. We fear for children and families who must live surrounded by crime, with few resources and, often, little to look forward to.

A Boston 10th grader shared with me some of the difficulties faced by low-income black teens like himself who see very little that's positive in their future. "I lived in Dorchester," he told me, "and my friends would say, 'Man, we ain't never going to leave here.' And they believe they're never going to get out because there are so many forces around them that won't let them rise up."

Some low-income teens feel trapped by the forces waiting to derail them and engulf their dreams—chronic unemployment and underemployment, crime, drugs, anger, and frustration—all limitations that can make them feel like giving in and giving up.

Some, like Mrs. Achebe, a supermarket clerk in Albuquerque, worry about the lack of supervision and monitoring of teenagers, particularly in unsafe areas. "Some poor folk tend to stop disciplining their kids," she told me. "They more or less let them grow up by themselves. They feel they don't have a chance in life anyway . . . and that's the wrong way to look at it. You can't give up trying to do better for themselves."

She, like many other parents, often directs her message of resistance to low-income black mothers, reminding them to keep a close and watchful eye on their children at all times, resist feeling resigned to a tough situation, and persist in trying to improve your family's life, no matter what.

Although instilling a sense of personal self-worth and self-esteem is critical for all our teenagers, it's particularly important to those who are economically shut off from the benefits of mainstream middle-class American life. It's easy to be dragged under and lost in our troubles and worries— dragged down so far that we begin to hate not just our circumstances but ourselves.

Sandra, a 42-year-old factory worker in North Carolina, gets frustrated with some of her low-income neighbors and friends who seem to have stopped trying. "Just because you are poor doesn't mean you should scrape and bow," she says. "The blacks around me who I would classify as low income, they're too comfortable in their setting and they don't want to get no better. They just don't want to rise above it. They don't feel like they're as good as the white person. They don't have the self-esteem."

Leo, a 19-year-old community college freshman, is the first member of his low-income family to have the opportunity to go to college, and the only one of his male buddies from his black neighborhood to do so. As he talked about why his fate turned out to be so different from that of his friends, he explained that his parents, and his father in particular, never allowed him to stop striving. Though poor, he always knew what was expected of him: good grades, responsible behavior, and respect. He believes that the same prescription can work for other low-income teens as well.

> They [parents] gotta keep giving them the initiative, the ambition to not be that way, because that's what my father did. He pushed me to the point where he didn't want me to lead the type of life that he had. [He told me] "It's not always like this. You don't have to be like this. Develop whatever it is that you have, so your life won't be that way."

The way Leo described it, his dad, like so many other black parents, uses his own personal stories of bad life choices, educational inadequacies, and other deficiencies to push and motivate his children, keeping them focused and setting their goals high.

Mr. Roberts, a 44-year-old father, summed it up when he explained, "We never had much money. We were definitely poor, but my parents saturated me with love and attention. And you can give that to a kid without a whole lot of money in the bank."

Like Mr. Roberts, many of us speak from personal experiences with poverty, and we want to share with the next generation what we've learned about raising children with little money. For example, 53-year-old Andrea Avery told me that when she went on welfare for a time in order to cover medical expenses, she intentionally made sure that her children didn't know the extent of her financial difficulties. That fact, she says, makes her proud. She thinks children should, if they can, be spared the full knowledge of family poverty. Don't dwell on lack of money, she advises, or at least don't share these troubles with your children, for too many black children are burdened with the facts of their poverty and deprivation. Allow them, instead, to be children, focusing on what they can control, including their own behavior, working hard in school, and being responsible. "You gotta struggle," she says. "I mean really struggle. But the things I'm talking about, like education, it don't cost anything."

Other parents offer heartfelt advice to parents struggling to raise families on little income. "Lift your children's expectations," said one. "Don't use race as a cop-out. The kids have to succeed in spite of it." "Be constructive," said another, concerned about a psychology of dependency caused by chronic unemployment and welfare. "Be contributors, even if it's no more than working every day." In addition to hard work, tenacity, and sacrifice, a single mother in West Philadelphia said she reminds her children every day that being poor is no excuse for not caring. "I stress the need to help others—that all of us should help one another whenever we can so no one struggles alone."

Some of the messages we want the poorest members of our group to hold onto tap our cultural legacy of survival, of finding inner strength through strength in the collective. One father, Mr. Harris, describes himself as a proud and strong black man who has weathered many storms. He wants low-income teenagers to heed the advice he gives his own two teenage sons: to always remember who they are and where they came from and to use that history to sustain them through the hard times. "Don't give up," he says. "Keep going. We come out of the womb fighting and struggling. We're the strongest people in the world. We're the only race in the world that they have openly tried to commit genocide on, and they still couldn't kill us off. We're still here, baby. And there's nothing in the world we can't do. You gotta keep encouraging these kids to do well."

Mr. Franklin distilled it when he told me, "The poor, especially single black mothers, should be applauded for doing a yeoman's job. [We need to] build on the structural skills that are necessary to achieve. Do well in school, resist peer pressure, avoid delinquent behavior, build inner strength, support each other, and reduce negative self-hatred."

When it comes to thinking about our middle-income families, we often cite very different concerns. Near the top of our list are the worries we have that center around what can happen to an unsuspecting black child who fails to remember the black folks' truths from home. We want these teenagers to know what they know—never forgetting the social and political knowledge of race and place, and the importance of being forewarned and prepared. We worry, too, about the erosion of psychic ties and social bonds across class lines. Our fears of racial disconnection lead many of us to believe that the parenting agenda of the black middle class, in particular, must repair these disconnects.

I interviewed Mrs. White, a 45-year-old mother of three, late one afternoon after work. I rode with her as she dropped her 15-year-old son off at the movies so we would have a few hours alone to talk, and sitting in Albuquerque traffic at rush hour allowed us plenty of time to do so. Divorced eight years before, Mrs. White had worked her way up to a position as shift supervisor at a large chain store. Her salary plus occasional child support allowed her family to live fairly comfortably.

It was important to her, she told me, to avoid shielding her children from trouble and pain. "We often want to spoil our kids because we don't want them to go through the pain of what we went through. But I think it's important for them to understand some of that pain. That they don't have things given to them on a platter because, as black children, and as black people, they will not get that same consideration when they go out into the world."

Mrs. White believes that even with higher education, training, and a stable income, there are certain things black families must never forget: that racism is alive and well; that they must always remember who they are and where they came from; that they must never sever their connection to the black community. Like other parents, she believes that black parents must find a balance between protecting their children against the malevolence of racism and preparing them for the eventuality of its effects. As a mother from outside Philadelphia explained, "Our children have to be told this is a racist society. To be on guard. Expect the unexpected."

Many middle-class African Americans, while heralding the opportunities that accompany increased racial integration, share a sense that in leaving the poorer black community for the suburbs, we have moved up and out of connection with blacks as a whole and away from black folks' knowledge, what we need to know to help us interpret and endure racial reality. Some of us have become estranged from our cultural traditions, our sense of belonging to a group whose survival has depended on our collective ability to resist social and psychological annihilation. Some of us have lost sight of the lessons of resistance, pride, and self-help culled from our social history and, finally, to the commitment to continue the struggle for social justice—the agenda of social activism.

Mrs. Patterson, who lives in an urban black neighborhood, told me that her black friends who live in largely white neighborhoods feel a certain tension in their family lives that she doesn't feel within her own family:

> They're very worried about the fact that their kids are not, in fact, in their community. They're outside of their community and they're constantly doing things with their kids to reconnect. They spent more time reinforcing their blackness than I did. Their kids come into the black community to get their hair done. Everything with being black, they come into the black community and then go back out to the suburbs. My daughter has several good friends who have moved out to the suburbs. [For one friend] it was almost like a day-to-day battle.... She'd go to school in a predominately white school system. White kids would be using the word *nigger*. And my daughter said to me, "You know what's so funny about it, Mom? I can go to the Boston Public Schools all day and never hear the word *nigger*." So this kid, living in a relatively affluent suburb, was hearing it almost daily. So I can imagine that her parents should have been doing something. I don't know if they did, but that's a strain.

Other parents talked about the stresses of understanding how to resist—and teaching children how to resist—racism in the suburbs, often disguised by a veneer of education and good breeding. The reality is that for reasons too complex for full discussion here, white teenagers in the suburbs, often taking the lead from black teenagers who use the term themselves, feel that it is okay to use the "N" word as well. But it's not okay, and suburban black parents bear the burden of intervening, explaining, supporting, and protecting when it comes to issues like this and myriad other issues that their urban counterparts might not face.

Middle-class parents often complain about their teenagers' excessive autonomy, their behaving as though their actions have nothing to do with and have no effect on other blacks. Although we want our teenagers to become resourceful, independent, and autonomous to the degree that they are able to stand on their own, make their own decisions, and chart their own paths, we don't want them to do this at the expense of their racial ties, by devaluing the bridges that carried them over, or even worse, by burning the bridges altogether so that others never make it across.

Michael, a 17-year-old in Raleigh, put it this way: "There's a tendency," he told me, "for some upper-class blacks to get in with the white crowd and get lost in what they are—to not know themselves. They should stay true to their heritage and not sell themselves out to the white race. Selling out means hanging with whites, not recognizing your own black brothers and sisters. Just feeling you are better than other blacks just because you are with whites."

Parents and teenagers alike told me we must resist adopting attitudes, values, and behavior that promote such racial disconnection. That black suburban children may grow to think they are different from, or even better than, other blacks (especially poor blacks) is, they believe, a direct violation of the kinship principle that researchers say is embedded in the African heritage of black people, which envisions a concept of self as existing primarily in relation to others, both within the family unit and outside of it. The value placed on interdependence and interrelatedness is a cultural and psychological resource that helps us maintain a sense of peoplehood and dignity, and ensures collective survival.

"Some of them," Mr. Walker said to me, "don't want to associate with some of their own kind. They say, 'I've made it, now you make it. And I'm not going to help you either.' I've seen some of these brothers and sisters. They make it, their status changes, they're making good money—but what are we doing? Have we forgotten where we came from?"

I talked with a father of three who worked in the maintenance department of a hospital in Philadelphia. He was on his lunch break, he said, and he was afraid of running overtime. He was also worried, he confessed, about saying the "wrong thing." But when we began to talk about child rearing among upper-income and middle-class African Americans, he came alive and stopped keeping track of time. At the hospital, he came in contact with all kinds of black workers—some well-paid professionals, others low-income hourly workers like himself. He was concerned, he said, that suburban black children whose parents have not helped them build strong black identities or prepared them for the realities of racism will be unable to make connections with other blacks. This lack of preparation, he believed, will make them more vulnerable to being taken advantage of by both whites and blacks.

> There's nothing to touch base with, no kind of way. There's no sense of being black, and they've become scapegoats. They get used because they've got that money—[and] this, that. They become easy targets. . . . The parents have got to tell them, "Sure this is fine, but you know, you are black, and you have to be able to relate to all types of blacks"

In the 1930s, the folklorist Zora Neale Hurston, an astute observer of the black social world, coined the phrase, "my skinfolks, not my kinfolks," signifying an important black folks' truth: that we are not all the same, that we don't necessarily all get along, and it's okay to be "my race but not my taste." A black child raised in a predominantly white environment without this knowledge may risk developing unrealistic, romantic, and idealized notions of connections across class lines, and is vulnerable to being taken advantage of by street-smart poor black people ready to capitalize on middle-class black guilt.

In Albuquerque, Ms. Allen, talking about how black middle-class parents raise their teenagers and how difficult it is to cross class lines today, complained,

> You must instill in them that they're not better than the next black. We might not have had the opportunity that they had, but we're still striving to get there. It might take us longer, but eventually we'll make it there. Some (middle-class blacks) are real snooty. They can't dress no better than I can, they can't look no better than I can, they

can't be as pleasant as I am. What's wrong with people nowadays? Especially blacks. I remember you just could drive up and down the highway, blacks see you, don't even know you, they be waving. Now everyone is getting a little higher than the next one.

Ms. Babson, from West Philadelphia, captured the sentiments of many others in her descriptions of the obstacles that hinder our connections across class lines. "I was raised to believe that we should be lifting as we climb," she said, echoing the motto of the National Association of Colored Women. She thinks of herself as someone who has moved up and out, and doesn't hesitate to admit that she is happy to be where she is. While she has fond memories of her old neighborhood, and the public housing project where she was born and raised, she is also quick to bemoan its decline, which she has witnessed firsthand in her position as a pastoral counselor. To her, certain conduct is inexcusable, and so are the surroundings in which many urban blacks live. "We've stopped ourselves before we've been stopped," she complains.

She told me the story of a friend who sacrificed and saved for many long years in order to make the down payment on her own home in a predominantly black neighborhood. Within months it was burglarized and vandalized, costing a great deal of money to repair. The terrible violation was by other blacks, not white people, she moaned to me. The thugs and thieves who are running us out, she said, are our own people. They've made us fearful of our own neighborhoods. To turn this terrible trend around, she suggests we start in the home.

"First," she explained, "parents must teach their teenagers the importance of standing upright. I mean by changing the environment—the party spirit, the drugs, the alcohol. It's tearing us apart. When your mind gets clear, you're going to get out there and sweep it up, and get those low-lifes out of your life. [Then you need to] help some marginal guy to have a good self-esteem so he could turn around and help you. [But] this stuff is not going on."

Maybe it wasn't going on in her life. But I found evidence that the very thing parents talked about as being important to their children's social and moral development—feeling racially connected across social class and regional differences—was indeed taking place. Those who believe it is important have found ways to instill these values in their own lives and are teaching them to their children in a number of useful, imaginative ways.

CARING AND CONNECTING

A job counselor I know works in a large agency that tries to place young adult women who were formerly dependent on government subsidies into full-time employment in the private sector. She is frequently frustrated by what she sees as clients' refusals to take and adopt her job-readiness suggestions. "They complain that my suggestions are too complicated and rigid," she says. "They say I'm just like the white counselors, only worse because I'm black. I guess they feel I shouldn't criticize them when they miss appointments or show up for work dressed like they've been partying all night. They think I look down on them like the white counselors sometimes do. And I don't. At least I try not to."

During an interview in a large urban high school in Boston, 16-year-old Dianne told me that she didn't know any middle-class black people, so she couldn't answer my questions about social class. Whether this was true is debatable, but her perception left me concerned. Those other black people were nowhere near her universe. She was not connected to them, nor they to her.

It used to be that our black doctors, teachers, store clerks, and unemployed maintenance workers all lived in the same neighborhoods. We went to the same schools and churches. We knew about each other's pasts, present-day constraints, and dreams for the future.

Today, however, we live in separate communities on the other side of town with our own kind—families of similar income and education—or in integrated middle- and working-class white neighborhoods. The black poor are all too often left to fend for themselves, sinking or swimming, all the while being blamed for every ill that plagues this society: out-of-wedlock births, teen pregnancy, youth delinquency, escalating crime, high-school-dropout rates, drug abuse, and decaying moral values. The black poor rightly feel unfairly blamed, rejected, and marginalized.

The situation creates an ugly and dangerous dynamic: attack before you are attacked, and hang on to what little you have no matter what. Anger and resentment cut across class lines, even within families. I heard stories of family members accusing other family members of thinking they are superior, or lambasting each other's values, lifestyle choices, and child-rearing practices. Maybe these incidents seem especially nasty because they are so personal and so important to us. The insult runs deep because we desperately crave the connection; we know that our survival is inextricably intertwined with its preservation.

The fear that blacks with the economic and social resources to do so will disconnect from poor blacks and from the black community as a whole (voiced by both poorer and better-off blacks) ran deep among the people with whom I spoke. It was usually cast in terms of loss, both at the family level and the larger racial collective, with an overlying sense of "if we don't take care of our own, no one else will," and a feeling that the fate of the black poor is closely tied to the fate of all blacks. Better-off blacks often acknowledge how easily they could imagine themselves as poor—"there but for the grace of God go I."

Cross-class challenges exist in black settings as well. One father, Mr. Franklin, whose family had slightly more money than others at his sons' school, described the pains he took to keep his children connected:

There was always a sense of difference that my kids felt that led me to try to let them understand their own group—and the outside group. As it happens, many black middle-class kids feel closer to white kids than they feel to other black kids. That has always been the battle in these mixed integrated settings. So it was always very clear to me that I had to push the positive. And then, unfortunately, my kids had a lot of hassles with kids who had home problems and other things, and I always had to mediate that, so they wouldn't feel hostile towards the black poor kids who were punching them, hitting on them, saying, "you look funny—you've got the wrong kind of hairstyle, you dress bad" My kids weren't necessarily stylish. So I've had to mediate issues of race and class differences within the group for my own children.

"Pushing the positive," mediating differences—Mr. Franklin's strategies for resisting the disconnect have relevance to any cross-class situation for blacks. But the resentment that some black have-nots feel toward black haves runs deep. As much as the black middle class looks back at the rest of the black community, saying, "Let me stay connected; let me help my children stay connected," a component of the poorer blacks left behind are understandably suspicious. And although it can be hard for middle-class blacks to imagine what it is that those who are left behind are trying to protect—a decaying infrastructure, crime, inadequate services—it's a response that is familiar and understandable when we think of it in terms of children, and adults as well, who are abandoned or betrayed by those close to them.

Once rejected, we often close up, fearing that connections will open us up to betrayal again. Those left behind need much, including opportunities to be exposed to middle-class values, attitudes, behaviors, and lifestyle choices. They need to be encouraged to think of us as one, and not to hold money, residential location, and educational achievement against the black middle class, or to prejudge, exclude, demean and devalue, question the racial allegiance of, or envy and resent, blacks with money, power, and resources. We all need to focus our energy instead on care of the extended self.

What all of us must do is work to resist the kind of excessive individualism that leads to disconnection, the kind described by Larry Mungin in *The Good Black,* his book about his experience as an attorney at a white law firm. Having shed his connections at the urging of his achievement-oriented mother (who saw them as not helpful to his climb up the firm's competitive ladder), he prided himself on his personal achievement, bending over backward trying to please the firm's white partners, only to discover that "in the eyes of his employers, there was no such thing as a good black." But for many middle-class blacks, connection with the black community as a whole—as opposed to roguish individualism—is seen as a moral imperative. As Fannie Lou Hamer said, "Whether you have a Ph.D., a D.D., or No D., we're in this together. Whether you are from Morehouse or No house, we're in this bag together." The resistance I'm talking about is a resistance to this sense of separation and psychic alienation, a disconnection that obscures the reality that the destiny of each individual African American is linked to the destiny of all other blacks. We know that in forging ties of mutual support, collective survival and racial progress can be achieved.

This connectedness is not simply an aspiration, it is a moral imperative. We find our strength—both cultural and individual—in the reservoir of racial identity. Connection sustains us, gives us purpose, energizes us, keeps us focused, allows us to bounce back when we fall, even gives us a reason to bounce back, and provides us with both a compass and a map.

It's also the right thing to do because we know that individual achievement does not necessarily bring about group advancement. When you hold connectedness firmly in mind, you can link individual advancement to group advancement and see group advancement as a source of individual hope.

"No matter what side of town you live on, your roots are still coming from the same place. We're all part of each other. Keep that pride in there," a Raleigh security guard, Bob Sealey, told me. "I've seen folks move up in the world, away from their roots. It's important not to let that happen. Try your best to stay in the black community, at least maybe the black church—to whatever ties you can hold onto."

Along with staying attached to a black church, parents talked about maintaining those ties that bind us together, connecting and reconnecting us in a variety of ways, and suggested a rich array of resistance strategies. They include viewing films, television shows, and documentaries featuring topics of interest to African American history and social life; making yearly visits to family in the South, or in major low-income urban areas; and enrolling their children in predominately black extracurricular and summer activities like camps, black softball leagues, and basketball teams. Others say they make rituals of telling the stories of their ancestors, emphasizing the connection of all blacks through a common heritage. Still others stress the importance of compensating for disconnection in the black community through reparative relationships, by remembering that all blacks are family, and acting on that knowledge.

These "reparative relationships" are intended to restore some of what has been lost through the rupture of the black community. One father, Mr. Lane, offered this description of a community badly in need of healing:

We used to know who the enemy was. Not only did we know who the enemy was, we knew who our friends were. We knew where our safe harbors were, and we knew where our strengths were. And it's kind of paradoxical to say it, but all of that was lost with the gain of integration. In many respects, we would have done better to have held on to some of the tenets of segregation. When we were segregated, we were decidedly in our own communities, we knew who we were in those communities, we knew who the good guys and the bad guys were in the community, and then we knew the threat from without. Because with those parameters, we allowed only so many negative things of our own to take place in the community.

Come integration, and in our pell-mell rush to be like everybody else, we gave up many of the things that had kept us strong through all of the bad times. [We lost] family—the idea that if my daughter went to somebody's house across town and did something wrong and somebody saw it, by the time she got back here, the phone call would have already come in, saying, "I whipped her because she did thus and so"' and "Thank you, Ma'am, I'll take care of it." And when she comes in the door, she comes and gets her butt hit. That doesn't happen anymore. In fact, not only do you not put your hand on somebody else's child, you're very careful what you say and to whom you say it. He may go home and come back with a family or a Molotov cocktail or an Uzi, or what-have-you. We had a sense of family that went beyond this house. We were all family. We all had responsibilities for raising, for rearing, for nurturing, for giving respect to. We don't have that now. There is little or no respect anymore. We have no respect for law and order. Of course, we didn't have that much respect before because we had no hand in making order. But now we have no respect for ourselves. The laws that we set up in our own structure—we don't have that anymore either. So loss of family—and I mean family in the broader sense—is our largest loss.

Mr. Ropes, a high-school math teacher in Boston, tries to make up for the loss of larger community family by stressing the now-even-more-critical importance of the smaller family unit to his sons:

The first thing is commitment to family. Personally, in my happiness and unhappiness in marriage, I've tried to show [my sons] that it's very important to be committed to family. I say that every child deserves a mother and a father. I lived that. I saw that. Even though my own parents were divorced, my grandparents were that mother and father throughout my lifetime. They made sure they were there at all the rituals of significance. And they made sure they told me . . . that I am part of them, and they are part of me, and we don't abandon any of us, okay? And that's the important thing I think I'd like to teach my children. It's important to be committed to your own family.

Most of us have in our memories powerful visions of racial connectedness, of the extended self that expands its moral community beyond immediate kin. Parents tell me that they want their children to learn about, internalize, and build on the proud African American history of struggle and resistance. These baby-boomer parents, who had their consciousness of social injustice heightened in the 1960s, see their lives and the lives of their children as tied to the promise of justice. Yet we know we are raising children in an environment in which moral codes of justice and equity are frequently violated.

Black people get angry at racism and the perpetrators of racism. And we also get angry at other blacks. When parents talk with me about racial connection, it is as much about community building as it is about dissipating anger and getting rid of frustration. We talk about needing to look at our own people in a different way, in ways that allow us to make sense of our strong feelings about what other members of the race are doing right or wrong. We are hungry for ways to think about other blacks in order not to feel bad about them, ways of understanding why we are in the position we are in.

We're not talking about replacing resentment and anger with pity or resignation. And we're certainly not talking about finding new excuses. We're talking about searching for accurate, appropriate, and useful explanations that help us find the understanding we need and the solutions that actually work. And we're talking about reconstructing the community that we've lost.

Black parents tell me they want to help their children develop systems of culturally based values that guide just and caring social behaviors and that give them the courage to take a stand when these values are tested or are in conflict with other important issues such as the law, respecting authority, and work policies. A 16-year-old Philadelphia boy told me the story of his aunt, who saw all black children as her responsibility, and took action on their behalf. She is a model of what today's black adults can and must do to keep the black community strong despite its disconnections. According to the story, the young man's aunt happened to be in a grocery when a couple who had their young children with them was arrested at the store for shoplifting. Loud, rude and indifferent to the plight of the young family, the police began talking about calling the department of social services to come take the children. The aunt intervened and offered to take the frightened and confused little girls home. When I asked the boy why he thought his aunt had taken responsibility for the children even though they were strangers to her, he said,

> She was trying to help them. Because it was a shame. The cop, it was a white cop, and he said, "We're going to have to leave the kids here and somebody's going to have to come and get them." And my aunt was like, "We'll take them." He said, "Don't you understand English?

We're going to have to leave them [to be picked up by social ser-
vices]". He was getting smart. My aunt didn't want to get smart with
him. So the lady [who was caught stealing] said, "I know them. They
can take my kids." So, we just took them to my house [and called
their grandma to come get them].

The boy's aunt, who obviously had a clear, strong sense of racial identity and obligation to her community, had needed to think fast and act de-
cisively, and she did, sparing the children further trauma at the hands of an
overwhelmed foster-care system that is too often insensitive to blacks. She
had an internalized, instinctive grasp of her place in the extended black
family at large and acted in a way that taught her nephew, and the family she
helped, the importance of acting on the community's behalf, even when it
means helping strangers.

Another mother, Sadie Walker, a social worker in a large urban area,
spoke about her exasperation with the social service system for tolerating or
ignoring the degraded conditions in which some black families live. When
she was having a particularly difficult time managing a case where children
were living in a filthy and abandoned crack house, she was shocked to hear
a colleague tell her that "some of those people like to live like that." "My response," she said, "was, 'Well, I'm raising the standard.'" She calls her colleague's attitude unethical, incompetent, and short-sighted. "Some people
are just too lazy to look at things. It's easier to get rid of something, to get it
away from you, to dismiss it, to discharge it. . . . They just haven't realized
that the same children they're treating today are the same adults we're going to meet 20 years from now walking down the street."

Mrs. Walker's story is a particularly compelling account of a black
woman who is not deterred by class barriers, and who sees her obligation
to connect with the poorest black children—to save and nurture the next
generation—as a moral imperative.

Connection and caring is, at its heart, about racial identity and moral
development. It's about what kind of people black parents want their children to grow up to be: compassionate, connected, and committed to working toward social justice and civil rights.

The moral values that are related to self-definition (who we believe we
are as individuals) and the values related to other blacks (who we believe we
are and what we should be about as a people) are deeply embedded in our
sense of racial identity and illuminate the connection between culture and

care. In order to be empowered, teenagers must build a strong and positive racial identity, grounded in a sense of belonging to a group whose very survival has been dependent on our collective ability to resist social and psychological annihilation. Developing such a racial identity—a racial self in connection with others—allows black teenagers to understand who they are; nurturing an ethic of care helps them to honor their connections to one another and to nourish the community, as well.

RESISTANCE STRATEGIES

Unhealthy (Short-Term, Survival-Oriented) Strategies

- For middle-class blacks, disconnecting from the black community by uncritically assimilating white values, failing to connect with lower-income blacks, and allowing our children to adopt the attitude that they are better than, or significantly different from, blacks who are less well educated or less financially secure

- Allowing our feelings (guilt, resentment, fear, self-righteousness) about our social status differences to blind us to one another's strengths

- Allowing our feelings about our social status differences to keep us from taking one another to task when we witness attitudes and behaviors that are harmful to the blacks who engage in them, or to other blacks or to future black generations

- For lower-income blacks, feeling hostile and suspicious toward better-off blacks and locking them out of the low-income black community, a strategy that is self-defeating because it weakens the black community as a whole and deprives poorer black communities of critical resources, including time, commitment, and money

Healthy (Long-Term, Liberating) Strategies

- Helping our children and teenagers understand, appreciate, and realize the concept of the extended self—that is, the importance of being connected with the black community as a whole

- Helping our children to learn to appreciate and respect differences within the black community

- Encouraging cross-class connections by enrolling black suburban children in black summer camps and extracurricular sports and activities, and by shopping, visiting, volunteering, and attending church in the black community

- Supporting black businesses and institutions

Psychologically Strong, Socially Smart

A psychologically strong, socially smart teenager knows to resist the notion that poor blacks "want to live that way," knows that blacks must take responsibility for their own communities, and understands the destructive power of disconnection in the black community. She can also act on a moral claim with confidence, taking responsibility and decisive action. He is not undermined by accusations that middle-class status and values are elitist or inappropriate for blacks and resists "othering" the poorest and most disenfranchised among us. Such a teenager is willing to act on the moral violation of disconnection by repairing relationships with blacks across class lines.

PART FOUR

SCHOOL RULES

A Philadelphia father described his daughter's struggle with, and his response to, an issue far too many black teenagers face at school: the low expectations that many teachers and administrators have of black students.

My daughter Tiffany is 14 now, and at this age you never know who you're going to meet at any given moment. Sometimes she's Miss Independence, other times she acts like she's scared to death to try anything new on her own.

We've always been really involved parents. We go to all the PTA meetings, all the parent conferences—my wife bakes cookies for the bake sales, you know. Tiffany has watched us deal with these schools over the years. If we had a question or a concern, boom—we're there in a flash. If we don't like the way a teacher does something, ring, ring, ring. Me or my wife, one of us is on the phone.

Recently we had this situation. Tiffany came home and she said, "Daddy, I'm in a new reading group and I don't think it's the right one for me." So I said, "Really? What's the problem?" She said, "Well, I used to be in a higher reading group, but two weeks ago the teacher moved a few of us around and now I'm in a lower group and I shouldn't be because I'm not being challenged." "Challenged"—that's the word she used. So I said, "So what do you want me to do about it?" "Talk to the teacher and tell her I should be in another group." So you know what I said to her? I told her, "No." She looked at me with this shocked look on her face and I repeated myself. "No. I'm not doing nothing. This is your problem and I expect you to take care of it." She started to protest and whine. "But Daddy, you're a teacher. You know how to talk to these teachers . . ." I said, "You do, too. And if you don't know exactly what to say, we'll talk about it and find the right words. But this one is on you. You are old enough and smart enough to handle this situation."

Now I don't know why that teacher switched the groups around. I do know that Tiffany feels she can work harder. And I want her to always remember that she has the power to get her needs met. Tiffany is smart; she's got her evidence, put the pieces together, and since she presented her argument to me, I know she has the ability to argue her case in front of a teacher. Right now she's nervous, and that's okay. I'll work with her, help her find the right words, make the best case. That I'll do. But I think that a large part of my responsibility as a parent is to help my child to be able to appreciate the value of working hard in school and to feel she has the power to make the school respond appropriately to her educational needs.

Schooling is an intensely charged issue for black Americans. Teenagers and parents alike recognize its critical importance—as a gateway to better jobs, better housing, and a strong, healthy, powerful black community. Teenagers and parents alike also recognize the obstacles that impede blacks' access to full and forceful education, like inferior resources, stereotyping, the low expectations that teachers and administrators often have for black students, and the quagmire of complacency into which too many blacks surrender. Parents know how important it is to teach their children to counter low expectations, resist complacency, and help their children reap the intellectual, financial, and social rewards of a strong and positive educational identity.

Tiffany's father is teaching his daughter how to resist responsibly. By placing the power to oppose her teacher's presumption of low performance into his daughter's hands, he has taught her how to appreciate and exercise her own power. In doing so, he helps her to replace a situation that had the potential to disempower her with an opportunity to be empowered.

Not long after I talked with Tiffany's dad, I heard a similar story from a teenage boy's perspective. Sixteen-year-old Antoine riveted me with the clarity of his understanding of his teachers' power. He was describing the day-to-day problems of attending his black urban school—loud noise, weapons checks, broken elevators, teacher and student frustration—when he blurted out, "My teachers that have a problem with me, they take it out on my brain." His summation was right on the money. The truth is, teachers possess astounding power: they can decide to teach black children or not to teach them. Possessing this power means possessing a weapon that can inflict permanent damage.

At 16, Antoine had a grip on the power dynamic, at his school and at schools across the country. He may even have been aware of the ever-widening gender gap that also marks the black educational experience, a gap that starts early on in school, and a gap that my female African American college students often observe and comment on. Black women significantly outnumber black men enrolled in colleges. And the ratio of black men to black women attending college is widening steadily. This not only takes a toll on black college women's social lives; it also perilously affects the economic future of black men, and ultimately black families. We know that the gap begins early, when teachers react adversely to boys' behavior (which is often rambunctious and loud, or marked by distractibility), responding with more negative attention, negative evaluations, suspensions, and referrals to special education programs than they dole out to girls. To compound the problem for boys, some of us black parents, perhaps because we are so worried about our sons' mere physical survival in a world that is intensely and increasingly perilous for black males, focus primarily on protecting them, neglecting to push them to raise their own standards and expectations.

The fact that over the past two decades something in our educational system has gone terribly wrong (for both black boys and girls, but particularly for boys) is well known in the black community, and the parents and teenagers with whom I spoke were eager to talk about it. Stories about school spilled out in every context—identity formation, what it means to be black, what parents wanted for their children, what they believed their children weren't receiving—even before I asked any formal questions about education. Education is a hot-button issue for African Americans. We know at the deepest, most visceral level that a strong educational foundation is critically important for blacks. It means better career and economic opportunities, the chance to make large-scale change in the black community, the opportunity to genuinely influence the power dynamic between blacks and whites. But at the same time we are profoundly suspicious of our country's educational system, which continues to be controlled by whites—a system that formally disenfranchised us for decades, and informally continues to do so.

This tension informed many of my talks with families. Parents and teenagers alike speak of the value of education, most often in terms like these: Even if they're poor, they can become whatever they want to be—if they get that background, that resource, that education. Black parents should urge their children to stay in school and learn as much as they can about anything and everything. If you're given the tools, then you can work with it.

Others see the need for each generation of blacks to exceed the last, and education is the means to that end. "If that doesn't happen," one father said, "we will perish as a race."

At the same time, parents and teenagers alike are acutely aware of the shortcomings of the system. Although some teenagers that I talk to describe themselves as academically strong, most teens I know describe their educational progress as marginally "okay," and some use even less positive terms. Their parents are even more disenchanted with their children's education. Most had been educated in the legally segregated schools of the South or in racially segregated neighborhoods in Boston and Philadelphia. By contrast, either due to desegregation bussing programs, or because they lived in integrated neighborhoods, their children were members of integrated school communities.

These mothers and fathers voice a profound distrust of a system that has actively participated in subordinating blacks. Many complain about the low expectations set for blacks by teachers and administrators. Others speak of the profound apathy and sense of complacency many black teenagers feel because of poor schooling. Still others talk about issues of identity that their children face at school, especially when they feel pressure to choose between performing well academically and fitting in with their black peers.

Parents find that designing resistance strategies in the context of school is particularly demanding, since it requires treading a delicate path between encouraging education and compliance to teachers' demands while at the same time inculcating the right degree of suspicion about the system.

Certainly the distrust is well founded. After all, generations of black slave children in America were not allowed to learn how to read or write for fear that they would use these tools to gain freedom, and even after emancipation, blacks were confined to separate and definitely not equal schools. And although the mandate of the U.S. Supreme Court in Brown v. Board of Education technically changed that in 1954, the parents with whom I spoke retained painful memories of the violence against, and denigration of, black students that became commonplace as desegregation took hold. Soon after the decision in *Brown* came down, W. E. B. Du Bois spoke of the tension that continues to haunt black parents today.

The decision, he said, confronted "[n]egroes with a cruel dilemma." On the one hand, "they wanted their children educated. That is a must, else they continue in semi-slavery." On the other hand, he continued, "with successfully mixed schools they know what their children must suffer for years from southern white teachers, from white hoodlums who sit beside them and under school authorities from janitors to superintendents who hate and despise them."

To fuel the distrust we parents already possess, for the past two decades the nation has crept again toward resegregation, especially with the conservative movement's relentless attacks on court-ordered bussing and affirmative action. Gone is the black history and literature movement that flowered in the 1960s and 1970s; and many of the black teachers are gone as well. Teaching, once the top vocational choice of African American college graduates, has dwindled in popularity, and the number of black teachers decreases each year. Moreover, black schools in low-income rural areas and the inner city have had their attention distracted from race-specific learning to more immediate concerns: children from broken homes; the effects of drugs, violence, and poverty; and the difficulties of maintaining discipline under circumstances like these.

Although some schools—public and private, predominantly white and predominantly black—are doing an excellent job of creating an environment where all students feel they belong and where expectations are high for all students regardless of race, many are not. And although some teachers are committed to changing the existing educational system to make sure the best is brought out in all children, too many are stymied by school administrations bent on maintaining barriers to change, focusing on the bottom line, and stalling, fearful of political backlash.

Statistics describe gross underachievement by black students, not just in low-income urban and rural schools, but now in more affluent middle-class schools as well. Reports show gaps in black achievement that seem to increase the longer children stay in school: gaps in standardized test scores, disproportionate dropout rates, and questionable mastery of basic skills upon graduation. We black parents have to question why it's always our children who fail in school, and many of us reject the notion that we are entirely to blame for the situation. Instead, we point to the color-blind ideology of racial innocence—the belief that if we don't talk about race, race won't matter—as part of the problem. Many others believe that white educational institutions consciously and deliberately hold blacks back, denying us access to tools that develop the critical skills that might put us at a true economic advantage, as well as to accurate information about our cultural history and the achievements of our forebears. Or, as one man in Raleigh put it, the schools have deliberately "trained us to be stupid."

Many of us resent the high cultural price we have paid for the privilege of attending integrated schools: the surrender of racial solidarity and culture in exchange for an opportunity that includes sharing space and taking instruction from those who often don't see blacks as worthy of full and fair inclusion. We feel the loss is profound: Gone is the richest mission of the segregated black schools: the creation of a set of educational practices and beliefs that were culturally relevant and specific to the needs of blacks. In its place stands unrelenting low academic achievement by black children across the country, and persistent patterns of underfunding and mismanagement of black schools, with high teacher-turnover rates, diluted curricula, and significant discipline problems.

Many black baby-boomer parents describe having attended what they believe were good, caring, educationally solid schools, where the teachers held the futures of their black students close to their hearts, and where they felt a sense of racial solidarity and common purpose. Teachers felt free to teach racialized messages about school success and failure, messages that started, "We as blacks are up against . . ." and "We as blacks must succeed because of . . ." and "A lack of education leads to our failure as individuals and as a people because . . ."

In private conversations out of the earshot of white colleagues and school officials, I've often heard African American educators privately complain about bussing and racial desegregation. Much like the parents with whom I spoke, they maintain that to successfully educate black students, to genuinely promote academic achievement, personal growth, and development in black children—particularly black males—we must redirect our efforts to achieve racial integration in schools and once again build our own educational institutions, separate from whites.

There is, of course, an inherent paradox in an argument that says we must return to the past to create fair, caring, successful schools for black children today. I've never heard an argument in favor of the underfunded, resource-poor, segregated black schools of the past. With the loss of those old segregated schools, however, we have lost a battery of caring teachers who had the requisite knowledge to teach black children well, to foster their self-esteem, and to expand their understanding of black cultural history. These were teachers who could recognize that cultural differences present both opportunities and challenges, who had the skill and the will to build upon cultural resources, and who recognized and understood the relationship between academic and personal development as well as social and moral development. They knew that black children need to possess a sense of efficacy—a belief that they possess the power to make things happen—and teachers like these worked hard to develop that power within.

The parents' descriptions of this loss reminded me of the story a relative once told me about her father, a black teacher in a black school in Kansas, who found himself fired from his teaching position immediately after the *Brown* decision. Maybe the law could require the school administrators to admit blacks to the same schools as whites, but they certainly weren't going to let any black teachers teach white kids. Just like that, he and many other black teachers were dismissed from their responsibilities of teaching black children. And gone with the black teachers were the essential lessons for black students about who they were in the world and how to take their place in it—stories of black achievement and history.

Even against this bleak background, we black parents know that to be psychologically strong and socially smart, our children must be well educated in order to get ahead. We continue to stress the importance of holding the bar high, and we expect our children to succeed, often invoking the same sorts of encouragement our own parents had provided to us. Most important, we maintain that our most critical task as parents is to instill in our children an unwavering belief in their own intellectual competence.

One father told me about an incident that occurred when his daughter, Marian, was in the sixth grade. Each year at her school, the teachers selected students to receive achievement awards. Marian had earned all A's throughout the middle grades, and she had the highest grades in the most academic subjects, a fact that was known to all because of the school's policy of making grades public. Nevertheless, when it came time to present the awards in a schoolwide assembly, Marian received only two of them. Both she and her parents were surprised and upset. After the awards ceremony, at a party organized by the teachers to recognize Marian as the top student of the sixth-grade class, her father took her aside to talk. "Dad," she told him, "I had the highest grades in all those areas. I should have gotten all the awards." "Yeah," he told her, "but you didn't get all the awards. And this is exactly what I been telling you about. Sometimes even when you achieve, you may not get what you are due, but if you don't achieve, you have no hope of ever getting it. So you're always handicapped, but that's your lot in life because you are black."

Marian's father used this difficult and painful event in his daughter's life to teach two essential lessons. First, that life is not always fair for black folks, but that's no reason to give up trying. And second, that you mustn't assess yourself by the criteria designed by others; you must always strive to do your best, know you've done your best, and hold on to that truth in the face of those who might suggest otherwise. While it might sound bleak, this harsh negative critique of the world set in motion the design of resistance strategies for coping with the unfairness of race and gender bias that empowered Marian. Rather than having a demoralizing effect, her father's truth-telling was ultimately liberating because it replaced negative critique with positive recognition.

The fact that the people who had changed the rules in the middle of the game were teachers—adults whom his daughter had trusted and her parents had told her to listen to and obey—was disturbing, but it is a fact of life for which black teenagers like Marian must remain ever vigilant. They must also resist becoming discouraged by such behavior, and instead should take a stand for educational excellence, personal achievement, and tenacity.

Another father, Bob Fraser, described with pride the way his daughter pushes herself. If she gets an 85 percent on a test, he says, she wants to take it again because she won't be happy unless the score is in the upper 90s. "I'm trying to be a fair, good parent," he says, "and not push her. At the same time, I'm saying, 'You're as good as the top student in that class. Don't be dragging in any inferior grades in this house. Your daddy is a teacher. We're top people and you're part of us. So you've gotta do it—you've gotta get those A's and B's.' And she hears that."

He explained that he was passing on the same messages about education that he had heard growing up in much harsher times:

I could remember my mother saying, "I'm not scrubbing these floors on my knees for you to come in here speakin' bad and talkin' in a way that does not say I'm sending you to school to get an education." My mother didn't have one herself, but she pushed and she's still pushing on me to excel and to do well. If I heard anything about race, it was "you're as good as the next person." And that's what I came up believing.

Parents and adolescents who talk about responsible resistance emphasize the need for teenagers to resist pressures by other teenagers—black or white—to treat academic achievement with disdain. In particular, they worry about the tendency of some blacks to equate academic achievement with "acting white" and something to be avoided. They worry as well about sliding into complacency: of black teens not bothering to resist the messages of their own inferiority. When we envision responsible resisters in our educational systems, black parents stress the importance of holding standards for black achievement high, even in the face of institutionalized low expectations. But underachievement by black students is not just the fault of careless teachers and institutional racism. Most disturbing of all is the disservice some black parents do their children when they emphasize athletic achievement, hipness, or entertainment at the cost of academic success.

I heard these strongly held ideas expressed by parents who were college graduates and by those who weren't, by teenagers in school and by dropouts who had recently returned, by pregnant girls and teenage mothers who were struggling to stay in school, and by achieving college students. But the theme raised most often had to do with the disastrous effects of low expectations—most often held by teachers and administrators, but also at times by peers and parents—and the urgent need we have as black parents to help our children resist and exceed them.

LOW EXPECTATIONS

Felicia, a 15-year-old from North Carolina, told me that her parents had attended all-black schools in the South. From the stories they told her, she felt sure that it was easier to be a black student in a pre-*Brown* segregated school than it was to be a black student in an integrated school today. "[I]t was easier," she said, "because they wouldn't be judged because they were black." The hardest part about being in school today, she told me, was dealing with the teachers' low expectations of blacks. "The teachers," she said, "they don't expect blacks to be smart. You have to prove them wrong. So you have to work hard and show them that you really are a different person than some of the rest."

Mrs. Freeport told me the story of her teenage daughter, who had been thoroughly engaged in academics when the elementary school she attended was all-black, but faced increasing difficulties as she grew older and the school became integrated.

My daughter was brought up basically with black kids. She had a tremendously good experience. By the time she was in the sixth grade, the schools were integrated. But with her personality, she didn't have any problems in terms of her teachers and her school-work, because she had black teachers and, even through junior high, we didn't face any problems with her. When she got into high school and went to an integrated school, she found that there was prejudice there. The teachers expected less of her and the few other black students in her class. [But] she would conceal things that happened to her. She wouldn't share them, because she didn't know what the outcome would be. We had to find out later.

Over time, the mother came to understand that her daughter was under attack in the predominantly white high school.

There was nothing that was done to her physically, but it was just that she was a part of the group of kids that were mistreated by the students. The white kids were ganging up on the black kids, because there were so few of those kids. Til she finally says, "Mama, I cannot stay at that school." And we started to question her at that point. "What is happening?" [The daughter described an incident with a dance teacher who forbade the black students from performing with the dance group.] She felt the tension with the teachers because she felt that the teachers were not giving [the blacks] adequate attention, and she was very withdrawn from them. We knew she was capable of doing her work, but it was like she just got so disinterested in it because the teachers didn't care anything about her. And they made a distinction in the homework with the black kids and the white kids. Especially in biology and science. Several times they had separate sets of homework, until we were made aware of it. They're always saying that black females are dumb in math and science and stuff.

After she had confirmed her daughter's claims, Mrs. Freeport decided to take action.

By that time, my pressure had started to rise, and so I went to the school. I'm not the kind of person who can sit back or go to the bottom. I go to the top when there's a problem with my kid.

Although the daughter's reaction to the problem (to be silent in the face of prejudice and mistreatment) was in keeping with where she was developmentally at that stage in her life, it's an example of a maladaptive resistance strategy—one that works in the short run only, to allow avoidance of immediate conflict, but it changes nothing and, if allowed to continue, can lead to depression and despair.

It's tough to take on the world at such a young age, and no one should expect her to. Mrs. Freeport's strategy—to first ask questions, gather evidence and make connections, and then, when it appeared necessary, to challenge the school directly and make herself visible and heard—is an example of a healthy resistance strategy that leads to empowerment and long-term change. She told me that with her younger sons she is even more intent on being a constant visible presence at their schools.

I'm more visible to them [the teachers], so they know that they're not going to get by with so much. I don't think it's overprotection. It's just that I'm more aware of the prejudice and what they can and what they can't get away with. And my concern is on education now—that they get the best they can get.

This mother understood that it is only by showing teachers that you care and are watching that you can require them to rethink their assumptions about black students, give them the attention and respect they deserve, and understand that mistreatment won't be tolerated.

Mrs. Freeport also told me about the tremendous value she places on open communication, and how it pained her that her daughter hadn't brought her concerns to her earlier. If she had, the mother told me, "I think I would have been able to go in and get a group of parents to say, 'Let's see what's going on.'" She encouraged her children to talk about racial matters and work together to solve problems, and planned to continue to do so, despite the difficult lapse with her daughter. She understood the value of preparing her children for incidents like the ones her daughter had endured.

Many of us parents know of the destructive assumptions teachers often hold about black students, the stereotypes of black children—all black children—as dumb and deficient. As a result, black children and teenagers often become withdrawn and fearful, falling victim to the "rumors of inferiority" that become self-fulfilling prophesies. Black parents sense as well that some teachers have low expectations for black children based on assumptions about the parents' sometimes low level of education. This is so even though research shows that parental education doesn't always correlate with academic performance in black adolescents (the same way that it does for whites).

As an educator and a mother of a black child, I have an insider's sensitivity to this issue. I know that not all teachers hold to the false and insulting stereotype of black intellectual inferiority. I also know that not all of the teachers who have low expectations of black students are white women and men. But it would be irresponsible and inaccurate not to identify and speak out about the fact that far too many education professionals insist on expecting less of our children and youth. It happens, and all too often. Why do the stereotypes persist and why do some teachers take to them so readily? One possibility is that teachers in large school settings have only a short time to connect with each child, to try to understand him as an individual and learn about his intellectual and social needs. When schools are overcrowded, teachers are overworked, and children have multiple and often extreme needs, making these meaningful connections can be terribly difficult. For some, holding on to the stereotypes can be a form of administrative efficiency. On the other hand, as recent research shows, even in well-funded schools with smaller class sizes, blacks don't always fare as well as their white counterparts. What we need are more educators, parents, and programs that target the "stereotype threat" of genetically based intellectual inferiority and low expectations by building black students' sense of competence and self-efficacy in the domain of academics.

Although these wrong-minded assumptions about the black intellect can serve to light a fire under some black students— "I'll show them I can succeed"—they can just as easily backfire, creating the negative, self-destructive attitude of "Why even try?"

Yet black parents are aware of characteristics that incite and reinforce the stereotype in teachers ready to receive it: black English dialect, a child's social class, the neighborhood he lives in, and who he hangs out with. At the same time, we know that "acting white" isn't the answer; staying involved and visible, and preparing our children for the inevitable, is.

Teenagers, because of their lack of experience, frequently need help from adults in discerning teachers' often-subtle expressions of prejudice.

A father, Mr. Ephat, and his teenage daughter told me about a time when the two of them together detected and countered the unfairly low expectations inflicted on the girl by her teachers, which nearly cost her the opportunity to achieve in an honors course, and which created in her a crisis of confidence, making her doubtful of her already-proven abilities. Although she had consistently received high grades in social studies for a number of years, her teachers did not place her in the honors curriculum for social studies in high school. Her parents, sensing that something was wrong, went immediately to the school to discuss the matter. Their daughter, for the first time in her life, lost confidence in her academic abilities. As she told me, she kept thinking to herself, "I can't do honors, I can't do honors."

The father was horrified by his daughter's response, because it brought home how easily a teacher's assumptions about black intellect can undermine even a previously confident student:

You have to be so careful as a black parent. Here we had a child who was confident that she was fairly bright and could do the work. And because of the teacher's recommendations, she had a little crisis in confidence. This "I can't" stuff—this is something that I'd never heard before. Now, I have no illusions that she was an across-the-board honor student in every subject. I knew that it would be tough for her, because I see how hard she works to make the grades that she makes. But I'd never heard this "I can't" before. And it was all brought up by the recommendations and how her teachers saw her.

At her parents' insistence, the girl's school counselor pulled her records and noted both her good grades and the fact that every year since third grade she had performed better than the year before. "Oh my God," the teachers admitted, "we *have* made a mistake." The girl was placed in the honors curriculum. This family's strategy, to take the school head on, helped their daughter resist internalizing an attitude of defeat, and saved her from languishing in a curriculum that would do little to challenge her.

The girl's reaction to the school's initial decision (anguished self-doubt) could as easily have been to give up, to mentally check out, or to put her energy, as so many students choose to do, into other activities—athletics, being a class clown, driving the teacher nuts—instead of academics. Black teens, who are so often victims of low expectations, can come to believe it and stop trying at all, or stop trying so hard, or apply themselves inconsistently, out of a fear of failure.

In *Souls Looking Back: Life Stories of Growing Up Black,* a book for which I was an editor and to which I contributed, there is a young African American college student whom I call Chantal. In her autobiographical essay she wrote that when she was a top student in elementary school, her teachers frequently told her that she was "different." Her mother advised her daughter not to accept this backhanded compliment as flattery and warned her to be careful of those who wish to see her as a "token nigger." The psychiatrist James Comer writes that in the perception of too many white Americans, "when Blacks achieve in significant numbers or in areas held to be beyond the group's capacity, it is threatening; and most problematically, it does not change the negative perception of the group or of blackness." Chantal's mother, like many other African American parents, recognized what Comer speaks of, and she was determined to teach her daughter how to identify and resist negative appraisals from the wider society, how to debunk its myths and filter out racist messages.

Sometimes parents feel compelled to take steps beyond challenging the teachers, staying visible, and socializing their children to recognize racism in school settings. One father told me that after years of conflict with his sons' school over the importance of holding high expectations and other related issues (proper teaching, good instructional materials, timely communication when his sons were having problems), he turned to home schooling. He was especially disturbed by the tremendous influence teachers have over students and the power imbalance that leads youngsters to believe that teachers always know what they're doing even when they don't. "In this instance," the father said,

> I had to exert a tremendous amount of parenting authority. I had to have my kids recognize that they're not going to submit to the authority of teachers who knew less than their father and mother, and that they should not trust their teachers as much as they normally would have, because we know different and we know better at home. The authority of home has to be much more important than the authority of schools.

Because he travels internationally as part of his job, he took pains to take his sons with him as much as possible.

I was trying to open their minds to the diversity and richness of experience that was not American. And in that sense I found that this was a parenting duty and that I was kind of shaping the world for them, that I wanted them to see, as opposed to the world that the schools were giving them.

This father's resistance strategy was twofold: first, to teach his sons to think critically about the quality of the education they were receiving rather than to blindly accept it (which is similar to resistance strategies for helping children and teenagers critique and understand the role the media plays in fostering racial stereotypes), and second, to clarify the importance of the home as the foundation for learning. Like many of the other parents, he had little confidence in the school's ability or commitment to delivering the kind of education black students need and deserve: an education that holds them to high expectations and respects their individuality as well as their collective strengths. Like the other parents, he was well aware of the power of schools to destroy confidence and interest and produce silence, self-doubt, disconnection, and suffering among black students. And he knew that only by resisting—in his case, taking the highly visible act of withdrawing his children from school and the less visible act of teaching his sons to critically examine the education they were receiving—could he empower them. Although his financial resources provided him with options that other black families may not have (including international travel with his children), it's important to remind ourselves that there are many other resources that can help enrich our children's lives that are close at hand and less expensive, including libraries, films, museums, and cultural events.

RESISTANCE STRATEGIES

Unhealthy (Short-Term, Survival-Oriented) Strategies

- Using silence and withdrawal as a way to avoid conflict

- Disconnecting and disengaging from school

- Succumbing to self-doubt

- Promoting achievement in areas like sports and entertainment at the expense of academic achievement

Healthy (Long-Term, Liberating) Strategies

- Instilling in our children an unwavering belief in their intellectual competence

- Setting goals high for ourselves and our children

- Having continued, open discussion as a family of all race-related issues, including those that have to do with school (especially stereotyping and low expectations of blacks)

- Staying visible, vocal, and vigilant at school, and teaching the importance of these traits to our children

- Teaching youngsters to critically evaluate the education they are receiving, rather than blindly submitting to the demands of a system that devalues them

- Remembering and emphasizing the importance of home as the base of learning and authority

Psychologically Strong, Socially Smart

A psychologically strong teenager resists self-doubt and self-silencing. She refuses to suffer alone and shares her worries or concerns with trusted adults, like her parents, who can intervene on her behalf. She knows that a teacher's low expectations can affect her self-esteem and that this is wrong. She has self-confidence, knows her strengths and weaknesses, and believes in herself and her ability to resist and to make change.

A teenager who is socially smart knows that not all teachers assume that blacks are intellectually competent. But he knows that most schools do have some teachers who will serve as allies and advocates for individual blacks, and who are also committed to helping advance blacks as a group. He knows to seek out teachers like these and to be willing to work with them. He also understands that sometimes—especially when school issues are involved— it is better to enlist adults as advocates rather than challenge the system alone.

COUNTERING COMPLACENCY

Not all the negative stories I heard about schools revolved around bad teaching. As several parents were quick to point out, not all underachievement by black students can be tied to low expectations for blacks held by teachers. We blame ourselves as well.

Many parents tell me that, to their regret, we blacks sometimes participate in our own oppression by failing to set our goals high enough. Parents and teenagers alike point out that students all too often become complacent about their schooling. That is, they are either satisfied with their educational progress (lackluster though it may be), or they have become apathetic and unconcerned about the consequences of school failure. Some parents and teenagers acknowledge that black teens appear clueless about the obstacles that confront them now and will continue to confront them in a society dominated by a white power base. We fear that too many black adolescents simply don't appreciate how important education is for our group, and we worry that the "stay-in-school" messages conveyed by the schools themselves in this post-civil-rights era have become homogenized and fail to stress, or even note, the special significance of the message for blacks. And they are afraid that the complacency is fed by other messages that do filter through, messages that say to our youth that education isn't really important, or that it's less important than other things. As one teenage girl, Francine, who was ashamed of the conduct and appearance of some black boys at her school, put it,

> They don't really show respect for themselves. I wish they would realize that they are going to need education, and they're going to need the people that they're hurting now—they're going to need them later. And they're going to need the education in order to succeed in life.

Francine is concerned that the "so what" attitude that these boys at her school had lapsed into prevents them from envisioning themselves in the future—from seeing themselves in the role of responsible men, caring for and financially supporting familie, and contributing meaningfully to the black community and larger society. As one father, Mr. Murphy, put it:

> As black people, we can't afford to be as complacent as we are today. We can't afford to be complacent about how we are viewed by the world, what we do and our effect on the world. I think we have to be very intentional about preparing our children for this society.

Another father, Fred Prentice, was deeply disturbed at what he saw as black teenagers failing to take advantage of the educational opportunities they are offered, and again, failing to understand how vitally important education is, especially for blacks.

> I get upset when I am in the school system and I see "poor" kids behaving like middle-class white kids. By that I mean the way they respond to activities that are presented to them, like being in the band or whatever. I feel that they neglect the same things I see a lot of middle-class white kids neglect. They don't take it serious enough. They don't see it as a ticket out. They don't see it as being an important part of their lives.

According to him, the white students who are slacking off now will be able to fall back on connections or other resources, but the black students won't. He, too, attributes this complacency to a lack of understanding of the realities of the future. He is deeply worried about the high numbers of underachieving black students in our high schools, young men and women who are headed toward dead-end jobs with low-end pay, unable to support their families or build their communities. His proposed strategy to help teenagers resist this complacency is to help them develop a racialized lens, a way of seeing themselves as part of a larger political and social struggle.

Fred Prentice feels fortunate to have had an upbringing that he feels many black teenagers today don't have, to have had teachers and parents who made him understand how important education is for blacks. Despite their own limited education (his mother was a high-school graduate; his father had only a third-grade education), his parents always emphasized the importance of school and of accomplishing something with your life. "The schools don't emphasize it today," he said.

> When I was coming along, I was fortunate because I got it twice. I grew up with kids who were as poor, or poorer than I was. When we were coming along, we got it first from the teachers. And some of us were fortunate, we got it again from our parents. The teachers would say things to us like, "If you're going to compete in this world . . ." And they were saying, "In this white man's world, you've got to be more than good, you've got to be this, that, and the other." It was a priority for the teachers.

Today, he says, things have changed:

It's no longer a priority for the teachers, because teachers are very satisfied now to let our kids do what they will. [They say to black kids] "If
you can do the , fine. If you can't do it, fine." There's not the same sense
that your future depends on it. If your future depended on it, and you
had that future at stake in your own heart, you wouldn't let them
fail—not in the ways they are failing. [If they failed], it wouldn't be because of neglect. It would be because they tried their best and they still
failed. But that's not what's happening now.

This dad, like many other parents, feels that too many teachers are disconnected from the schools and communities they teach in, and from their
students as well. The problem isn't just in the suburbs, where white or many
black middle-class teachers may not know the black students they teach—
because the students are bussed in, or because the students aren't part of the
community. The problem also exists in city schools because so many teachers live outside the community or in parts of the city far away from where
they teach. Although they have daily interactions with the same students,
they don't get to know them the way teachers did when Fred Prentice was
growing up, at a time when teachers tended to live in the communities in
which they taught, or at least visited the families of their students at home.
(A parent in a low-income neighborhood laughed when I asked her if a
public-school teacher had ever visited her home. "Of course not," she said.
"They're too afraid to visit, or don't care to.")
Compounding this lack of connection by teachers is a lack of accountability for the futures of black students that appears to be built into the system. When Fred Prentice was in school, black teachers couldn't disengage so
readily from their students' failure. They knew that if their students failed to
learn, they would cripple the black community as adults. As members of the
same community as their students, they felt a more immediate stake in their
futures—in helping to prevent the difficulties (increased violence, drug
traffic, and delinquency) that would have an immediate effect on the teachers and their families as well.
Many of us, along with our children who are enrolled in some schools,
are made to feel like interlopers. This happens most often in the suburban
school, where our children say they feel out of place, uncomfortable, or disadvantaged. Because they feel they can never fit in, some resort to complacency and stop competing academically. Celia Pinkney, a mother in a
Boston suburb, told me that it was disturbing to see black students at her

daughter's school "acting out" when the white students seemed so serious about their schoolwork:

> You'd see a bunch of white kids in a little huddle, studying for a test or something, or talking about an exam that's coming up or a science project. And then you'd see ours chasing some boy, jumping on his head, fighting and talking loud. Believe me, I'm not making this up. I don't even want to have to repeat it, but this is what I see.

The black kids' behavior makes Mrs. Pinkney angry. And although she understands it as a reaction to being unable to fit the norm at the school they attend, she wants them to overcome their complacency and make the norm of achievement their norm, too:

> I think it's kind of an acting out because they need to feel comfortable. The parents don't live in the area. They know there's a big gap in the area, so they're not going to fit the norm which here is, "We're going to achieve. And we're going to have the best grades." That's the norm. And that's what I want to see our people feel in the same way. And I don't like group standards and ethical behavior and morality and excellence in grades associated with "this is a white phenomenon." It's a people phenomenon and we are people too.

When I asked her where she thought the black students had learned their behavior, she told me that she thought they had picked it up from older black teenagers and young adults who had similarly discounted and devalued their education. She was sure that these bad attitudes were not grounded in the larger black community. Her husband, on the other hand, had a different take on the issue. The black kids' behavior, he said, "[i]s taught by a white racist system that would like to eliminate the economic competition and [in order to do so] they have created this awful thing called 'black' and they try to make you act like that, and then we're dumb enough to get out there and start doing it."

He's not alone in his judgment. Research shows that black students today are buying into the destructive notion that the concepts of ethics, morality, and excellence are white ones. Opposition to acting white is a kind of socialization perspective that many of today's black teenagers hold toward authority and toward economic and political oppression. Many feel forced to decide between racial identity and Eurocentric definitions of academic success. The conflicts they face are both ideological and developmental as they struggle to "balance conflicting needs to define themselves within their cultural frame versus fitting in or doing well in school."

This attitude can take root in any school (integrated, predominantly black, suburban, urban, or rural) where the school culture allows, or even condones, such ways of thinking. White curriculum materials, ability-tracking programs that in effect segregate students by race and class, a school climate where only the academically successful students receive positive attention and praise and academic underachievers (often minority students) are ignored and derided, all breed cultures in which minority students reject school success. Such cultures lead to a disconnect—the students' refusal to identify with school—which results in poor academic performance.

A mother of a teenage girl told me how important it is to make sure our children know that although we as parents are there to provide support, we can't—and shouldn't—do the real work for them. She told me about the time she attended a student seminar at her daughter's school in recognition of Black History Month. The students in the mother's group were black. One of the them told her, "You know, these white teachers, they're flunking me and they're doing this and they're doing that."

> "Well," I said, "do you do your homework every night?" and he looked at me and said, "No." So I said, "well, that's your responsibility. [And] if after you've done your homework, and you've studied, you come back and tell me this white teacher still flunked you, I'll come back. I'll come to battle them down to the wire. I will fight with you all the way down the line. But first you've got to deliver."

This mother could have agreed with the student that he was a victim, but she chose not to. Instead she challenged the victim characterization, a challenge all the more powerful because she, the challenger, was black. Rather than endorsing the teenager's feelings of victimization and complacency, she took them head-on, educating the group in the importance of reading a situation, and naming it as racism only if it truly is. Racism exists, she told them, and must be countered, but laziness is not racism.

These feelings of alienation and complacency are probably compounded by the developmental fact of life that junior high and high school are times when cliques kick in and social comparisons become important. They are also times when the social and psychological implications of ability tracking systems are fully entrenched, making intellectual differences (or perceived intellectual differences) even more pronounced. And when the numbers are great enough, black students do band together. This can be for emotional or social support, which is to the good, because it allows black students to gain a better sense of who they are. But it can also contribute to an "us versus them" mentality, especially if the blacks already feel alienated and angry, and a spilling of collective venom on white students through teasing, sarcasm, and interference with other students' learning. For some students at this age, however, fitting in—especially if they're attending a school where they don't feel comfortable—is far more important than doing well.

But complacency—equating school success with acting white, slacking off, pressuring other blacks to reject school, refusing to participate in "white" activities like going to museums or the library—is a thoroughly ineffective, maladaptive way to deal with devaluation and alienation. In the short run it may make students feel better; it's easy and it offers a ready identity tied to the images of black success that dominate the culture—that is, blacks as cool and hip, blacks as athletes and entertainers. But what the teenagers who lapse into complacency don't realize is that this attitude is perilously close to the identity that too many school personnel expect of blacks: that we are simply not as smart as the white kids. And the strategy fails dramatically in the long run; it marginalizes black students, turns teachers off (even those teachers who do truly wish to improve the educational status of our youth), and does nothing to change the wrong and deeply embedded assumptions that many teachers hold about blacks. Worst of all, it reinforces them.

It can be hard to understand why our teenagers might buy into the stereotypes so readily, and harder still to acknowledge that sometimes they really do believe the stereotype and internalize the inferiority. Some, we hope, are simply unaware of what they're doing. Once we wake them up, we hope, they will come to their senses and refuse to buy in. The long and the short of it is that our black teenagers are lost and searching for role models of African American achievement that they can relate to. They need models of blacks with integrity who achieve intellectually and possess a black identity that is proud and comfortable, but who still can have fun. Our job as parents is to supply these models for our youth.

Parents who want their children to resist internalizing low expectations and intellectual laziness need to emphasize three simple ideas: first, that if black people under much worse circumstances have painfully and success-fully struggled to get an education, you can, too; second, that if black peo-ple under much worse circumstances have struggled to make certain you can get the best education possible, then you must participate and achieve that goal as a moral imperative; and third, to turn your back on education is to participate in your own oppression.

By teaching the history of black folks' struggle for education, often by sharing our personal stories of what family members have had to endure to gain admission to our nation's schools and colleges, parents teach their chil-dren that they are connected to a long line of people who have refused to al-low others to shape their destiny. We can also teach our children that they have a personal and collective responsibility to honor that connection and to do their best. Finally, we must communicate to our youth, clearly, precisely, and repeatedly, the paramount importance of education. I believe that this message is most powerful when delivered as a racialized one: that because they are *black*, it is critical that they devote to their education every ounce of their determination, strength, and energy. As part of this ongoing teaching, parents also need to be brutally honest with their teenagers about the grave consequences of an inadequate education for black people: poverty, social and political disenfranchisement, and further marginalization. They must make their children aware of the dominant culture's insidious message that a black teenager's future work won't require advanced education or training; that the larger society expects blacks to work in service professions as order-lies, security guards, clerk-typists, and at menial and manual labor. They need to know that society doesn't expect black people to use their brains.

Parents who are determined to raise their children to resist becoming complacent about their schooling must also be prepared themselves to re-sist the attitudes of other African Americans who devalue education. It is frightening to contemplate the teenagers and their families who have lost their motivation to improve their educational status, or who aren't hurting enough to push themselves harder or to figure out how to navigate a system that isn't pushing them hard enough. But the situations that are particularly difficult to comprehend are those where black parents actually enable their teenagers to be academically unsuccessful. I fear for the children of these parents and for the black community as well.

One mother, Bridget Reed, told me about her exasperation with black parents who don't take education seriously themselves and make it easy for their children to buy into racist notions of intellectual inferiority. A single mother, she had worked her way through college and saw the urgency of staying on top of her own daughter's education. If she could choose a single thing for blacks to work toward together, she told me, it would be education.

> Education is just a low, low point for black people. I don't think it's as important as it should be. I mean, it's just that a lot of black parents do not particularly push their kids to do well. Like my sister-in-law; she got D's in math. And my brother [her husband]; he got D's in math. So now their daughter has D's in math. And that's okay, you know—it's not even a question for them. They would never think, "What can we do to make her get a C?" It's just too much of that "it's in the genes being a dummy" stuff.

She offered this practical advice:

> If you know you didn't go to school and you didn't learn enough to be able to help your kids with some new math, I suggest you find somebody out there who can. Find out who's the smartest kid in the class and make friends with his mother. That way, when they come over, their kid can help your kid, or whatever. But a lot of black parents I know, they don't even try to get tutors.

She went on to describe things she had done with her young daughter as she grew up: trips to museums and libraries, and reading aloud at home. Friends and relatives, she said, had told her these activities were "too white."

> What's wrong with taking your kids to the museum? There's nothing wrong with it. Why does it always have to be barbecue pits in the park? The best party, the best dance. Why can't it be like something more positive? All that body rhythm is great, but we can't all be dancers and make a living out of it.

Ms. Reed saw her sister-in-law's complacency as affecting her daughter in areas other than school, as well. She says that when the girl announced that her mom "showed me how to get all the men, so I ain't got to worry," she was horrified. What if the man she caught with her hip ways turned out to be poorly educated, unemployed, and unemployable?

When she returned to the subject of her niece's D's in math, she was outraged:

> If you can stand up there and dance with your kids and play games with your kids and show them how to be hip, and show them how to be cool, why the hell can't you show them how to learn?

The problem is that some black parents settle for too little. We may say all the right things about our children's education, but we behave as though we ourselves don't really believe them. D's and C's are passing grades so why worry? For some, the attitude arises out of feelings that "if it was good enough for me, it's good enough for them," or we project our own perceived deficiencies on our children: "I wasn't good in school so why should I expect my kids to be?" In some cases, it may mean that a parent, driven by shame and guilt over her own school experiences, unconsciously doesn't want her child to succeed too much—at least not more than she has. In others, it may be too hard to have to think of their children as smarter than their parents—at least not in the basics. Knowing that your child can do algebra or write a research report and you can't, can be tough to take. To avoid the feeling of shame, the parent devalues the source of the feeling. "School doesn't matter." "Don't even try to do well."

Some parents unwittingly support school failure by adopting the "bad genes" theory. A father might say, "I wasn't good in math, so I don't expect my son to be either" (and that's okay with me). This attitude is dangerously close to notions of racial genetic inferiority—that intelligence is immutable and unaffected by effort. Parents who think like this are, I believe, unaware of the implications of this line of reasoning.

In addition, some parents may refuse to take part in activities that might enrich their children's educational achievement (visiting museums and libraries, and attending lectures and plays) because they feel those activities are "too white." This could well be the reason why there are often so few blacks at cultural events and activities. If you are a black adult for whom crossing over feels dangerous, you may choose to stay put, even at a cost to your children. It's not that blacks don't see the value of these activities, or that they are nonintellectual or anti-intellectual. It's just that for many, it feels too treacherous, too hard to be the first to or the only one.

It's tough to be the only black eighth grader enrolled in an art class at the museum, or in a swimming class at the YMCA, especially if your black peers are not supportive; and it can be hard as well for the parent who stands by waiting in a crowd of all-white parents. Parents need to take a deep breath and dive in, summoning their courage and maintaining an unwavering focus on the good that can result for their children.

Complacency is an insidious issue for blacks. An attitude of doing just enough to get by, adopted because it's easy to adopt, can just as easily become a habit that influences other areas of life as well. The complacent attitude, with its deemphasis of education and its overemphasis of dance, popular culture, and being slick, is short-sighted and makes no positive change for blacks. Although historically we blacks have valued and adopted being cunning and slick as survival strategies, we did this because there were precious few other options available in the past. Today, especially with regard to education, the strategy is dysfunctional. Systems have changed, yet for far too many of us the old approach—getting over and getting by—hasn't.

Teenagers who do just enough to get by (to pass the test or the class or receive a diploma) haven't internalized the message that they will inevitably be in competition with white people, as well as many other potentially well-trained and better-educated nonblack people, and that getting by won't necessarily get you ahead, or even get your foot in the door. They will vie for employment and advancement with people who have certain unearned privileges and the advantages that go with those privileges—like being assumed competent and trustworthy until proven otherwise.

When it comes to our children's schooling, we must be explicit about race, creating and delivering messages about intellectual development and academic achievement in racially specific ways. Chances are that by adolescence our children have already heard the rumors of inferiority; most have been threatened head-on by the stereotypes of black intellectual incompetence. Having heard the rumors, they must know what to do with the information. It isn't healthy to ignore information like this, or to deny that the stereotype exists. That kind of response leads to psychological vulnerability, anger, fear, and escapism. And the more a child fears the stereotype, the more powerful it becomes.

The parents and teens with whom I talked agreed: the healthy response is to resist the stereotype. To do this, we must teach our teenagers the facts. They must know in their hearts that rumors of black intellectual incompetence are not true, despite what they hear from school officials reporting black students' low SAT scores, or, in many schools, their low achievement grades. We must teach them that achievement is directly tied to effort. You work hard, you achieve more. It's that simple. It's not about genetics; African Americans are not intrinsically less able.

We also need to teach them to understand the origins of the stereotypes—that they are the creation of those who wish to maintain existing systems of oppression and domination. Once again, this is a black folks' truth: the idea that for some people the only goal is to maintain whatever power they possess. And one way to maintain that power is by discrediting "the other." These attitudes are part of the ideology of many American institutions; they are even woven into the fabric of many of our schools. Finally, they must understand how to effectively navigate around and across the racial barriers built into the system, keeping in mind that the system is so well entrenched that some of us African Americans end up believing the stereotypes about intellectual inferiority ourselves. And they must beware: some of those who are settling for low achievement may indeed be their friends. They must know that only by resisting the stereotypes, aiming high, and applying themselves—diligently, every day—will they reap the educational rewards to which they are entitled.

RESISTANCE STRATEGIES

Unhealthy (Short-Term, Survival-Oriented) Strategies

- Emphasizing achievement in sports, entertainment, and popular culture over academic achievement

- Avoiding academic involvement and success as "acting white"

- Adopting a complacent attitude—that is, doing only enough to get by (pass the test, pass the class, get the diploma)

- Believing you are limited by "bad genes"

- Settling for low achievement in school

Healthy (Long-Term, Liberating) Strategies

- Presenting constant messages to children of the critical importance of education for blacks; helping them understand the disadvantages for black teenagers and young adults associated with low achievement, now and in the future (low-level jobs mean low income, difficulty raising families, inability to buy what you want and need, and few prospects for financial stability in retirement); knowing this means internalizing the message on an individual level as well as taking to heart what it means at a group or community level

- Teaching children to recognize and repel stereotyping of blacks as intellectual inferiors and believing, instead, in their intellectual competence; understanding that the notion that we are intellectually inferior is socially constructed to prevent us from competing economically

- Teaching children to develop a racialized lens: to see themselves as part of a larger political and social struggle

- Providing children with models of intellectual black achievement, from the public arena and from close by (family, coworkers, community members)

- Taking steps to ensure academic success at school: holding standards high, finding tutors, risking the discomfort of being the "only one" at museums, libraries, plays, and other events in order to enrich your child's education; making clear that they must apply themselves and persevere, with a full understanding that for a black teenager, getting the very best education possible is the most important task in life; emphasizing that part-time jobs, athletics, parties, dating, and learning to drive are secondary to schooling, which must be paramount

- Staying vigilant, visible, and involved at school; intervening when a child is mistreated; and letting teachers and administrators know directly that you will not tolerate unfairness or disrespect

Psychologically Strong, Socially Smart

A psychologically strong teenager knows that education is essential. He works hard, stays focused, and knows that he's in school to learn and gain skills. He resists family patterns of failure and underachievement, and he knows to get help when he needs it.

A socially smart teenager knows that as a black person she can't afford to be complacent. She knows that the risks of complacency are severe: low-level education, low-level jobs, permanent low-income status for oneself, family, and community. She knows her enemy (a system that's designed to keep blacks subservient) and resists participating in her own oppression.

SHAPED BY SCHOOL: EDUCATION AND IDENTITY

Black parents and teenagers have much to say about the interplay of schooling and issues of identity, about the effect that an educational setting can have on a student's sense of self, as an individual and as a member of a racial group. Some of the stories were positive; others were negative. All of them demonstrated the critical effect that feeling part of a group, or not part of a group, can have on knowing who you are. Clearly, wherever teenagers are thrust daily in close quarters with other people—students and teachers, blacks and whites—is a crucible in which a sense of self is formed, for better or for worse.

Diane, a ninth grader, told me how happy she was after she transferred to a public exam school in the heart of the city. An exam school is one that requires that students pass an entrance exam for admission. These schools tend to enroll and graduate high-level students. This school was filled with students who, like her, took education seriously, and in so doing taught her a tremendous amount about being black and smart. She told me what the change meant to her:

> Well, I met a lot of other black girls, you know, who had really good images and stuff and who never gave up. And they knew where they wanted to go, they knew where they came from, and things like that. That was really helpful. As opposed to some of the people who I went to school with before. They were like, "I'm here because they made me come, and I'm not going to do nothing while I'm here."

For Diane, studying among other blacks who were equally intent on achieving served as nourishment to her soul, providing her with a sense of support and community that the complacency at her previous school had not.

Other stories I've heard are not as positive. One mother told me a different story about her son. Although he had what she called "brains" and "book sense," and didn't smoke or drink, she was worried that he didn't have enough of a sense of himself to say, "Get off my back," or "Stay away from me; I don't need your cigarettes," if he were pressed hard enough. "He takes a lot from his peers," she said. "The other kids call him 'nerd.'" She said that when she pointed out to him that he had no friends, he responded with, "Well, I don't need a lot of friends, Mom. They get you into trouble."

This mother was understandably concerned. A peer group of other achieving black teenagers could have provided her son with a foundation of power, the comfort of numbers, a stronger base from which to resist. Alone, he would be easy prey for complacent or disconnected teenagers; it might well be easier to join them than to resist.

A mother in Boston, Susan Lyons, told me about her 11-year-old daughter who attended a predominantly white suburban school and who, from earliest childhood, had taken her schoolwork and grades seriously. Then, when she was in fifth grade, her grades plummeted. "All of a sudden," the mother said, "we didn't know what had happened. And all the little white girls who used to call or come around, or who she would visit—all that was out." All this happened at the same time a group of black children from another part of the city enrolled in the school.

Luckily, a sensitive black teacher saved the day. She called the Lyonses to a meeting at school, and, as Susan remembers it, told them,

> Your daughter is a very lovely girl and she's having an identity crisis. And I think you should know that she's chosen to be with the black kids, you know, as an identification thing, and not be with those who were affirming [her] doing their homework and taking school seriously.

Mrs. Lyons was outraged at the situation:

> I said, "I'm not living in this town, paying this much money for this kind of school, to have my kid want to play around just because the other kids are black". I don't care about the color. I really don't. I said, "I want her to be prepared to go to college. And she's not going to be prepared if she doesn't get good grades."

She and the teacher came up with a plan: to make her daughter's seating in the class conditional on her grades. They would move her away from the seating block where this group of black students sat. If her grades went up again, she could move back to the area with her black friends. But she could stay there only if she kept her grades up.

I asked the daughter to talk about what happened with her black friends after she was forced to separate from them.

> Well, they, I mean, they just went back to their norms—where you know [they said], "You're white." I was white because I was hanging around with whites. So they ignored me, and I ignored them.

Mrs. Lyons acknowledged that the girl had been in an extremely difficult situation,

> because consciously she did have to choose. And what we said was, "There are blacks who are just as serious about school as you are. Unfortunately, these are just not the ones."
>
> So we tried to still affirm the race, and let her know that people just had different choices, and that at this point in their lives they chose to play and get C's. And that she couldn't afford to do that. [We told her] "You are a person and that has to take precedence over any color identification."

The parents recognized the important part the black teacher had played in the experience. When I asked the mother if she thought a white teacher would have been as responsive to the problem, she said no, she didn't think so. Mr. Lyons added,

> There are a few white teachers that I see who may have been as sensitive to what was going on as the black teacher was, but for the most part, the white teachers probably would have just thought that [our daughter] was just one of those [academically lazy] black kids and put her in that category. There's unconscious prejudice, and there's stereotyping, even with the white teachers that I like. It comes up and you say, "My God, we have to do something." It's still there.

This story shows a clear, fascinating interplay of bad resistance and good resistance strategies. The new black students' adoption of a complacent, underachieving attitude in response to their new white environment, and the girl's decision to sacrifice her academic status in order to take on the racial identity that the black group dictated (and be part of the group) are both short-term survival strategies. Fortunately, in response, both the teacher and the mother reacted with healthy resistance strategies: The teacher recognized the daughter's developmental need for racial identity and affiliation and took immediate steps to communicate this need to her parents. The mother took fast action as well, working with the teacher to stop the conduct that threatened her daughter's future. The point she made of affirming to her daughter her racial connection—reminding her that there are other academically successful black kids out there, and that she was not alone—was a brilliant final strategy.

Another mother described her daughter's brush with academic failure and how she had helped her surmount it. She was in her first year of boarding school in New England, and she was having a hard time academically. The mother was afraid her daughter, who had always received good grades in the past, was attributing her difficulties to the fact that she was from a single-parent, working-class black family and had attended a city school. As the semester progressed and her struggles with the subject matter intensified, her daughter started to doubt her own abilities, having convinced herself that she had entered boarding school with an inferior educational background. The mother knew better:

> But, what I tried to do is tell her, "The problem is you didn't study. You just did your homework, and beyond that you made absolutely no effort." And now she can see, you know, because now she calls me and tells me, "Mom, I did my work and now I'm studying more in the library."

The daughter continued to work hard and, at her mother's urging, stayed to repeat the year. The strategy was a success: the daughter raised her grades and her self-confidence and was nearly an honors student when I talked with her mother. The most critical part of this mother's very effective resistance message was about gaining power and control through effort and hard work, refusing to allow her daughter to buy into the notion that she was inferior, or a victim of her previous schooling.

As active, involved parents, we can (and should) encourage our schools to create learning environments where black students can feel comfortable being both black and smart. A teacher I know told me the story of an all-black school where the superachievers have turned both the "acting white" stereotype and the stereotype of the academic nerd on its head. These academically successful students have developed their own style of dressing and acting. They are not copying the white nerd look, nor the sitcom character "Urkle the dweeb" look—the goofy oversized glasses, the plastic pocket protectors, the high-water pants pulled up over the waistline. Instead, their clothes are fitted, neutral, slightly retro, and urban—an image that's both consistent with the broader aesthetic of the school culture and uniquely black. By doing this, the achievers made sure they weren't singled out as freaks, or as white wanna-be's. They are perceived as the smart kids, which is fine with them. In fact, they feel proud of the image of being black and smart. They can integrate those two identities because they are in a school culture that supports black students' success. Most important, the image of the successful black student in this institution is an indigenous creation; it evolved from, and found a secure home within, the culture of the black students themselves.

RESISTANCE STRATEGIES

Unhealthy (Short-Term, Survival-Oriented) Strategies

- Identifying with peers who deemphasize academics and cut classes

- Feeling victimized by inferior schooling, and internalizing notions of incompetence

- Succumbing to the erroneous belief that a person can't be both black and smart

Healthy (Long-Term, Liberating) Strategies

- Teaching children that they have the power within themselvesd toachieve academically, if they expend the effort

- Teaching teenagers that identity is not to be externally imposed (by whites or other blacks) but internally defined

- Finding and involving your children in groups of achieving black youth who value education

Psychologically Strong, Socially Smart

A psychologically strong, socially smart teenager has a positive attitude toward education, and at the same time maintains her racial connection. She stays focused on what she must do in order to succeed: stay in school and resist the pull of friends who avoid schoolwork. She has developed the ability to negotiate the school world, be it predominately black or predominately white, while developing a strong racial identity and sense of self. She looks for friends who will support her in this effort and is mindful that not all black social groups will have her best interests in mind. She knows that black students have special needs and face special challenges in school. She musters her energy and talents in order to be ready, willing, and able to develop intellectually, despite the obstacles.

SPIRITUALITY

A Source of Strength and Purpose

For parents, the connected themes of faith, spirituality, and commitment to the struggle for social justice arise as antidotes to depression, nihilism, and despair. Parents and teenagers alike recognize—and revel in—the power of the spirit to lift them, to allow them enough strength not just to go on, but to go on growing and flourishing and to resist in the face of racial injustice.

One 17-year-old told me how hard it is for his mother to keep from being overwhelmed by the idea that some blacks are lazy—"that they don't want to work for stuff." Once she thinks about it, he says, "She blows it all out of proportion. The small percentage, or whatever percentage it may be—it really weighs on her mind more than the other ones who are working hard." Thinking about the situation we are in, worrying about poverty, racism, and social inequities can wear on you, just as it wears on this boy's mother. Some of us are angry about where we are, or, as in this mother's case, where other blacks are. So much seems out of our control.

It is easy to despair, and despair is a powerful, painful emotion, with the potential to cloud our judgment and trap us in a place where we are simply unable to do what we need to do in order to move ahead. Some of us, as one mother told me, start to feel that there's just no point in resisting. But we can't allow ourselves to despair. As she says, "They feel they're not going to have a chance in life, because they come from this or that background, and that's the wrong way to look at it. No matter what background they come from, they shouldn't give up trying to do better for themselves."

Teenagers tell me that faith is important and that parents can help their children sustain it. As Susan, a 16-year-old, told me, "My mother says that if some people give you a hard time, just pray about them and say, 'I'm not going to give in to whoever, whatever—you know.'" She also told me that the most important thing her mother ever told her was "to believe in yourself and keep the faith and believe in God. That keeps me positive." Another young man, Sean, told me that his mother says, "As long as you put God in it, it'll work."

Many parents agree with Mrs. Robinson, who talked about the importance of developing spiritual and ideological beliefs that provide meaning to life. She said, "I rely on my Upper Being more so than anything, because I feel like he gives me courage to overcome a lot of the obstacles in my life."

And the black church itself speaks to our blackness in ways that no other institution can. As Carolyn Johnson says, "The black church allows the freedom to practice in a natural way the fundamental expressions of blackness. . . . talking back, call and response, testifying, spirit dancing, releasing and replenishing—being unabashedly black—were and are the mainstay of cultural communion in the traditional black church." The church serves other valuable purposes as well. To Mary Pattillo-McCoy, "the black church culturally and religiously binds together the black middle class and the black poor . . . [it] retains a collective ethos and a correspondence of practice that stretches across class groups."

One college-educated dad in Philadelphia, Mr. Michaels, describes the lessons of faith that he learned as a child, reinforced at the historically black college he attended, as the very lessons he still taps to keep on keeping on. "I think our strength is coming from the black church," he said. "You get your exposure there. I remember the first day at college. I went in and was sitting there and the dean of men said this. He said, 'You follow these two pieces of advice and you'll make it through [college] and you'll make it in life.' The first piece of advice was to keep your faith in God and go to church when you can. The second piece of advice was to associate with people you can learn from. That was it. I don't think there's any more than that."

The black church helps us in countless other ways as well. It serves as an extended home space where African Americans of all ages can feel both secure and free to teach and learn the lessons of black community. It is where as children we learn the lessons that help us "hold on": the sustenance of prayer and music, the healing and energizing power of spiritual assistance, the pleasure and importance of meaningful rituals. For those of us who feel isolated from the black community in other aspects of everyday life—at work, at school, or in our neighborhoods—it provides a black peer culture for socializing, dating, and just plain small talk that affirms and blesses our blackness.

For our youth, the black church also provides an opportunity to learn and practice skills that will later help them serve and influence the larger community. In the shelter of the church, they can learn leadership, develop their communication skills (reading, writing, and speaking), and take on responsibilities appropriate to their age group, whether it's helping prepare a snack for toddlers, ushering, or leading a fellowship group. Here they have the opportunity to join in community-service activities and to observe and understand the importance of supporting the church and community with money. In our churches, through communing and worshipping with young and old, our children also develop a lifelong respect for their elders and an appreciation of the gifts and strengths of every age along the life span. And here they have the opportunity to join in a multitude of extracurricular activities that will enrich their lives and develop their skills, such as choir, Boy Scouts and Girls Scouts, field trips, and—for older teenagers at many black churches—college visits.

A mother in North Carolina shared a story from her childhood about growing up surrounded by women who lived their faith. I asked her to talk about some of the things her parents taught her that helped her know what it is to be black.

> Things like teaching me about living. Just getting together. People in your area, your neighbors, sharing with each other, good times and bad times. What was getting through to me when I was young was that there's a lot more going on than I know about. I would hear them complaining about their troubles, and how we just had to be strong and just give it to the Lord. They believed in giving everything to God. And my goodness gracious, as a young child, I didn't see what He was doing to soothe the situation. When they came, they were troubled, but when they left our house, it was always as if they were more at peace. My grandmother was troubled too, but I didn't know that until they came. And I'd hear her go back and forth with them about the things that she was unhappy about or displeased about. I was like, 'Oh. I didn't know that.' It was a learning experience. I guess now you would call it a kind of psychological self-help group.

This mother describes an important function of faith: its ability to restore us, reenergize us, bring us peace. Within this communion of women we can see black people's long legacy of leaning on one another, getting strength, sharing burdens, turning it over to God. Practicing our faith in this manner gives us the energy to come back and deal with the troubles of the world once again. Collectively we can find the strength to endure. We can use our faith to help one another hold on.

The psychologist Nancy Goldberger, talking about how black women see and experience their relationship with God, emphasizes the liberating, strengthening aspect of the fusion of God with the self: "There is a sense of God as someone who listens as well as directs and dictates, who frees as well as expects obedience. Furthermore, God is experienced as 'in me' (not external); thus the person's voice can be God's voice. The orientation to God as authority coexists with a strong sense of self, experienced as a distinct and particular person who can and should be known by God and by other people on her own terms."

The vast majority of the African Americans with whom I spoke would describe themselves as Christian. A very small minority said they found themselves drawn to the Muslim religion, or at least read the Koran, and one or two parents described themselves as religious, although they had chosen to make a break from the religious denominations they had grown up in. Most of us try to attend church regularly; we use the black church to socialize and to keep our children connected to the church community (especially blacks who live in predominately white suburban neighborhoods). We also recognize the social needs met by the church and participate in community services coordinated at the church, like food pantries, clothing drives, and mentor programs. Beyond this, and most important, we feel a deep spiritual root that embraces far more than formal religion. It is by tapping this root—by plugging into this source of strength—that we African Americans reconnect continually with what is often deepest and most central to our experience.

I feel that black baby boomers these days, like their white counterparts, are seeking a renewed sense of spirituality—for guidance, solace, and purpose. Clearly some of this search is related to our approaching middle age, and some of it is tied to living in a culture that feels so rootless and individualistic. The search for spirituality and the return to organized religion is about recovery as well, recovery of the faith many of us grew up with and from which we later turned away.

This return to spirituality is occurring in a number of ways. We are re-connecting with the religious teachings we absorbed growing up, or, if we had been disenchanted with organized religion in the past, we're bouncing around, introducing ourselves to various different religious practices and beliefs, trying to find a good fit. Some of us are taking our search for a spiritual center away from traditional organized religion altogether, re-creating spiritual practices from which we can draw strength, usually incorporating prayer and other church rituals at home, or in the communion of friends. Thus, black baby-boomer parents and our children participate in positive and fulfilling ways within a variety of church and spiritual cultures today.

Today black people, as well as many other Americans, are seeking to uncover our essential spirits, which appear to be buried in the daily battles of living: dealing with racism, sexism, negative media images, paying bills, raising kids alone, loneliness, and social isolation. In this sense black people are in recovery—not necessarily the 12-step type of recovery (although many blacks are in those programs as well) but recovery from the defeating situations and negative thoughts so many of us are struggling to overcome.

Today's return to faith must also be considered against the backdrop of civil rights activities, organized and energized in the black church, that were part of the black baby boomers' childhood landscape. This is where many of us learned our moral values and learned to apply lessons about morality to our social condition; it is where we learned the importance of mobilizing the community to right the wrongs of legalized segregation. The church was a natural place for us to be in communion with one another, to renew and sustain our faith, and, especially in the civil rights years, to engage in political activism. Even our church songs were transformed into songs of freedom, as in "Ain't gonna let nobody turn me 'round"—songs that energize our spirit and affirm our dreams.

We need to encourage our black teenagers to share in this bounty. We must convey to them the importance of keeping their faith in God and help them acquire the tools that will allow them to use spirituality to lift them up, invigorate them, sustain them in hard times, and help them determine the direction they need to pursue. In addition, they need to acquire what Carolyn Johnson calls "holding on tools." The two most important "holding on tools" mentioned by the parents and teenagers with whom I talked were prayer and spiritual music. The Bible and attending church services were close behind.

PRAYER AS A SKILL TO BE LEARNED

Research has shown that prayer is the single most important coping response among African Americans. It not only endows us with the strength to meet personal crises, it reduces stress, particularly for African American women, who have been found to pray more often than men. Studies show that people who pray have better mental health than people who don't pray. One of the greatest gifts we can pass to our children is an ability to pray and an understanding of its power. Teenagers who know how to pray—to sit quietly, spending quality time with themselves, learning to listen to the voice inside—will learn to remember to "know what they know." They will have the stillness and capacity to stay in touch with the truths with which they were raised: black folks' truths. They will be able to tap into the lessons from our legacy of resistance—the struggle and hard-won success—and will ultimately be better able to resist healthily, effectively, knowingly. We must help them to know that a power exists that is benevolent, loving, and available in times of need.

So much of the power of the black church lies in its music, in the messages of the old Negro spirituals that speak to the spiritual legacy of resistance, providing the lift that exhorts us and allows us to rise above hardship. It reminds us that although the struggle is never-ending, odds can be surmounted and "trouble don't last always." Our music is yet another conduit of the oral tradition that carries our history of resistance. Making each song our own, we rejoice in and share our lived experiences of overcoming adversity by continuing to sing the songs that have sustained us so well for so long, and by telling and retelling our personal tales of perseverance, struggle, and resistance.

When one woman began her story with a short, familiar verse from a popular gospel tune whose last line proclaims, "Nobody told me that the road would be easy, but I don't believe he brought me this far to leave me," she showed that she had made the song's message of resistance her own. At one point in her life, she told me, when she attended a college whose campus newspaper demeaned black students and faculty, she drew the strength to resist from the words of the same song. Her resistance strategy, to turn her resentment into a force that propelled her to persist, was smart, self-affirming, and ultimately liberating.

As we all know, loud music and constant chatter are part and parcel of teenage culture. Taking the time to sit still and silent, praying, may not be a skill their peer group encourages or endorses. And although some people may say it is possible to teach young people to be quiet, adolescent culture is competing against us on this one. The loud, dominant back beat of hip-hop and the raucous, verbal sparring of rap are hard to struggle against.

Oddly, many teenagers and young adults have told me that they don't necessarily have to be in complete silence in order to be contemplative. My college students tell me they write powerfully emotive poetry while listening to Lauren Hill or select cuts from any number of contemporary R & B, hip-hop, reggae, and rap artists. They use poetry as a way to get in touch with their feelings and music as a way to access those feelings. But maybe their ability to find stillness within noise is not so odd after all. Black worship traditions have certainly never been known for their quietness. Our cultural past encourages entry into the worship service in loud, celebratory ways. Call and response, testifying, spirit dancing—all are examples of our uninhibited "expressive release." This isn't to say that black teenagers shouldn't get quiet. The task is to incorporate the ability to become contemplative or thankful into the music our teenagers listen to today. The enormous success of Kirk Franklin, the Winans, and many others in today's hip-hop gospel music tradition, shows that our teenagers can be encouraged to love God, to give praise, and to do what's right in a pulse and rhythm that speaks to them and helps them get in touch with themselves and find out what they want and where they should be going.

PURPOSE

During a long conversation a 10th grader at a Philadelphia public high school, Omar revealed a startling aspect of his past. We had been talking for some time about his life, and about the school he had dropped out of the year before, but to which, after much thought, he had returned. His year away from school had been a mind-opening experience. Not only was he able to learn the hard lesson that without a high-school diploma his earning potential was pretty low, but he also went through a powerful identity conversion process, coming to terms with who he is as a black male, and making key decisions about what he believes. He also decided to abandon his identity as a drug dealer. The turning point, he said, had been his introduction to Islam. "Sometimes religion fails us, you know," he said. "In some ways it tells you to have all these morals and it don't make no sense. But going to Muslim churches and going into black bookstores, and going to the library, you know, I learned more about myself. And I don't need this [selling drugs] to make me feel like I'm good, or feel like I need to make money now."

He told me that he now knew that he could—and should—make money legally, but that first he would need to continue his education. I reminded him that many people are spending much time, energy, and resources trying to find ways to reach teenagers like him, hoping to convince them to turn away from the drug scene. Many of these people feel they are fighting an uphill battle, that they are losing to the pull of the drug trade, to the fast money and excitement. "So you're saying that knowing more about yourself, taking the time to learn about your cultural background did it for you?" I asked. "Yeah," Omar told me.

> It can do it for a lot of people. I mean, I read that in the sixties people like the Black Muslims used to go around, and they'd just snatch drug addicts and prostitutes off the streets, and they used to take them somewhere and like build them up, build up their self-esteem. Teach them about theirself. Empower them. And when they came out, they were a different person. That way they were helping the community instead of hurting it.

As he has learned more about who he is, his belief system has developed. Islam has empowered him to look at himself as a black man, and to make sense out of what it means to be a man in this culture. There are many who argue that Louis Farrakhan and the followers of the Nation of Islam put forward a very powerful message about black manhood and provide a path by which men can learn to integrate their spirituality with their race and gender. Like this young man, several of the black teenagers I spoke with in the Philadelphia schools were attracted to the notion of purpose persented by Farrakhan and his clear articulation of what blacks should be about, be committed to, or avoid. For this teenager as well as for many others, the message of Islam spoke to his emerging sense of black male identity and to his desire to form a coherent sense of values and determine his personal purpose. It gave him an understanding of who he was and what he should be about. He found his strength and his ability to be a part of the community, and he was able to stop his destructive ways, this time in a non-Christian context.

The psychologist James Marcia says that when adolescents make a commitment to values, goals, and behavior, they achieve a sense of identity. Knowing who they are and what they believe can be, as it was for our 10th grader, a powerful, life-changing event. Parents and other adults have a role to play in this aspect of identity formation. The African Americans I talked to identified as most critical the task of helping their teenagers to gain a sense of life purpose, and the two moral values that they felt aided that quest were the development of a sense of justice and a sense of care and connection.

Garrett, a 14-year-old, told me that his father helps him in this process by making certain that he reconnects by remembering the past. As he said, "My father tells me repeatedly that he knows I'm going to make it, and when I do make it, don't forget where I came from. 'Your family [he says], we struggled . . . together, and you're the first one that's probably going to branch out and stop that struggle. And don't forget our people that struggled before us.' So it's a constant reminder of what I went through to get to where I am."

This father sees himself on an upward social trajectory, which he attributes to his own efforts and those of family members. He wants to make certain that his son never forgets where he came from. He wants him to know that not only is it important to honor the past—those who worked to make your success today possible—he also wants him to understand that yesterday's struggles make today's success that much sweeter.

This struggle to achieve, or, for so many of us, to simply hang on and survive, is inextricably tied to a teenager's sense of life purpose. But it means more than just individual advancement, or teaching teenagers how to value personal responsibility or stand on their own two feet. Parents and teenagers today say the struggle is for group advancement as well, and to achieve that goal will take all of us, our collective will focused unwaveringly on collective action.

For today's black families, racial connection is an overriding concern. When parents tell me about developing a life purpose, they mean a collective purpose: determining and acting on what we want as a people, and what we want our children to be working toward as members of the black race. As the philosopher Audrey Thompson says, for black people, "caring means bringing about justice for the next generation and justice means creating the kinds of conditions under which all people can flourish." Black parents believe that they should be socializing their teenagers to acquire the collective will to bring about systemic change because, as they see it, that's the only way all blacks will be lifted.

When black baby-boomer parents talk about this issue, they appear to be taking their cues from the 1960s, a period in which we as a people engaged in massive collective social action. Tired of being treated as second-class citizens, tired of the injustice, believing we were entitled to be treated as God's children with dignity, fairness, and awareness of our intrinsic worth, we were willing and able to fight to make that happen. That was the prevailing discourse at that time. Unfortunately, it isn't now. Nevertheless, it seems to me that African Americans truly feel a need to resurrect that sixties' sense of purpose and commitment to social change. And even if it's a very long time before the revolution takes to the streets again, there is one critical thing that can and must be accomplished today: to help our teens internalize the struggle, to commit to a system of values, and to construct a sense of self that gives them direction, keeps them focused, and ultimately gives meaning to the struggle.

The process of gaining self-awareness, of coming to understand who you are and what you should be about, never takes place without struggle. While struggle is hard, it is necessary to the building of strong individuals and strong communities. But it must take place under the watchful, caring eye of the community. For struggle that takes place apart from community often leads to despair. Helping black teenagers to overcome helps provide them with life purpose, and allows them to deal with the confusion, resentment, anger, and bitterness associated with their devalued status. It enables them to hold onto a strong self-concept, develop their self-esteem, and retain and maintain their dignity.

Simply stated, the message is: stay connected, because connection is the foundation of a morality of care and community. We want our children to grow up and be able to look into the eyes of another black person and say, "You are me, I am you." We want them to be attuned to issues of social injustice, not only when they are victimized but also when they witness injustice to others, and to know what they can do to fight it. We want them to be able to say, "This is wrong, and I will do what I can." We want them to feel confident that they can make a difference.

Today's black baby boomers have not lost sight of the fight for justice and freedom that we so vividly remember from our youth. We have internalized this piece of history, a history that many of us shared in creating, as a history of black resistance. The stories about race and perseverance and about fighting back (so many of which were shared with me) provide the framework around which this generation's own identities were constructed. The challenges and the victories of the civil rights movement became the processes of struggle and triumph we have identified with and are passing to our own children.

Spirituality anchors racial identity, providing hope and purpose. When we teach our children to tap this source, we are not only nurturing religious and moral values; we are also helping our children learn that to be black and to be able to survive today, at the dawn of a new century, requires a hard-won, tenacious resistance of the psyche—a resistance that recognizes the interdependency of African Americans with each other, with the history that shaped our faith, and with faith itself. For resisters resist with body, mind, *and spirit.*

A CALL TO ARMS

As the black baby-boomer generation, we carry with us a real, gritty, and hard-won sense of resistance and aspiration forged in the promise and upheaval of the 1960s. It is our responsibility as parents to draw on that resistance and pass it on, as a precious gift, to our children, who face pressures different from the pressures we faced as teenagers, but just as insidious: the new, covert racism, and the ubiquitous influence of the media that undermines their feelings of pride and effectiveness. Perhaps there will soon be a reawakening of the social justice movement that so many of us believe our country desperately needs. Until then, we must continue to resist in the ways that are helpful, real, and within our control. We must endow our children with the skills and strength to resist from within: from their psyches, their spirit, and their souls.

Some people argue that there's a vast generational divide between the hip-hop generation and us, their black baby-boomer parents. Many of us see our children's generation as egocentric, vulgar, and unfocused. Many of our children, in turn, see us as out-of-touch sellouts. But this generational divide disappears when it comes to issues of racism, because racism affects all African Americans, young and old, everywhere and every day. There's much that we baby boomers can teach the hip-hop generation about the struggle to lead rich and meaningful lives in the skin we're in. And it is our responsibility to do so.

Each of us has our own personal stories of successful resistance and a stock of cleverly crafted strategies, invented and reinvented over the years, that have allowed us to stand up to the pernicious effects of racism and take a stand for healthy, strong, and spiritually centered black individuals, families, and communities. This collective wisdom is ours to share with the next generation, not as a static, fixed knowledge base ("I did it this way so you have to do it this way, too"), but as a living, infinitely malleable kind of wisdom. We black baby boomers are savvy and experienced; we are well aware that racial realities shift with time. It is our job to work with our teenagers, to build with them a base of knowledge about their racial reality that is grounded in their present-day experiences—a foundation upon which they can learn to accurately assess a racially linked situation: read it, name it, oppose it, and replace it if need be. Our children need both the spirit and the tools to resist in healthy, responsible ways. All it takes is our time, energy, and patience.

When it comes to parenting for resistance, maintaining silence about racial matters carries a high cost. The parents and teens who can best envision and put into practice effective resistance strategies are those who talk together often about their racial reality, share ideas across the generations, and build upon their knowledge in developmentally and age-appropriate ways. I have found that the children from these families possess a priceless repertoire of healthy, effective resistance strategies, and the wisdom to know when and how to apply them.

We must talk with our teenagers every day and with all our hearts. We must listen well, discuss thoughtfully, and guide them through the process of challenging and testing assumptions. We must help them stay focused, committed, and able to maintain a sense of optimism about our racial reality.

The social change our country so fervently needs will come about when, and only when, we are willing to work to make that happen. In the meantime, there is much that we as parents can control within ourselves: our attitudes, our will to persevere, and our own behavior. If we want these attributes for our children, then we as adults must be willing to maintain them in ourselves. Our children are watching us, learning from us, and taking their own social cues from what they observe at home. When they see us asserting ourselves, committing ourselves to social justice, caring for others in our own communities as well as in the larger multicultural communities in which we live and work, and crossing the racial divide with courage and integrity, they are learning. When they see us advocating for better schooling for African American children, loving who we see in the mirror, acting toward each other in civil ways, honoring and embracing the tremendous diversity within our group, and respecting and appreciating nonblack people the way we ourselves wish to be respected, then we increase the chances tenfold that our children will grow to be loving, strong, resistant, and resilient adults.

It is critical that we give race a central, unabashed focus in our child-rearing practices. No one else will do this teaching for us. We, as parents, must help our children understand who they are and what they face. Because only if they are forewarned and prepared will they be able to circumvent the barriers that continue to exist in this society.

Make no mistake: being racially conscious is not the same as being racist. I am not arguing that black children should grow up to commune with and care only about other blacks. What I'm saying is quite the opposite. I'm saying that our children need the tools to engage successfully with an ever-widening range of people and groups outside of the black community. To accomplish this, we must begin by helping our children love themselves. Only then will they be able to extend the principles and practices of love, caring, and justice to the larger human community.

Finally, we must imbue our children with an unwavering sense of mission and of purpose. And although we must encourage them to find and pursue their own individual paths, we must also teach them to remember their connection to those who struggled and sacrificed before them, to their own families and communities, and to the next generation of black children for whom they will soon be responsible.

In today's multicultural environment, many black people are coming to recognize and embrace their multiracial origins, rejecting the "one drop" rule that used to define who is black. Some blacks today don't want to be defined by a single ancestry. Some see the black–white dichotomy as little more than a polarizing myth, and perhaps it is. And maybe a day will come when we will no longer need to talk about racial differences, power, and injustice. I'd like to think that the baby-boomer generation, with its feet still warm from the heat of the 1960s, will be the one that brings us closer to the elimination of racism. By equipping our children with self-love, courage, and the ability to analyze and respond thoughtfully and appropriately to racism and perceived racism—by raising a generation of socially smart, emotionally strong, spiritually connected, and responsible resisters—we can take an enormous and real step toward that day.

RESOURCE GUIDE

BOOKS

The Black Parenting Book. Anne C. Beale, Linda Villarosa, and Allison Abner. Broadway Books, 1998.

Black, White, Other: Biracial Americans Talk About Race and Identity. Lise Funderberg. Quill, 1995.

Developing Positive Self-Images and Discipline in Black Children. Jawanza Kunjufu. African American Images, 1997.

I'm Chocolate, You're Vanilla: Raising Healthy Black and Biracial Children in a Race-Conscious World. Marguerite A. Wright. Jossey-Bass, 1998.

Raising Black Children: Two Leading Psychiatrists Confront the Educational, Social, and Emotional Problems Facing Black Children. James P. Comer and Alvin F. Poussaint. Plume, 1992.

"Why Are All the Black Kids Sitting Together in the Cafeteria?" And Other Conversations about Race. Beverly Daniel Tatum. Basic Books, 1997.

WEBSITES

http://www.black families.com/living/parenting/
  The site covers a number of issues including health, finance, parenting, and family relationships. Updated regularly.

http://www.saafe.com/
  SAAFE is a clearinghouse for single African American fathers to obtain services and information on parenting.

http://www.black parenting.com
  The Black Parenting website is the official web site for *The Black Parenting Book*. It is an on-line guide to raising African American children in the first five years.

http://afroamculture.about.com/
  The website is self-described as "the network of sites led by expert guides." It offers net links to a large number of interest areas specific to African Americans.

FEATURE FILMS AND VIDEOS

Amazing Grace. 1991. 60 mins. Written and narrated by Bill Moyers, this documentary uses the hymn *Amazing Grace* as a vehicle for looking at black religion and the black civil rights movement. [PBS]

Amistad. 1998. 152 mins. The film version of the *Amistad* slave ship revolt and trial. [FF]

The Autobiography of Miss Jane Pittman. 1974. 110 mins. History of the black experience in the U.S. as seen through flashbacks into the life of a 110-year-old former slave. Key periods are presented: slavery, Reconstruction, the Jim Crow decades, and the civil rights movement. The film is based on the Ernest J. Gaines novel of the same name. [FF]

Buffalo Soldiers. 1997. 120 mins. All-black cavalry regiments were created by Congress in 1866. This movie presents an accurate portrayal of the life and context of these soldiers. [FF]

The Color Purple. 1985. 154 mins. The film version of Alice Walker's book about the life of a poor black girl in the South from 1909 to 1947. [FF]

Do the Right Thing. 1989. 120 mins. Spike Lee's story of conflict in perceptions of the American experience between black Americans and immigrants and children of immigrants. [FF]

Eyes on the Prize I, America's Civil Rights Years (1954–1965). 1987. *Eyes on the Prize II, America at the Racial Crossroads (1965–1985).* 1990. Award-winning documentary of the history of the modern struggle for civil rights for black Americans. [PBS]

Glory. 1989. 122 mins. A film that chronicles the story of the 54th Massachusetts Regiment in the Civil War, the first black voluntary infantry unit. [FF]

Hoop Dreams. 1994. 169 mins. The film traces the lives of two outstanding black basketball players and their families through high school and their dreams of playing in the National Basketball Association. [FF]

A Raisin in the Sun. 1961. 128 mins. The film tells the powerful story of a black American family in the 1950s. It is based on the 1959 play by Lorraine Hansberry. [FF]

Roots: The Triumph of an American Family. 1977. Total time: 12 hours. An ABC miniseries, the odyssey of one family is used to tell the story of black Americans from slavery through Reconstruction. The sequel, carrying the story from Reconstruction through the 1970s, is *Roots: The Next Generation,* made in 1979, total time: 11 1/2 hours. [FF]

REFERENCES AND NOTES

Introduction

xi. *The truth is that although:* "Reducing the Risk: Connections that Make a Difference in the Lives of Youth." Division of General Pediatrics and Adolescent Health, University of Minnesota, Minneapolis, September 1997, p. 34.

xii. *Some social scientists, such as Stephan and Abigail Thernstrom:* Thernstrom, S., and Thernstrom, A. M. (1997). *America in Black and White: One Nation Indivisible.* New York: Simon & Schuster.

xii. *Others, following the lead of William J. Wilson:* Wilson, W. J. (1978). *The Declining Significance of Race.* Chicago: University of Chicago Press. See also Wilson, W. J. (1987). *The Truly Disadvantaged: The Inner City, the Underclass and Public Policy.* Chicago: University of Chicago Press.

xii. *"unfairly infringes on individual autonomy":* Wilkins, D. B. (1996). Introduction. In K. A. Appiah and A. Gutman (Eds.), *Color Consciousness: The Political Morality of Race.* Princeton, NJ: Princeton University Press, p. 7.

xiii. *in our schools, and in our homes:* For example, President Clinton's Race Initiative.

xv. *had the highest blood pressure:* Krieger, N., and Sidney, S. (1996). "Racial Discrimination and Blood Pressure." *American Journal of Public Health, 86*(10), 1370–1380.

Chapter 1: Spanning Two Cultures

6. *wrote in her autobiography:* Wade-Gayles, G. (1993). *Pushed Back to Strength: A Black Woman's Journey Home.* Boston: Beacon Press.

10. *In the home is where children first learn:* Harrison, A. (1985). "The Black Family's Socializing Environment: Self-Esteem and Ethnic Attitude Among Black Children." In H. P. McAdoo and J. L. McAdoo (Eds.), *Black Children: Social, Educational and Parental Environments.* Newbury Park, CA: Sage Publications. See also Harrison, A., et al. (1990). "Family Ecologies of Ethnic Minority Children." *Child Development, 61,* 347–362.

11. *this family cultivated a myth:* Stone, E. (1988). *Black Sheep and Kissing Cousins.* New York: Penguin Books, p. 99.

20. *The writer Toni Morrison has said:* Burrell Information Services. (1999, January

31). CBS News Transcripts, *60 Minutes,* "American Writer Toni Morrison Talks About Her Life."

21.   *for wearing the mask* was *a strategy:* Jenkins, A. H. (1982). *The Psychology of the Afro-American: A Humanistic Approach.* New York: Pergamon Press.

30.   *"the cold realities of rising housing prices":* Newman, K. S. (1993). *Declining Fortunes: The Withering of the American Dream.* New York: Basic Books, p. 187. For an interesting discussion of black baby boomers and generational identity, see Bowser, B. P. (1989). "Generational Effects: The Impact of Culture, Economy and Community Across the Generations." In R. Jones (Ed.), *Black Adult Development and Aging.* Berkeley, CA: Cobb & Henry.

Chapter 2: Parenting Black Children Today

32.   *It means working to raise a child:* Edwards, C., and Whiting, B. (1988). *Children of Different Worlds.* Cambridge: Harvard University Press.

32.   *It also means providing guidance:* Real, T. (1997). *I Don't Want to Talk About It: Overcoming the Secret Legacy of Male Depression.* New York: Scribner.

32.   *The kind of parent the person will be:* Brooks, J. B. (1998). *Parenting,* 2d ed. Mountain View, CA: Mayfield Publishing.

33.   *the "interdependent stage":* Galinsky, E. (1981). *Between Generations: The Six Stages of Parenthood.* New York: Times Books.

33.   *"My personal problem":* Giovanni, N. (1994). *Racism 101.* New York: William Morrow, p. 35.

34.   *Psychologists tell us:* Okun, B. (1984). *Working With Adults: Individuals, Family and Career Development.* Pacific Grove, CA: Brooks/Cole Publishing.

34.   *The developmental tasks of these years:* Ibid.

36.   *The psychologist Barbara Okun:* Ibid., p. 224.

39.   *In her study:* Peters, M. F. (1985). "Racial Socialization of Young Black Children." In H. P. McAdoo and J. L. McAdoo (Eds.), *Black Children: Social, Educational and Parental Environments.* Newbury Park, CA: Sage Publications.

39.   *This preparation includes presenting alternatives:* Ibid.

39.   *Michael Thornton and his colleagues:* Thornton, M. C., Chatters, L. M., Taylor, R. J., and Allen, W. R. (1990). "Sociodemographic and Environmental Correlates of Racial Socialization by Black Parents." *Child Development, 61,* 401–409.

40.   *Phillip Bowman and Cleopatra Howard:* Bowman, P., and Howard, C. (1985). "Race-related Socialization, Motivation, and Academic Achievement: A Study of Black Youth in Three-Generation Families." *Journal of the American Academy of Child Psychiatry, 24*(2),132–141. See also Branch, C., and Newcomb, N. (1986). "Racial Attitude Development Among Young Black Children as a Function of Parental Attitudes: A Longitudinal and Cross Sectional Study." *Child Development, 57,* 712–721; and Marshall, S. (1995). "Ethnic Socialization of African American Children: Implications for Parenting, Identity Development and Academic Achievement." *Journal of Youth and Adolescence, 24*(4), 377–396.

40.   *In other studies, the psychologist Margaret Beale Spencer:* Spencer, M. B. (1983). "Children's Cultural Values and Parental Child-Rearing Strategies." *Developmen-*

tal Review, 3, 351–370. See also Spencer, M. B., and Markstrom-Adams, C. (1990). "Identity Processes Among Racial and Ethnic Minority Children in America." *Child Development, 61,* 290–310.

40. *the importance of personal strength:* Spencer, M. B., Swanson, D. P., and Glymph, A. (1997). "The Prediction of Parental Psychological Functioning: Influences of African American Adolescent Perceptions and Experiences of Context." In C. D. Ryff and M. M. Seltzer (Eds.), *The Parental Experience in Midlife.* Chicago: University of Chicago Press, p. 339.

42. *As the writer Adrienne Rich:* Rich, A. (1975). "Women and Honor: Some Notes on Lying." In A. Rich (Ed.), *On Lies, Secrets and Silence.* New York: Brunner-Mazel, p. 186.

Chapter 3: The Bricks and Mortar of Building Strong Children

51. *As the psychologist Adelbert Jenkins has said:* Jenkins, A. H. (1982). *The Psychology of the Afro-American: A Humanistic Approach.* New York: Pergamon Press, pp. 13–14.

55. *We are also incorporating previously denied:* Parham, T. A. (1989). "Nigrescence: The Transformation of Black Consciousness Across the Life Cycle." In R. L. Jones, (Ed.), *Black Adult Development and Aging.* Berkeley, CA: Cobb & Henry.

Chapter 4: Teaching Strategies for Healthy Resistance

58. *the kind of deep inner faith:* Paris, P. (1985). *The Social Teaching of the Black Churches.* Philadelphia: Fortress Press.

64. *Reading involves paying close attention:* The guidelines listed below are adapted from the work of Deborah Meier, founder and past principal of Central Park East Secondary School in East Harlem, who calls them "habits of mind." They have been adopted by educators across the country for use in a wide range of academic disciplines, including literature and the social sciences, and are intended to help students critically analyze what they are learning. Meier writes, "The fundamental aim of CPESS is to teach students to use their minds well and prepare them to live productive, socially useful and personally satisfying lives. The school's academic programs stress intellectual development. Five 'habits of mind' are stressed: (1) to help students learn to critically examine evidence; (2) to be able to see the world through multiple viewpoints—to step into others' shoes; (3) to make connections and see patterns; (4) to imagine alternatives (what if? what else?); and finally (5) to ask, 'What difference does it make, who cares?' These five are at the heart of all our work, along with sound work habits and care and concern for others; habits of work and habits of heart. The curriculum affirms the central importance of students learning how to learn, how to reason, and how to investigate complex issues that require collaboration, personal responsibility, and a tolerance for uncertainty." From *The Senior Institute Handbook,* Mission Statement, Central Park East Secondary School, New York City (1991). Cited in Nathan, L. (1995).

"Portfolio Assessment and Teacher Practice" (Doctoral dissertation, Harvard University). Ann Arbor, MI: UMI Dissertation Services, p. 67.

70. *Here are some questions*: The guidelines listed are adapted from the work of Deborah Meier, founder of the Central Park East Secondary School, who calls them "habits of mind." For more information, see notes on p. 267

74. *as a protective buffer against the negativity*: Peters, "Racial Socialization."

76. *a collaboratively constructed knowledge base*: Goldberger, N. R. (1996). "Cultural Imperatives and Diversity in Ways of Knowing." In N. Goldberger, J. Tarule, B. Clinchy, and M. Belenky (Eds.), *Knowledge, Difference, and Power: Essays Inspired by Women's Ways of Knowing*. New York: Basic Books.

76. *trust themselves as sources of knowledge*: Ward, J. V. (1996). "Raising Resisters: The Role of Truth Telling in the Psychological Development of African American Girls." In B. R. Leadbeater and N. Way (Eds.), *Urban Girls: Resisting Stereotypes, Creating Identities*. New York: New York University Press.

82. *The psychologist Martin Seligman*: Seligman quoted in Brooks, J. B. (1998). *Parenting*, 2d ed. Mountain View, CA: Mayfield Publishing, p. 78. See also Seligman, M. (1990). *Learned Optimism*. New York: Pocket Books.

Chapter 5: Growing Up Female

92. *the children surveyed are not optimistic*: Spratling, C. (1994). "Black Children Facing Worst Crisis Since Slavery-Advocate Says." Knight-Ridder/Tribune News Service, Report on the Children's Defense Fund, the Black Community Crusade for Children poll commissioned with Peter D. Hart Associates.

95. *The American Association of University Women's study*: American Association of University Women. (1991). "Shortchanging Girls, Shortchanging America: A Call to Action." Washington, DC: AAUW. See also the AAUW Report (1992). "How Schools Shortchange Girls." Washington, DC: AAUW Educational Foundation and National Educational Foundation.

95. *Similarly, the September 1997 Commonwealth Fund*: The Commonwealth Fund. (1997). *Survey of the Health of Adolescent Girls*. Louis Harris and Associates, New York, NY.

97. *The sociologist K. Sue Jewell*: Jewell, K. S. (1993). *From Mammy to Miss America and Beyond: Cultural Images and the Shaping of U.S. Social Policy*. New York: Routledge, Chapman & Hall, p. 168.

107. *most important virtue that a woman can possess*: Lakoff, R. T., and Scherr, R. L. (1984). *Face Value: Politics of Beauty*. Boston: Routledge & Kegan Paul.

108. *social role of ugly duckling*: Grier, W., and Cobbs, P. (1968). *Black Rage*. New York: Basic Books.

109. *As Sonja Peterson-Lewis and Shirley Chennault determined*: Peterson-Lewis, S., and Chennault, S. (1986, Winter). "Black Artists' Music Videos: Three Success Strategies." *Journal of Communication, 36*, p. 113.

109. *and their dark skin is unattractive*: In a study I conducted with my colleague Tracy Robinson, we found that, overall, among black teens we surveyed, there was a positive relationship between satisfaction with skin color and self-esteem. However,

it was also clear that colorism, or stereotyped attributions and prejudgments based on skin color, may be a double-edged sword for black teens, affecting both those who are perceived as "too black" and those who may not be seen as "black enough." For example, the teens who saw themselves as very dark skinned, or very light skinned, were least satisfied with the way they looked as compared to the teens who were somewhere in the middle. Lighter-skinned teens, possibly concerned about being perceived as stuck-up, unduly favored, or secretly wishing they were white, reported that they wished they were darker. The darker-skinned teens, perhaps seeing their own dating, marriage, and career options diminished, expressed a desire to be lighter.

113. *increase among black girls within a 15-year period:* Gortmaker, S. L., Dietz, W. H., Sobol, A. M., and Wehler, C. A. (1987). "Increasing Pediatric Obesity in the United States." *American Journal of Diseases of Children, 141,* 535–540.

113. "Changes in Self-Esteem in Black and White Girls Between the Ages of 9 and 14 Years. The NHLBI Growth and Health Study." *Journal of Adolescent Health,* 23(1), 7–19.

113. *negative social pressure about being overweight:* Kumanyika, S., Wilson, J. F., and Guilford-Davenport, M. (1993). "Weight-Related Attitudes and Behaviors of Black Women." *Journal of the American Dietetic Association,* 93(4), 416–417.

114. *"having the right attitude":* Ingrassia, M. (1995, April 24). "The Body of the Beholder. White and African American Girls' Body-Image Differ." *Newsweek,* p. 66.

114. *rates equal to white rates:* Striegel-Moore, R., et al. (1995). "Drive for Thinness in Black and White preadolescent girls." *International Journal of Eating Disorders,* 18(1), 59–69.

Chapter 6: Obstacles to Creating a Positive Identity

117. *their racial identity unfolds as well:* Harter, S. (1990). "Self and Identity Development." In S. S. Feldman and G. R. Elliott (Eds.), *At the Threshold: The Developing Adolescent.* Cambridge: Harvard University Press. See also Spencer, M. B., and Markstrom-Adams, C. (1990). "Identity Processes Among Racial and Ethnic Minority Children in America." *Child Development, 61,* 290–310.

121. *The psychiatrist James Comer says:* Comer, J. P. (1995). "Racism and African American Adolescent Development." In C. Willie, P. P. Rieker, B. Kramer, and B. Brown (Eds.). *Mental Health, Racism and Sexism.* Pittsburgh: University of Pittsburgh Press.

121. *rejection of all things white:* Ibid., pp. 163–164.

125. *Her commonsensical experience is echoed by research:* Phinney, J. S. and Aliperia, L. L. (1990). "Ethnic Identity in College Students from Four Ethnic groups," *Journal of Adolescence, 13*(2), 171–183.

142. *In Beverly Daniel Tatum's words:* Tatum, B. D. (1997). "Why Are All the Black Kids Sitting Together in the Cafeteria?" And Other Conversations about Race. Basic Books.

143. *According to Nielson Media Research:* Nielson Media Research in New York City, data reported in Fisher, C. (1996). "Black, Hip and Primed to Shop." *American Demographics, 18* (9), 52–57.

143. *That's well above the national average:* Ibid.

143. *In 1997* Time *magazine reported: Time* magazine sidebar. September 1, 1997, p. 25. See also *A Different World: Children's Perceptions of Race and Class in Media.* A survey conducted by Lake Sosin Snell Perry & Associates and Motivational Educational Entertainment (MEE) for Children Now. Los Angeles, 1998.

Chapter 7: Dating, Family Formation, and Crossing Over

156. *"techniques for interacting with other people":* Rice, F. P. (1999). *The Adolescent: Development, Relationships, and Culture.* Needham, MA: Allyn & Bacon, p. 273.

162. *Finally, we need to help our daughters:* Most husbands and wives are similar in racial backgrounds, but mixed marriages are on the increase. Since 1970, interracial marriages in American have quadrupled, affecting over one million couples, or approximately 2 percent of the married population (U.S. Bureau of the Census, 1996). Research also suggests that younger black women may be more willing to cross racial lines and date white men, or men outside of the black community. See Blakely, R. (1999, July). "Dating White: When Sisters Go There." *Essence,* p. 91. Interracial marriage among African American women has increased from 20,000 in 1970 to 100,000 in 1995. See Mills, C. (1999). "Black Women Speak Out About Their Interracial Relationships." *InterRace, 45,* 4–7.

Chapter 8: Spending and Financial Good Sense

171. *"30% less likely to have savings":* Malveaux, J. (1998, October). "Banking on Us: The State of Black Wealth." *Essence,* p. 101.

172. *topped $400 billion annually:* Ibid.

173. *family turmoil caused by debt:* Harris, F. (1998). *In the Black: The African American Parent's Guide to Raising Financially Responsible Children.* New York: Fireside, p. 146.

176. *selling "hot" goods:* Furry, M. M. "Children Manage Money Too." *http://www.black families.com.* Furry reports that as of February 1999, statistics regarding unemployment of black versus white youths 16 to 19 years old showed the following rates: black males, 32 percent; black females, 27 percent; white males, 12 percent; white females, 11 percent. This can be attributed to the lack of well-paid work for black teens, the reluctance of many black teenagers to take the low-paid jobs that are available, and racial discrimination. When young blacks do find work, it is more likely to be part-time. In addition, the inflation-adjusted earning of all young men who work full-time has dropped by one-fifth since 1979.

Chapter 9: Dissing, Boys, and Destroying the Ties That Bind

182. *As the psychologist Ann Ashmore Hudson says:* Hudson, A. A. (1997, October 26). "Dangerous Dozens: Where's the Romanticism in Talking Trash?" *Boston Globe.*

182. *"was the kiln in which I was fired":* Wilson, A. (1996). Interview. *American Theatre,* p. 15.

186. *powerlessness and economic isolation:* Staples, R. (1985). "Changes in Black Family Structure: The Conflict Between Family Ideology and Structural Conditions." *Journal of Marriage and the Family, 47,* November, 1005–1013.

186. *inconsistent performance of their own fathers:* Taylor, R. J., Chatters, L. M., Tucker, M. B., and Lewis, E. (1990). "Developments in Research on Black Families: A Decade Review." *Journal of Marriage and the Family, 52,* November, 993–1014.

186. *detached from others:* Majors, R. G., and Billson, J. M. (1992). *Cool Pose: The Dilemmas of Black Manhood in America.* New York: Lexington Books.

188. *The player's game is sexual conquest:* Oliver, W. (1989). "Black Males and Social Problems: Prevention Through Afrocentric Socialization." *Journal of Black Studies, 20*(1), 15–39.

188. *As Sisela Bok has written:* Sisela Bok, quoted in Brelis, M. (1999, May 9). "Looking at Littleton Means Seeing the Corrosive Effects of Humiliation." *Boston Sunday Globe.*

188. *Arising from a sense of vulnerability and powerlessness:* Pierce, C. M. (1995). "Stress Analogs of Racism and Sexism: Terrorism, Torture and Disaster." In C. Willie, P. P. Rieker, B. Kramer, and B. Brown (Eds.), *Mental Health, Racism and Sexism.* Pittsburgh: University of Pittsburgh Press. In the NBA, feelings of disrespect can be so powerful as to cause men to risk their livelihood over it. During the endless NBA strike of the 1998 season, I impatiently wondered why overgrown, overpaid athletes making an average salary of over $300,000 a year as rookies would grouse about respect. But exploitation has a long memory. Black men with few other employment options have labored with their bodies so white men can profit, and with little acknowledgment or respect for their sacrifice and work. Instead, they are seen as overgrown black men making lots of money but too dumb to know how to handle it properly. Thus they are undeserving and unworthy. I now understand the strike better as a symbolic recovery of respect for black men.

188. *see the gun as an instrument of self-respect:* Gilligan, J. (1996). *Violence: Our Deadly Epidemic and Its Causes.* New York: Putnam, p.

188. *And the violence isn't only against others:* Shaffer, D. (1995). "Worsening Suicide Rate in Black Teenagers." *American Journal of Psychiatry, 151*(12), 1810–1812.

189. *"collective upward social trajectory":* MacLeod, J. (1995). *Ain't No Makin' It: Aspirations and Attainment in a Low-Income Neighborhood.* Boulder, CO: Westview Press, p. 130.

192. *"the pampered and prosperous middle class":* Feagin, J. P., and Sikes, M. P. (1994). *Living with Racism: The Black Middle-Class Experience.* Boston: Beacon Press, p. 6.

193. *Even when we enter the job world:* (1997, June 27). Black per capita income overall is still only 56 percent of white income. *Boston Globe.*

204. *"there was no such thing as a good black":* (1999, January 18). Barrett, P. M., and Chamber, V. Review of *The Good Black,* by L. Mungin. *Newsweek,* p. 56.

Chapter 10: School Rules

215. *Black women significantly outnumber black men:* (1999, Spring). Special Report. "College Degree Awards: The Ominous Gender Gap in African American Higher Education." *Journal of Blacks in Higher Education,* 6–9.

215. *The fact that over the past two decades:* Kunjufu, J. (1989). *Developing Self-Images and Discipline in Black Children.* Chicago: African American Images.

217. *The decision, he said, confronted "(n)egroes with a cruel dilemma":* W.E.B Du Bois, quoted in Weinberg, M. (1977). *A Chance to Learn: The History of Race and Education in the United States.* New York: Cambridge University Press, p. 87.

217. *and many of the black teachers are gone as well:* Teaching, once the top vocational choice of African American college graduates, has dwindled in popularity, and the number of black teachers decreases each year.

217. *Statistics describe gross underachievement:* Belluck, P. (1999, July 4). "Reason Is Sought for Lag by Blacks in School Effort." *New York Times.* p. 1.

218. *the schools have deliberately "trained us to be stupid":* Note: Carter G. Woodson wrote that American schools intentionally "mis-educate the Negro," stating that the identity of the black students is intentionally distorted and misrepresented in the curriculum's Eurocentric approach to education and history.

219. *understood the relationship between academic and personal development:* See research on caring, committed segregated black schools in Siddle Walker, Vanessa (1996). *Their Highest Potential: An African American School Community on the Segregated South.* Chapel Hill: U of NC Press, and research on black teachers in Michele Foster (1997). *Black Teachers on Teaching.* NY: New Press.

223. *The destructive assumptions teachers often hold:* See Steele, Claude, M. "A (1997). Threat in the Air: How Stereotypes Shape Intellectual Identity and Performance." *American Psychologist,* 52, 613–629; and Steele, Claude M.(1999, August). Thin Ice. "Stereotype threat and Black College Students." *The Atlantic Monthly,* pp. 44–54. In these works on stigmatization he argues that there can be a devastating effect to black student performance caused by the negative-ability stereotype threat, which states that blacks do not belong in the domain of academic and intellectual excellence.

224. *"rumors of inferiority":* Howard, J., and Hammond, R. (1985, September 9). "Rumors of Inferiority." *New Republic,* pp. 18–23.

224. *On the other hand, as recent research shows:* Belluck, "Reason Is Sought."

224. *target the "stereotype threat":* Steele, C. (1999, July). *Atlantic Monthly.*

224. *building black students' sense of competence and self-efficacy:* Howard, J. (1995, fall). You can't get these from here: the need for a new logic in education reform. *Daedalus,* 124(4), 85–92

226. *it does not change the negative perception:* Comer, J. (1995). "Racism and African American Adolescent Development." In C. Willie, P. P. Rieker, B. Kramer, and B. Brown (Eds.), *Mental Health, Racism and Sexism.* Pittsburgh: University of Pittsburgh Press, p. 160.

226. *Souls Looking Back.* Garrod, Ward, Robinson, and Kilkenn. (1999). *Souls Looking Back: Life Stories of Growing Up Black,* NY: Routledge.

232. *Research shows that black students today:* Fordham, S., and Ogbu, J. (1986). "Black Students' School Success: Coping with the Burden of 'Acting White.'" *Urban Review,* 18, 176–206.

232. *"balance conflicting needs to define themselves":* Murrell, P. (1993). "Afrocentric Immersion: Academic and Personal Development of African American Males in Public Schools." In T. Perry and J. Frasier (Eds.), *Freedom's Plow.* Boston: Beacon Press, p. 251.

Chapter 11: Spirituality

248 *As Carolyn Johnson says:* Johnson, C. (1987). "Communion in Spirit." In G. Gay and W. L. Baber (Eds.), *Expressively Black: The Cultural Basis of Ethnic Identity.* New York: Praeger, p. 316.

248. *To Mary Pattillo-McCoy:* Pattillo-McCoy, M. (1998). "Church Culture as a Strategy of Action in the Black Community." *American Sociological Review, 63*(6), 768.

250. *The psychologist Nancy Goldberger:* Goldberger, N. R. (1996). "Cultural Imperatives and Diversity in Ways of Knowing." In N. Goldberger, J. Tarule, B. Clinchy, and M. Belenky (Eds.), *Knowledge, Difference, and Power: Essays Inspired by Women's Ways of Knowing.* New York: Basic Books, p. 348.

251. *Even our church songs:* Pattillo-McCoy," Church Culture," p. 771.

252. *Studies show that people who pray:* Jackson, A. P. and Sears, S. J. (1992). "Implications of an Africentric Worldview in Reducing Stress for African American Women." *Journal of Counseling & Development, 71*(2), 184–190.

255. *As the philosopher Audrey Thompson says:* Thompson, A. (1998). "Not the Color Purple," *Harvard Educational Review, 68*(4), 533.

256. *For struggle that takes place apart from community:* Robinson, T., and Howard-Hamilton, M. F. (2000). *The Convergence of Race, Ethnicity and Gender: Multiple Identities in Counseling.* Upper Saddle River, NJ: Prentice Hall.

PERMISSIONS

Portions of this work first appeared in part in the following published articles and book chapters:

Janie Victoria Ward, "Raising Resisters: The Role of Truth Telling in the Psychological Development of African American Girls," in *Urban Girls: Resisting Stereotypes, Creating Identities*, Bonnie Leadbeater and Niobe Way (eds.), New York, NY: New York University Press, 1996.

Tracy Robinson and Janie Victoria Ward, "'A Belief in Self Far Greater Than Anyone's Disbelief': Cultivating Resistance Among African American Girls," in *Women, Girls, and Psychotherapy: Reframing Resistance*, Carol Gilligan, Annie Rogers, and Deborah Tolman (eds.). Binghampton, N.Y.: Haworth Press, 1991. Article copies are available from The Haworth Document Delivery Service: 1-800-HAWORTH. E-mail address: getinfo@haworthpressinc.com.

Janie Victoria Ward, "Cultivating a Morality of Care in African American Adolescents: A Culture Based Model of Violence Prevention," in *Harvard Educational Review*, 65:2 (Summer 1995), pp. 175–188. Copyright © 1995 by the President and Fellows of Harvard College. All rights reserved.

INDEX